PRAISE FOR *I WOULD MEET YOU ANYWHERE*

"An intimate, deftly told story illuminating adoption's complications and losses, *I Would Meet You Anywhere* is sure to move anyone who has ever felt rootless, questioned their place within their family, or longed for deeper self-understanding."

—Nicole Chung, author of *A Living Remedy*

"Susan Kiyo Ito is like a surgeon operating on herself. She is delicate, precise, and at times cutting with her words. But it is all in service of her own healing and to encourage us all to be brave enough to do the same in our own stories."

—W. Kamau Bell, author of *Do the Work! An Antiracist Activity Book*

"In the intimate pages of *I Would Meet You Anywhere*, Ito yearns to learn of her parentage within the confounding context of closed adoption. As Ito plots a path to locate and know the birth parent who forsook her, we experience the pain of diminishing the self in order to be seen. An exquisite memoir of mothering and daughtering amid racial and generational differences."

—Julie Lythcott-Haims, author of *Real American: A Memoir*

"*I Would Meet You Anywhere* is a roller-coaster ride of an adoptee's search for her birth mother, which swerves and takes on speed the moment she has been found. Ito's investigation into her origin story takes her deeply into issues of identity, culture, convention, and history—and motherhood, in all its choices, losses, emptiness, and fierce love. *I Would Meet You*

Anywhere is a brave, compassionate, and necessary memoir that bears witness to how we let go, when we hold on, and how families are not just born but chosen."

— Rahna Reiko Rizzuto, author of *Hiroshima in the Morning*

"If it is possible to feel all the emotions in a single book, this is it. Determined to no longer be the secret or the 'wild inconvenience,' Susan Ito writes with grace, courage, and wonder. *I Would Meet You Anywhere* is a cinematic, breathtaking journey of family, identity, and secrets: an instant classic in adoption literature."

— Lee Herrick, California Poet Laureate

"*I Would Meet You Anywhere* is the poignant memoir of Susan Kiyo Ito's search for her birth parents. Ito's story opens the door to Japanese American adoptions with insight and understanding into the complexities of family, identity, and choice. A rich and compelling read."

— Gail Tsukiyama, author of *The Brightest Star: A Novel*

"My heart waxed and waned as I witnessed Ito navigate fraught interactions with her biological mother. This deeply moving memoir grapples with where the biological family fits amid a cacophony of secrets and longing all too often faced by adoptees."

— Angela Tucker, author of *"You Should Be Grateful": Stories of Race, Identity, and Transracial Adoption*

I WOULD MEET YOU ANYWHERE

MACHETE
Joy Castro, Series Editor

I WOULD MEET YOU ANYWHERE

A MEMOIR

SUSAN KIYO ITO

MAD CREEK BOOKS, AN IMPRINT OF
THE OHIO STATE UNIVERSITY PRESS
COLUMBUS

Library of Congress Cataloging-in-Publication Data
Names: Ito, Susan, 1959– author.
Title: I would meet you anywhere : a memoir / Susan Kiyo Ito.
Other titles: Machete.
Description: Columbus : Mad Creek Books, an imprint of The Ohio State
    University Press, [2023] | Series: Machete | Summary: "A memoir
    about one woman's search for her birth parents, exploring complicated
    relationships with family, the legacy of WWII internment on generations
    of Japanese Americans, and the challenges adoptees often face in learning
    their own histories"—Provided by publisher.
Identifiers: LCCN 2023017253 | ISBN 9780814258835 (paperback) | ISBN
    0814258832 (paperback) | ISBN 9780814283066 (ebook) | ISBN 0814283063
    (ebook)
Subjects: LCSH: Ito, Susan, 1959- | Adoptees—Biography. | Mothers and
    daughters. | Racially mixed women—Biography. | Birthparents.
Classification: LCC HV874.82.I86 A3 2023 | DDC 306.874—dc23/eng/20230706
LC record available at https://lccn.loc.gov/2023017253

Cover design by Nathan Putens
Text design by Juliet Williams
Type set in Adobe Palatino

Dedicated to my parents,
Masaji and Kikuko Ito

Three things cannot long stay hidden: the
sun, the moon, and the truth.
—the Buddha

A people without the knowledge of their past history,
origin, and culture is like a tree without roots.
—Marcus Garvey

CONTENTS

PREFACE

I was never supposed to tell this story. It is challenging to write, and publicly share, a story which holds a secret at its core. I have been that secret my whole life. I have also been writing about it for more than three decades. This book represents an excruciating tug of war between my own wanting to know and wanting to tell, against the forces of that secret.

Perhaps because I have lived with my existence as a secret—and because so many details of my own life, heritage, and history have been kept from me—that the need to know about and tell my story has been consuming. I have done my best to relate my own story, which is inextricably tangled with the lives of others. In this work of creative nonfiction, I have worked diligently to change names and other identifying details so that those who do not want their story public may remain anonymous. The risk of telling this story comes at a great cost, but the cost of not telling it is equally painful. As Maya Angelou wrote, "There is no greater agony than bearing an untold story inside you."

This book is focused on a particular aspect of my life. Readers who know me will recognize that much has been omitted. My life includes many facets and experiences that do not show up here. This is not meant to be a comprehensive autobiography.

I have strived, to the best of my ability, to treat everyone mentioned with as much compassion and forgiveness as possible. There are no heroes or villains in this story, other than institutional ones.

It is my fervent hope that readers will find resonance, comfort, strength, and validation in these pages: adopted people, birth/ first parents, adoptive families, multiracial people, those who have struggled with hard reproductive decisions, those who have experienced intergenerational repercussions from war and other trauma, and anyone who has grappled with issues of identity, family, and belonging.

Thank you for joining me.

PART 1

I WOULD MEET YOU ANYWHERE

My clogs squeaked in the snow as I approached the Holiday Inn in an unfamiliar, wintery city. I searched the lobby for an Asian woman but didn't see one. Was she already here? Was she going to show up as planned? Or had she bailed on me, reenacting the ghosting of two decades ago? The note in my pocket just said, "Holiday Inn, noon on Saturday, room under the name NOGU-CHI." I sidled into the restroom to brush my hair and practice making a cheerful/intelligent/sensitive/mature face in the mirror. At twenty years old, I was still sometimes mistaken for a middle schooler. Suddenly, my outfit of jeans, mock turtleneck, sweater, and chunky clogs seemed wrong. Too casual? Too college student? I *was* a college student. But maybe I should have dressed up more.

"Hi," I said to my reflection. "Hello. I'm Susan. Hello!" I arranged my face into a variety of expressions: smiling, solemn, in between. I pushed back a tsunami of anxious tears. Then it was time.

I walked through the lobby to the hotel's front desk and spoke her surname. Our name. My original name from the papers my adoptive parents had wrangled out of a county clerk only months ago. *Noguchi.*

"Room 1211. She's expecting you," said the red-haired clerk with a badly knotted tie. He pointed toward a bank of elevators.

The doors pinged open on the twelfth floor, and I edged slowly down the hallway. I paused in front of each door. 1207. 1209. I stopped in front of 1211. My watch read 11:58. I brushed the fake wood laminate door with my knuckles. Time ticked like a tiny bomb on my wrist. Two minutes to twelve. One hundred and twenty seconds. I stood with my palm against the door, watching the hand sweep its way around once, twice, a little blade slicing away at the time. I recited a little rhyme in my head. *I would meet you in a house. I would meet you with a mouse. I would meet you in a room. I'd meet you at exactly noon.* At five seconds to twelve, my hand curled into a loose fist and knocked twice. Then I stepped back, breathing hard.

The door opened. I half expected a blinding light and that I would step over the threshold into an abyss. But on the other side was an ordinary hotel room, and a Japanese woman my height stood in the doorway.

She was my birth mother.

I took in her ink-black hair, razor straight, with a sharp line of bangs above her eyebrows. No pin curls or foam rollers for her, no beauty-parlor perms like my adoptive mother. My heart pinched, thinking about that mother, oblivious back in New Jersey. I blinked and stared again at the soft rounded blip of her nose, her full lips. Her face, her rounded cheeks, looked familiar. She wasn't smiling.

Her eyes took me in. They moved over me, head to toe, quickly, expressionless. Then she spoke. "You must be Susan." Her voice sounded professional.

"Yes."

She stepped aside to let me pass. "I hope you don't mind that we've met here."

"Oh, no. Not at all." A giggle bubbled up from my gut and once again, my mind rhymed. *I would meet you in a car. I would sit inside a jar. I would meet you—anywhere.*

I scanned the room. Two double beds with gold quilted spreads. Suddenly, I was exhausted. I wanted to lie down. I wondered if we might take a nap, side by side. Two rounded chairs like parentheses perched next to the huge glass windows.

"Let's sit by the window," she said.

I awkwardly pushed the chairs together, then apart, trying to arrange them so that the sun, shining through the white winter sky, wouldn't glare in either of our faces. For a moment, I considered heaving myself against the glass, flying through shards of window into the swirling snow.

Finally, we sat facing each other. I chewed my lip. "I don't know what to say," I murmured.

"Neither do I." Her voice was cold. It wasn't a "me too" comment of solidarity. It was more like, then why are we wasting our time here?

I shrank into my chair. *She hates me.*

I fiddled with my envelope of photos and papers, my show and tell. "You probably would like to know how . . . how I found you."

GO FOR BROKE

I grew up in Park Ridge, a small town in northern New Jersey, within walking distance of the New York state border. My parents were Masaji and Kikuko Ito, and we lived in a pale-green ranch house on Summit Street. They had adopted me when I was three and a half months old. We were the only Japanese Americans in town and the only Asians until I was in third grade and a Chinese American family arrived. My parents each had two brothers; my grandparents, uncles, aunts, and cousins all lived in nearby counties. Every Sunday, we drove into Manhattan to our church, which attracted Japanese American families from every borough and nearby state. My mother had been born and raised in Brooklyn and my father in the Bronx. This church had been the center of their community since they were children. Life felt split in half: weekdays, we were immersed in white suburban life, and weekends, we connected with our Asian roots.

My cousins were like weekend siblings to me. We gathered in each other's backyards on weekends, while the uncles hammered away on home improvement projects and the aunties stuffed inarizushi "pillows" and served them alongside hotdogs and potato salad.

I rarely saw other Asian faces in our town, and I wasn't used to seeing them in the media either. We didn't have access to the infinite television and cable channels that are now available around the clock. Our viewing was limited to the four major networks, and our choices were laid out for us in the weekly *TV Guide*, which arrived in our mailbox once a week. I loved the *TV Guide*. I read all the Hollywood gossip and trivia and pored through every day's listings, marking the shows I wanted to watch with a red pen. My mother was a television fanatic. My father worked as a traveling salesman, away from home for weeks at a time, and the television helped distract her from her loneliness. She mostly watched sports—baseball and football—or game shows or reruns of *I Love Lucy*. Another one of our favorites was *The Courtship of Eddie's Father*, which featured Miyoshi Umeki, one of the few Japanese American actresses of the time.

"Miyoshi is on!" we called to each other, as if she was a family friend.

One listing that I always kept an eye out for was the 1950s movie *Go for Broke*, which we all referred to as "Daddy's war movie." It turned up once or twice a year, usually in the wee hours of the morning, 2 a.m., a late-late show. The first time I remember seeing it, I was only eight. My mother came to wake me with a fake candle with a light-bulb flame in a brass holder. The yellow light fell around my bed in a buzzy, buttery circle.

She handed me my glasses, and I blinked through the sleepy sand in my eyes. It was strange being up in the middle of the night. The house was quiet and hollow. Our footsteps echoed in the black tunnel of the hallway between our bedrooms and the living room. I could see myself reflected in the picture window, snug in the fluffy pink bathrobe I'd received when I'd had my tonsils out the year before. She tucked my red plaid baby blanket over my shoulders.

My father was, luckily, not on the road that night. Often, he was driving through North Carolina, Georgia, Tennessee, selling souvenirs to gift shops along the interstate. But this night he was home, and he joined us in his blue-striped seersucker robe. My mother set a bowl of rice crackers on the folding TV table, with tea and hot chocolate in china cups. My father fiddled with the rabbit-ear antenna on top of the console, and the movie crackled into view.

The broadcast glowed in black and white, though we had a color television. Big script letters filled the screen: Van Johnson, the big star! I recognized him because Lucy in *I Love Lucy* was always trying to get his autograph or to talk to him. She and her best friend, Ethel, swooned over Van Johnson, though I didn't understand why. He was blonde and bland looking. But it impressed my father that he was in *Go for Broke*.

"Big star," he nodded. "Big deal that they got him to sign on," he said. "He was a good man to do this, to be in a movie with a buncha nihonjins."

He didn't look like a good man to me. In the opening scene, he portrayed an army officer who had just found out he was going to be in charge of the 442nd regiment, made up entirely of Japanese American soldiers. "I'm not going to be stuck with a bunch of Japs," he scoffed.

I flinched. My parents' mouths tightened a bit in the flickering light. My father patted my leg. "It's okay, Sus, they have to have him say that, to make it realistic. Some fellas actually said things like that."

"I thought you said he was a good man."

"The *actor* is a good man. He's playing a prejudiced guy." He patted me again. "Just watch, though. He'll change."

"How many times have you seen this movie?" I asked.

He counted on his fingers. "Four, five times? First we went to the premiere. That was a big night, Rascal. Van Johnson came himself. The VA sponsored it, and they had a big party after. The Shudokai church cooked, all kinds of nihon-no-mono, a big cake. 'Go for Broke' in the icing. They let veterans like me, Uncle Yo, Uncle Kiyoshi, all in for free."

He cleared his throat and gazed into the darkness of the hallway.

My mother clapped, a sharp short noise. "Hey, enough you two. Pay attention."

Parts of the movie were funny. We laughed when the soldiers played a joke on the Van Johnson sergeant. They called him bakatare—baka!—behind his back, and he didn't realize they were saying he was stupid. The hair on my arms quivered at that word. It felt like a secret swear word, and I loved that the mean officer was getting the brunt of it. A number of funny Japanese in-jokes popped up throughout the movie. I felt like I was watching people I knew—men from the church or my uncles. I had never seen my family on a screen. The 442nd soldiers were short and fast, and it made them valuable. I'd heard my father say those words 4-4-2 a hundred times, but never understood until that night what he meant.

Four four two. Those magic numbers. Hero numbers. He had told me many times about how he'd fought in Italy during the war, how he had carried a hundred-pound radio on his back. He was an anomaly, a short Japanese American with a Brooklyn accent who spoke Italian. When we went to eat in Little Italy, he ordered in enthusiastic, fluent Italian, startling the wait staff. He had absorbed the language over three years, and after his death I discovered a huge leather photo album filled with tiny black and white snapshots of his life in Italy. He had befriended many Italians and was taken into homes by families who fed him. There were photos of beautiful women too. Later, my mother told the story of the blonde Italian woman who had showed up at their apartment door when they were newlyweds.

"I told her to look me up if she ever came to America," my father stammered. "I didn't think she ever would!" They turned the bewildered woman away, who apparently wasn't expecting my soldier father to have a wife in New York.

My father told me that the 442nd was the "most decorated" unit in US history. I didn't know what decorated meant, but I took it to mean they had gotten a lot of medals. Beautiful, shining decorations on their uniforms like purple hearts, ribbons, and stars. I imagined my father bejeweled and shimmering. I didn't understand that decoration equaled death, more deaths per unit than any other.

I didn't understand that so many soldiers had enlisted from

desert camps where they had been imprisoned with their families, from infants to elderly issei like my own grandparents. My parents had not told me about the Japanese American incarceration—that more than a hundred thousand people had lived behind barbed wire for years. Japanese Americans on the East Coast had largely avoided that fate, and I suppose my parents were reluctant to discuss it, though I didn't know it at the time. I didn't learn about the camps until I was in college.

What I also didn't know then was that my birth mother had been a child in one of those desert camps, that she had lived in barrack shacks with her siblings and parents. What I wouldn't realize until many years later was that those camps, and the war, were the driving factors behind my existence. My birth mother's family had lost everything—their home and business on the West Coast. They had nothing to return to when the war was over, so they took an offer to be sponsored by a church in a tiny town in the Midwest. Their family was an anomaly, an aberration, and although they were treated kindly, they were perpetually foreign, perpetually outsiders. There were no other Japanese people to date or marry. Given this status in the community, it's not a surprise that my birth mother kept her private life a secret and that I, a half-white child, was the result. When I trace the events that led to my conception and birth, to my adoption and my life as I know it, I always end up coming back to that camp.

I was unaware of all of this, watching the 442nd that night on my living room television with my parents. We watched the Japanese soldiers tricking the Germans, rescuing the Lost Battalion in France. The famous battle looked like a glorious run through the forest, leaping over logs, the soldiers grinning and hooting as they charged uphill. The ones who were shot twirled in midair and collapsed silently to the ground. Van Johnson was incredulous at what the nisei soldiers pulled off. They were great! Unbelievable!

I jumped on the couch, throwing pillows in the air. "Go for broke! Go for broke!" My parents laughed. "Calm down, Rascal."

I declared it the best war movie I had ever seen. My heart was pumping with pride for my father. In the final scene, the American flag fluttered while FDR awarded medals to the soldiers. My mother applauded. "Jouzu ne. You did good, Ito." She picked up the dirty dishes from the TV tray.

The men of the Lost Battalion, the white soldiers, filed past the 442nd soldiers, shaking their hands and thanking them for their lives. One of the tall hakujins reached out to a nisei from Honolulu. "Aloha, little guy," he said, and wiggled the man's nose.

My father reached over abruptly and turned off the television. "I don't like that," he said gruffly. "That part bugs me." He touched his own nose like he was brushing off an insect.

It was almost three in the morning, and I was struggling to stay awake. "Yoi-sho. Time to go neh-neh. Again."

He pulled me up by both arms. On the way to my room, we passed a photograph in the hallway of my parents long ago, sitting on a park bench. My father in his army uniform, crisp looking. Decorated with so many pins on his pocket. His hair thick, black, and glossy. My mother snuggled next to him on the bench. He sighed, and we stood looking up at their smiles, their heads so close together.

THE PLACE I CAME FROM

Don Leadon was the object of every junior high girl crush: he had honey blonde hair that swooshed over his forehead and blue eyes like a cloudless sky. He was the first boy to wear a flowered button-down shirt. He emulated the stars on Rowan & Martin's *Laugh-In*, with their groovy style clothing, bell bottomed pants, and long hair.

My mother brought up his name one day when we were having our after-school snack. She worked in the front office at my elementary school, and she knew things that other mothers didn't know. When I was a student there, I had been allowed to pass through the swinging saloon doors to the inner sanctum of the secretaries' desks and help her with various tasks. I'd stack and count milk money nickels or turn the handle on the mimeograph machine until her workday ended at four o'clock. Then we'd drive home in our station wagon. Now, I went to the junior high in the center of town. She had been offered a job there, but she declined, and I was glad to be independent. I walked home on my own, and we met in our kitchen after school for a snack.

"Don Leadon is adopted too, you know," she said casually. She pulled a bobby pin from her permed black curls and separated the tines with her teeth.

My heart surged. It startled me to hear his name, especially paired with that word—*adopted*—that always made me feel conspicuous and strange.

"He came from the same place as you."

"The same place?" I couldn't fathom what she was talking about. New Rochelle? She had told me I'd been born in New Rochelle, the same town that Dick Van Dyke lived in on television.

"Spence-Chapin."

I repeated the words after her.

"The adoption agency. Where we got you. Don Leadon came from there too."

My head spun. *The place I came from. Where they got me.* I didn't know the difference between an adoption agency and an orphanage. I had seen pictures of rooms with high windows, filled with white metal cribs, rows of babies whose cries floated up to the ceilings. I had been in one of those places. With baby Don Leadon. Had we been there at the same time? Had his crib been next to mine? Did we recognize each other's voices from long ago?

Of course, we were not there at the same time, but I didn't know that. There were no rooms full of cribs. Spence-Chapin was only a momentary stopping place, a place of exchange and commerce. It was the place where my adoptive parents drove to "get" me, wrapped in a pink blanket damp with spit-up. It was the place where papers were signed, their signatures wet.

"Do you know anything about her?" My voice was dry and painful in my throat.

"Who?"

This was awkward. I didn't want to say the word. I shrugged.

"Oh, you mean your mother?" It was bizarre to hear my mother referring to someone else as "your mother." In her thick Brooklyn accent, it sounded like "muthah."

I sat silently, managing the smallest nod.

"I think we heard she was in college. An art student? Something like that. That's how come you're so artistic, you know." My mother had enrolled me in extracurricular art classes from the time I'd been in preschool. We had driven to larger towns in Bergen County so I could form creatures from papier-mâché or learn to paint with black sumi ink. She'd been nurturing my nature, and I hadn't even realized it.

"Do you know her name?" It felt terrifying to even ask the question.

She shook her head. "Nah. They don't tell the adoptive parents that stuff. All we knew was that she was nihonjin, the father was hakujin. That's why you're hanbun-hanbun." Half and half. Sometimes people remarked, "Susan doesn't look nihonjin," and my mother's response was always, "She's hanbun-hanbun." Eyebrows were raised, and it usually stopped the conversation.

Sometimes my mother jokingly called me a mutt. I didn't laugh. The only other half-Japanese person I knew was a girl at our Japanese church. Her mother was nihonjin-from-Nihon and her father was Black. At church, my mother would nudge me with her elbow. "There's Patricia." As if we belonged together, in some Half-n-Half Club. I was jealous of her though. She *knew* what her two halves were. Anyone could see her mother in her eyes, her father in her skin. But I was a mutt.

I rode my low-slung bike with the banana seat and V-shaped handlebars to the town library and surreptitiously looked up the subject ADOPTION in the card catalog. I had left behind the low-shelved juvenile section of the library to explore the vastness of the adult section. I learned how to use the card catalog to research my school projects on insects (cicadas, which both fascinated and terrified me), wolverines, and Antarctica. I loved the glossy blonde wood of the card catalog drawers, the orderliness of the Dewey decimal system, and how the coded numbers translated into specific areas and shelves of the library.

It had taken me years to understand that not everyone was adopted and that babies did not magically appear in cribs. My friends' mothers had swollen with pregnancy, and I had learned at age ten, shockingly, about the details of reproduction from the

"Breeding Your Keeshond" chapter of our dog book. My heart stuttered in my chest as my fingers walked through the cards.

A. AD. ADOPTION. *The Search for Anna Fisher,* by Florence Fisher. I wrote down the book's number and pursued it, like a treasure hunt, through the stacks. I pulled out a thick book with a green cloth cover. On the first page, the epigraph shook me. "Oh why does the wind blow upon me so wild? Is it because I'm nobody's child?"

My stomach roiled. *Nobody's child.* I wasn't nobody's child. I was my parents' child. But the understanding that I had been born elsewhere, to other people, and given away was beginning to flicker in my mind.

I turned more pages. Florence Fisher's words took my breath away. Each chapter heading featured a brief quote by anonymous "adoptees." I had never heard this word before.

I'm sure you can understand my wanting to see someone in this world who is actually flesh and blood, related to me. —an adoptee

I raise Irish setters, and it's a little disturbing to know that I can trace their pedigree further than I can trace my own. —an adoptee

I feel lost and floating. —an adoptee

I slammed the book shut. I felt nauseated from excitement, dread, curiosity. I checked the book out and slipped it between the pages of a *Tiger Beat* magazine, like contraband. I didn't want anyone, especially my parents, to know I was reading it.

Don sat in front of me in homeroom, so the next day I tapped him on the shoulder. "My mother told me you were from Spence-Chapin." I said it like a secret code, like a password. As the words escaped my lips, I was struck by a sudden fear: What if he didn't know that he was adopted? I held my breath, waiting to see if I had just shattered his life.

There had never been a time that I hadn't known I was adopted, that I came from Elsewhere. It was written on my skin, in my eyes, in the shape of my hands, that I was different from my parents.

It wasn't as obvious with Don and his family, but if you looked closely, you could tell. Nobody in his family had brilliant blue eyes like his.

He stared at me. Don Leadon had never really looked at me before, and it opened up a balloon of happiness in my chest.

"Why?" he said. "Why would she tell you that?" He scowled.

I swallowed. "Because that's where I'm from too."

Suddenly the vast emptiness of my early life was populated by one other person. Don Leadon and I were alumni of that baby place, and if he had been there, maybe I hadn't been alone. We might have spoken to each other, in a coded baby language without words.

"Yeah," he said quietly. "Yeah, that's the place."

I got up and took a long drink at the water fountain. I tore a strip of notebook paper from my binder and wrote in small letters. *Do you think you will ever look for your real parents?*

He wrote on the back, *probably,* and then balled up the note and tossed it over his shoulder onto my desk.

In the back of the adoptee book, there was an address and the name of an organization that Florence Fisher had founded: ALMA. The Adoptees' Liberty Movement Association. It sounded dangerous, radical. I wrote them a letter and carried it to the post office, the tang of the stamp bright on my tongue. *Please help me,* I wrote. The typewritten response, which arrived at my house a few weeks later, said that ALMA supported my quest to know my origins but that they couldn't legally help me until I was eighteen.

I imagined myself as an eighteen-year-old, driving in a blue convertible with an older, even more beautiful Don Leadon. We would have a map and a cooler full of cheese sandwiches. The road that stretched before us would be long and infinite, like a cartoon road, a red arrow darting across the shape of the country, in squiggles and loops. We would take to the road, when we could drive, and find our original families together. He would drive with one hand, his other hand holding tightly onto mine.

NOT A JAPANESE GIRL

"Hold still. You're wiggling too much."

I squinted into the dusty full-length mirror in my mother's bedroom and tugged at the stiff red and gold obi, a gilded girdle, around my kimono-draped body.

"Let me finish your hair." My four-foot-ten, rough-speaking mother talked around the black bobby pins between her lips. She stood on a metal stool, fussing with my hair while I shifted my weight back and forth. I was eighteen.

Around us lay a mountain of crumpled blue paper we'd tossed on the floor while unwrapping my new waitressing uniform. The inner layer, snowy cotton underthings, had dozens of pea-sized buttons and long fabric ties. Then the elaborate flowered kimono, two layers of obi (one stiff and cardboardish, the other a gold braided rope), the divided white tabi-socks that went between my toes and snapped up the ankle. The final elements were a pair of slippery wooden geta shoes and the headpiece, a layered ornament that rained silk mums and butterflies over my sculpted hairdo.

"*How* much did this stuff cost you? Ikura?" We had both been shocked that my contract demanded I purchase the special undergarments and pay a monthly rental fee for the kimono and obi. I could feel the pride underneath the complaint, and I knew that it made her happy to see me dressed this way. The last time I had worn a kimono—an outfit sent by relatives in Japan—I'd been five years old. My father had snapped a photograph of me posed in front of our Christmas tree, holding up a silk fan.

"You nervous?" She stepped back and squinted.

"Yeah. I'm afraid I won't be able to understand anything. My nihongo isn't all that good."

"Well. Only worry if they start calling you baka." She laughed, a sharp bark, and jerked her palm up so fast that I ducked, almost losing my balance. My stomach tightened. *Baka* meant stupid. She had called me baka throughout my childhood. Whenever I saw my mother's lips tighten into that "b" sound, I knew what was coming.

"Whatsa matter? Thought I was going to hit you?" *Well, yes.* The men from our church joked that even though she was the smallest girl in their Brooklyn neighborhood she was the toughest and could beat up someone three times her size. I'd felt the back of her hand on my skull more than once.

"You better go. You don't want to be late."

I eased down the front steps of the house and folded myself carefully into her Gremlin hatchback.

"You be careful and don't drive too fast," she warned. "What time you be home?"

I looked at the spindly arms of the dashboard clock. "Maybe around midnight . . . ?"

"So late!"

I shrugged. "We're supposed to help clean up."

She frowned. "Okay. But none of this midnight business on a school night." I was earning summer credits at the local community college before my sophomore year. School nights were still sacred.

I had enrolled in a class called "Psychology of the Family." I had thought it sounded interesting and, hopefully, easy. The required hard science courses in the physical therapy program at Ithaca College had nearly beaten me down. The psychology instructor, a plump, dimpled family therapist, had assigned us a ten-page paper on any aspect of family life. I scribbled on the signup sheet: *adoption.* The idea of studying a subject that had defined my own family both fascinated and terrified me.

I checked out some books on adoption in the college library: *Lost and Found. The Adoption Triangle.* I was a point in that triangle between birth and adopted families. One book highlighted case studies of people who had searched for their birth families in England, where records were open to adopted adults. There were many unhappy outcomes. One woman had found her mother in a mental institution—she'd had a breakdown shortly after relinquishing her baby. Another adoptee's birth mother had died by suicide, another had been a victim of incest, and another realized that she had been raised by an aunt—believing all along it had been her mother. I wrote in my journal: *It's too much. I'm a part of all this. I'm involved, involuntarily.*

It was unsettling, but I couldn't stop reading. I pored guiltily through the pages after my parents had gone to sleep. Did I really want to seek out the unknown side of my own triangle? What would I do if my search ended in a graveyard? Or an asylum? I had raised the idea with my college boyfriend and friends. *We don't want you to get hurt,* they had said. *Why do you want to do this?* But I had so many questions. They stabbed at the inside of me. It hurt.

As I drove, I spoke my response aloud in the empty car. *I don't care. I want to know.*

My waitressing job was an hour north of our little town, across the New Jersey border at the last exit on the parkway. I drove up the long curling driveway to the Gasho restaurant, past the stone garden, the koi pond with the red bridge, the Japanese maples with their star-shaped leaves blazing around the entrance of the old farmhouse building. *Authentic Japanese woodwork,* the glossy brochure said. I loved to repeat that in my head. *Not a single nail or screw used.* I loved the dark knotted wood of the ancient building, tied together with rope, its beamed shapes fitting together perfectly like a giant puzzle. I loved the way the waitresses glided smoothly over the carpet, holding their trays high. I was in awe of the fierce, deft comedy of the chefs and their gleaming knives, their hands flashing over the steel grills. My parents had brought me here for birthday dinners or after a good report card. Now I would be on the inside.

I stumbled through the front entranceway, clutching my kimono sleeves.

"Ito-san!" The manager rushed toward me.

"Hai, Hattori-san!" The butterflies trembled on my headpiece.

He seemed angry. His lips tightened, on the verge of *baka*. "*Never* front door, Ito-san! Back door! *Kitchen* door!" His face shimmered with perspiration. "Front door is for customer only!"

"Very sorry, Hattori-san, gomen nasai . . ." I backed up and turned to walk around the building. How was I supposed to know these things?

"No, no, too late for go around. You go through kitchen now, but next time, *back* door!" He grabbed my arm. "You find Hideko-san, she tell you what to do."

Hideko-san, the older head waitress, was stocky in her black and gold kimono. She appraised me with a frown. "Hair not so good color. Maybe you find better color in box, neh? Chisai bit darker."

"You mean . . . you want me to dye my hair?"

"M-hm. Maybe look better." I understood what she meant. Maybe more authentic.

The smell of miso and green onions floated in the steam of the kitchen. Prep chefs shouted in Japanese, and the dishwashers sang along with Spanish on the radio. I followed Hideko past huge steel kettles of miso soup, enormous rice pots, steamers of green tea, salad dishes lined up on the countertops.

"You make twenty salads, put in refrigerator. Then make more." Hideko-san leaned over the freezer and gestured at the ice cream tubs. "You no eat *any*thing, not ice cream, not gohan, not any piece of salad. You get meal food in between lunchtime and dinnertime. You take food, we take off paycheck." Her voice was steely. "You go now. Tables five, six, seven. You take care of customers."

Show time. I filled a basketful of steaming face towels, pressed my shoulder against the swinging metal door, taking careful steps over to Kimi, the hostess. "Ready for table five."

Kimi smiled, her tiny teeth perfect. "You look cute in your outfit." She ran her manicured, coral nail down the reservation list. "Five. Why don't you take . . . Marsh. Party of six."

I gathered menus and called into the smoky din of the cocktail area. "Marsh?" A woman with champagne curls waved enthusiastically. "That's us!" She held up a glass of emerald Midori on ice. Three couples followed me to a horseshoe shaped table.

"Welcome to Gasho." I picked up the hot rolled towels with wooden tongs and laid them on their open palms. The customers opened the steaming towels and pressed them into their faces, making small sounds of pleasure.

The senior Marsh, a man with slick hair the color of french fries, licked a dot of beer foam off his upper lip. "Just a minute," he said.

"Yes?"

"If you're Japanese, I'll eat this towel."

"Excuse me?" My face heated up, prickling my cheeks.

"The brochure says this is place is authentic, that the farmhouse was built in Japan."

"Yes. It was shipped here from Osaka." I was trembling. The heavy, rope-wrapped beams hung over our heads.

"Oh, yeah? And where were *you* shipped from?"

I felt the blood draining from my face. I imagined it seeping out my soles, leaving me standing in a puddle of tainted, half-authentic liquid.

Who was I to think I could get away with working here? That by dressing up in this costume I could pass as Japanese? Even if I'd been adopted by two Japanese parents, I'd never be the real thing. I hugged the basket of limp wet towels to my chest.

"I *am* Japanese," I whispered hoarsely. "Half Japanese."

"Huh." Marsh picked at his molar with a carved wooden pick. "Listen, maybe we should just switch tables."

His wife looked around with panicky eyes. The two other couples in their party fiddled with their chopsticks, gazes down. "Ed. We're fine where we are . . ."

His beer glass came down hard, sloshing liquid. "*Damn* it. I go out to a Japanese restaurant, I expect a Japanese girl." He gestured toward Kimi, her silky black hair swishing as she led another group toward table eleven.

Kimi is from Korea, I said silently. Not a Japanese girl.

I bowed stiffly. "I'll speak with my manager." I didn't even want to think about what Hattori would say. I found him pacing back and forth near the bar.

"Gomen nasai. Hattori-san, the people at table number five are requesting a . . . a window view. To see the koi pond."

He wiped his face gruffly, then glanced at his watch. "Twenty-minute wait."

"Hm." I looked at the floor.

"Tell them wait in bar, I give drinks on the house."

"Hai. Thank you, Hattori-san."

After I delivered the offer to switch tables, the group followed me back to the bar. Marsh was happy. "Not bad! Free drinks!" He rubbed his hands together. "I'll take one of those hot sakes."

When I returned with the tiny cups, I heard him mumble to his wife. "This one oughta get a job at McDonald's."

The wife stared at me with helpless eyes.

I took a long moment to look the man full in the face. "Enjoy your dinner."

But he had given words to my deepest fear, that I wasn't really Japanese, or not Japanese enough. He was right. I wasn't authentic. And the other half of me was a mystery.

Hideko-san handed me a yellow plastic bucket with a sponge and spray cleanser. "You clean lady bathroom. Busboy clean man bathroom."

I couldn't believe I was scrubbing a toilet in a gold kimono, woozy and nauseous from hunger and ammonia.

Dinner, served on paper plates, consisted of a scoop of rice topped with scrambled egg. Hideko sorted dollar bills onto a table, clicking a calculator with the end of a chopstick. Finally she distributed envelopes. "Tip money."

I ripped the envelope open and counted twenty-nine dollars.

"Um. Hideko-san? I think maybe there is a mistake?" I held out the bills.

"No mistake."

"But I collected . . . I'm *sure* . . . almost two hundred dollars."

Hideko picked up the calculator. "All tips go in kitty pot. Add up, then half go to chef team. One-eighth go to busboy team. Rest go to waitress team. Divide in senpai order."

"Senpai order?"

Shizuko gave me a look that said *unbelievably baka.* "I first, I was here since day of opening. Next, Furuki-san, then Emiko-san. Keep going to kohai, last person come to Gasho."

"That's me."

"Hai."

"So, even though I collected almost two hundred dollars in tips tonight . . . this is it?"

"Hai. Oyasumi nasai, Ito-san. We see you tomorrow."

"Oyasumi nasai." I felt tears at the back of my throat. This was usually an affectionate goodnight between family members, but tonight it felt like a slap. Twenty-nine dollars, plus the three-dollars-an-hour base pay, wasn't even enough to pay for my kimono rental.

As I left, Kimi handed me a Gasho brochure, folded down and secured with a hair tie. "Miss Susan" was scribbled on the front. "Someone left this for you," she said.

My car sat lonely under one of the floodlights. I collapsed in the driver's seat and unfolded the odd little package. Inside was a twenty-dollar bill and written across the top: *Sorry for the trouble earlier. You didn't deserve it. —Mrs. E. Marsh*

I added the twenty to my tip envelope and put the key in the ignition.

The Thruway was a long glowing caterpillar of red lights, crawling slowly past an accident on the side of the road. I drove with the windows down, the night air biting through my clothes as I blinked to stay awake. The bones in my feet throbbed from clenching the smooth wooden soles of the geta, from rushing on tense legs the length of the dining room. After the Marsh debacle, the rest of my customers had been pleasant, jovial, tipping generously. I had counted in my head as I collected it from small plastic trays: nearly two hundred dollars. All of it went into the "kitty pot," as Hideko had instructed.

When I crossed the border back into New Jersey, my little town would be fast asleep. But the back window overlooking the driveway, my mother's room, would be glowing through the vinyl shade. I knew she would be sitting up, her hair in pin curls. The deck of cards would be spread across the bed. Alert as a fox, she would hear my car, would recognize it before it turned onto Summit Street. By the time I pulled into the U-shaped driveway, she would be stepping into her rubber zori and opening the front door. It wouldn't matter to her that I'd come home with a flimsy envelope with a fraction of my earned pay, or that I'd been insulted by a drunk hakujin. She'd be there to run hot water into the bathtub, to untie the knots at the back of my obi, and to hang the kimono on a wooden hanger for the next day.

SEARCHING

In the fall of my junior year of college in upstate New York, I was nineteen years old, a legal adult. I realized that I didn't need to wait anymore. I had spent the summer reading as many books as I could find about adoption. I was ready. I wrote to ALMA and received a flyer of upcoming events, including their next "How to Search" meeting in New York City.

I rode the Greyhound bus from Ithaca to Manhattan. I didn't tell my parents. They probably imagined me sitting on the dock of the rented house I shared with two roommates, my books beside me, the leaves in a riot of color around Cayuga Lake. The silver bus I was riding passed their exit—*our* exit—on the New York Thruway. Paranoid, I ducked my head down, as if they were standing at the side of the highway, searching for my face.

I had no idea how they would respond to knowing that I was joining this organization, going to a meeting to learn about searching for my birth parents. We had only discussed my adoption a few times. I didn't want to hurt their feelings. But I was burning to know more about who and where I'd come from. Who were the people who had made me? And why had they given me up?

I headed to Greenwich Village, to my friend Ken Shiotani's tiny apartment on Christopher Street. Ken attended the Japanese church and was like an older brother to me. He was a brand-new lawyer and had an orange-bearded roommate named Dan.

Their place was even smaller than my dorm room at Ithaca:

two cell-like bedrooms with barely enough space for a bed in each one, a miniature kitchen with a small table and two folding chairs, a bathroom where you sat on the toilet to brush your teeth in the sink.

I was excited for my first meeting of the Adoptees' Liberty Movement Association. I had been wanting to join them ever since I had been thirteen and read the memoir of their founder, Florence Fisher. Their name sounded revolutionary: I imagined adoptees, bandanas tied around our faces, charging into the Hall of Records. Demanding our birth certificates, the names of our parents, all the vital secrets that had been kept from us so long.

Dan and Ken's place was my hideout, and I loved the roughness of it, the roar of street noise from the Village outside, the creaking, ancient stairwell that led to their door. Nobody but they knew where I was.

Even though they were just a few years older, they felt like true adults to me, with their real-life jobs, newspaper editor and public defender. Ken poured little glasses of their homemade Kahlua, which we drank with Velveeta cheese and crackers. Dan, wearing a fluorescent yellow apron, had crafted a casserole of canned tuna and macaroni. They brought out a basket of instruments, including a guitar and accordion, and we improvised, laughing. I tapped alongside on a xylophone. We talked about my ALMA meeting the next day, and they peppered me with questions about my adoption. Their interest and support warmed me.

After dinner, we meandered through the Village and visited bars, listening to flamenco music, Irish music, jazz. We climbed the metal pipes of children's playgrounds and hung upside down, playing under the streetlights until nearly dawn. I hooked my elbows through their arms and skipped between them. I felt free, giddy with possibility.

In the morning, Ken cooked a bowlful of scrambled eggs and left early for the law library. I showered under a sprinkling of meager, tepid water, and Dan walked me to the subway and offered to ride uptown with me to my meeting. I didn't refuse. Suddenly, I felt weak with nerves. We arrived at East 46th Street and climbed the stairs to daylight. He kissed my forehead.

"Courage," he murmured and disappeared back down into the roaring subway tunnel.

I rode a jittery elevator to the second floor and entered a room filled with folding chairs and people holding cups of coffee and tea. The sound of excited voices was deafening. I clutched my purse and notebook to my chest. Stacks of literature were strewn across a long table, and I picked up a few pastel-colored flyers. Each was imprinted with the ALMA logo of a mother holding an infant and the words, *The Truth of his origin is the birth right of every Man.* I found an empty chair and sat down, reading slowly, the words blurring in front of my eyes. I scanned reprints of newspaper articles, featuring photographs of people embracing. "Happy Reunion." "Registry Proves to be Vital Link for Mother and Daughter." "The Need to Know." I tried to focus and read the stories, but I could barely sit still in the chair.

A woman with short, sculpted dark hair pointed at the seat next to me. "Occupied?"

I tucked my legs in to let her pass. "Oh, no."

She stuck her hand right into mine. Her fingers were long, unhesitating, and strong. "Are you an adoptee?"

I blinked. Nobody had ever asked me this question so directly before, out loud. Adoptee. I nodded. "I guess I am."

"When's your birthday?" She opened her purse and applied burgundy-colored lipstick.

This made me laugh. "August 11, 1959. And—my name is Susan."

"Oh, right! I'm sorry." She smacked her palm on her forehead. "I always forget to ask that first. I'm Dana. Dana D'Agostino. Hey, I'm a Leo too, but a few years older. I just started coming here a few months ago, and I haven't gotten very far. Are you searching?"

"I don't know . . . I think so?"

"Welcome to the club."

The program started, and we turned to the front of the room. A speaker pounded the podium and shouted, "We need open records! It's our right!" The audience clapped and called out "Yeah! Yeah!" I wasn't sure what "open records" meant, but the crowd's emotion revved up my heart.

Next, a panel of people who had searched for and found their biological relatives spoke about their experiences. *Natural families,* they said. Was my family unnatural? Boxes of tissue and miniature photo albums of the reunited kin, their faces pressed together, passed from hand to hand. I stared at the people in the photos. They looked so happy. They did resemble each other. Would I ever have a photograph like that? A picture of someone who looked like me?

Dana honked her nose into a tissue. "Look at this." She passed me a Polaroid snapshot of a woman holding a little girl on her lap. Another woman, with graying hair, but the identical smoky blue eyes, forehead, sharp chin, stood behind her. *Three generations finally together,* was scribbled below. They all had the same color eyes, the same little chin that could fit into a shot glass.

"Let's get into the same group for the search workshop." Dana claimed me, holding my sleeve with her long fingers, and I felt grateful to have a new friend. I spotted a sign that said LDA. "What's that?" I asked. "Mormons?"

"No," said Dana. "It stands for Late-Discovery Adoptees. People who didn't know they were adopted until they were adults."

"Wow." I couldn't imagine. My parents and I didn't pass as biological relatives; my adoption was conspicuous. Some of the people at the LDA table were as old as my grandmother.

"Some of them didn't discover their adoption papers until after their adoptive parents died!" Dana exclaimed. "Their whole lives. Nobody told them."

I shook my head. "That is so messed up."

In one corner of the room, a black posterboard with names and photos was surrounded by candles. "Those are adoptees who didn't make it," a tall balding man said sorrowfully. "Did you know that adoptees are four times more likely to die by suicide?" I didn't.

Huddling in small circles on folding chairs, we exchanged stories. Many of them were upsetting: stories of abuse, physical and mental. I was stunned at what I was hearing.

"My parents used to scream that I wasn't worth the money they paid for me."

"When I was a teenager, my mother said I was a whore like my birth mother."

I heard stories about sexual assault, about racist grandparents, and worse. I began to understand how random luck had brought me into my family. Black and Asian adoptees talked about being adopted into white families and being the only people of color in their schools, their neighborhoods. I suddenly appreciated my Japanese extended family, our church community, my parents' friends.

We had the option to meet up with a "search angel." Dana and I stood in line to speak with the open-records activist. We watched as others handed over their vital documents, and he shuffled through them, giving advice, pointing the way. I had empty hands. No papers, no precious manila envelope. All I had was the paltry information I'd known all along: the date of my birth, the city where it happened. The name of the agency that had brokered the deal: Spence-Chapin. I had my parents' word that my biological mother was Japanese and my own face that told me that my father was not.

Dana walked me to the elevator. "Do you think you'll come back next month?"

I looked over her shoulder at the crowd of adoptees still in the room. She nodded toward them. "These are our people, huh? I mean, they get it."

I nodded. Our people. "Yeah. I'll be back."

ONE OF THESE THINGS IS NOT LIKE THE OTHER

"She came over and did the white-glove test," my mother told me. Their adoption social worker, Crystal Breeding, literally donned white gloves and ran her finger along every surface of their home. At the time of their home study, my parents were living in a brick apartment building in Fort Lee, New Jersey, in a small cluster of Japanese American families. There weren't many of what my mother called "Oriental babies" available for adoption in New York city in 1959. The social worker had discouraged them from adopting a white infant, and they agreed it would be best to wait for a better "match."

They waited ten years. Finally, they got a call from Crystal Breeding. "We've got a half-Japanese baby," she said. My parents sped over the George Washington Bridge.

Nineteen years later, I called Information to get the number for Spence-Chapin. They were still in business. I asked for Crystal Breeding. My father carried a little snapshot of her holding me in his wallet. Both of us were smiling. But by this time, Ms. Breeding had long retired, and I got an appointment with a social worker named Nancy.

I paused before a brass door plaque with *Spence-Chapin* engraved in simple lettering. I tried to imagine my parents repeatedly walking through these doors over the span of a decade.

My father in his navy-blue church suit, my mother in a wool skirt and good nylons, her hair freshly permed. Every year, they climbed these marble steps. I wondered if my mother shed tears when they told her time and time again, no, not yet, sorry, keep waiting.

Finally, Crystal Breeding handed me to them, wrapped in a pink blanket. I was 106 days old. I had spent two months in the hospital where I had been born, gaining weight after my premature birth. Then I stayed in a foster home for five weeks. Why? Why, when my parents had been waiting for ten years, did I go into foster care for over a month? Years later, I learned that foster homes were waystations where children were fed but not coddled, where they were conditioned to quell their own crying. Docile babies, the agencies learned, were more satisfactory products. My parents, like many others, were pleased and astonished that I was such a "good baby" who never cried.

Nancy, the social worker, met me where I waited on a wooden bench. She was tiny, with salty hair, a dove-gray suit, and eyeglasses on a gold chain around her neck.

"Let's go upstairs to my office," she said and led me into a small, clanking elevator. She held a manila folder against her body with both hands. I stared at it. The story of my beginnings was in that folder. She saw me looking, and her fingers tightened.

We walked down a hallway with black and white hexagonal tiles. In her office, she gestured to a chair on the opposite side of an immense oak desk, a barrier the size of a casket. Both of her hands were flattened, palms down, on the folder, until I sat.

"Let me say what a pleasure and a joy it is to have one of our own babies return to us!" she said. "You're a Spence-Chapin alumna!"

This is an adoption agency, not a college, I wanted to say. But I held my tongue.

She leaned back into her chair. "Tell me. What was adopted life like for you?"

I was startled. I hadn't expected this. Would my response

determine if or how much information I would receive? I spoke carefully. "My parents were—*are* wonderful. My life was good."

She scribbled on a yellow pad. I imagined her writing. PARENTS: WONDERFUL. LIFE GOOD. "When did they tell you that you were adopted?"

"What?"

I don't remember ever *not* knowing. For many years, I believed it was the way all babies came into their families. They were "gotten," as I had been, from some baby place, a place like this. There was a disconnect between coming from the baby place and actually being born.

I said, "When I was very young."

"And how was it, growing up with Japanese parents?" She put her finger on a line in my file. I wondered if it said, *Half-Caucasian baby placed with Oriental parents.*

"It was fine. Except . . ." I looked out the window, at the white winter sky, the gray and brick buildings across the street. The rough song of traffic rose up.

"Except?" She looked at me over her eyeglasses.

"Sometimes, I wished I wasn't different from them. I wished I was all Japanese. It was just too—obvious." I looked at my big, square un-Japanese hands, the fine dark hairs on my knuckles.

I remembered a high school friend once singing that *Sesame Street* song, "One of these things is not like the other, one of these things just doesn't belong," and then pointing at the family portrait on top of the piano. *Hey, just like you.*

"Obvious?"

"That I was adopted."

"You didn't like being adopted?" She was beginning to bug me. I was the one who had come with questions, and now I was being interrogated.

"I didn't *mind* being adopted. But I hate all the questions people ask. Like—What are you? What's your other half? Who are your real parents?" I glanced at the folder on her desk. "I mean, that's why I'm here. For answers."

"Of course. Well, first of all, let me tell you that the information I have gathered is what we call 'non-identifying information.'" She hooked her index fingers in the air.

I squinted at her.

"That is, I can give you rough details about your background, but no specific names or places."

My eyes smarted, and I nodded. This is what the ALMA search consultant had warned—that agencies would only divulge vague or non-identifying information. I had really been hoping for more. I had hoped she would have seen what a fine, intelligent adult I had grown into and would give me all the details from that folder.

I slumped in my chair. "Okay."

"You might want to take notes." She opened the file.

"Oh!" I had expected to be given something. Papers. I scrabbled in my purse and pulled out a tiny notepad, no bigger than a matchbook. She slid a pen across the desk.

She scanned a page with excruciating slowness. "First of all. Your mother cared very much about you. She had great concern for your well-being."

Okay. *And you know this how?* It sounded like boilerplate language to me.

She ran her finger down the page. "You were born on August 11, 1959."

"I *know*."

Nancy skimmed the pages, spoke a few words, then flipped the paper and scanned the next one. She was just picking up crumbs to toss at me across her desk.

"Your birth mother was of—Japanese descent. She was five feet four inches tall and weighed 125 pounds." My heart jumped. Those were my measurements, exactly.

She went on. "She was college educated and working as a professional in the Midwest. She was twenty-seven years old at the time of your birth."

Twenty-seven! I thought she had been a student. My adoptive mother had told me that my birth mother was a college student, too young to keep me. But twenty-seven! A professional! Twenty-seven was old enough to be a mother. My skin prickled with a vague pain.

And what was this about the Midwest? I had been born in New Rochelle, in Westchester County, home of Dick Van Dyke.

"Wait, wait. What do you mean, the Midwest? What state?"

She pursed her lips. "I can't be more specific than that."

"Why—was I born in New York?"

"I can't tell you that."

I groaned. "Go on."

"Her parents were both born in Japan." Just like all four of my adoptive grandparents. "Her family was originally from the West Coast, but after World War II, they were relocated to—the Midwest." I scrawled notes. *West Coast — WAR → Midwest.*

"Does it say anything about my father?"

"He was of Caucasian descent. He was five feet ten inches, with dark hair and a stocky build."

"Could you be more specific? I mean, what *kind* of Caucasian?"

"I'm sorry, no." She kept skimming and reading. "I can tell you that his father made a living as a mortician. His mother was a homemaker, and he had a sister who was a schoolteacher." I scribbled onto the tiny pages. His sister. I had an aunt!

She told me that I had stayed in the hospital from August 11 to October 19, and then I had come to Spence-Chapin. I had stayed in a foster home in Queens for five weeks.

Foster home? "The foster mother reported that you enjoyed being propped in a corner of the couch to watch the activity of the rest of the family."

The rest of the family? What family?

". . . You went home to your parents at the end of November, right after Thanksgiving. Your adoption was finalized in January." She closed the folder and smiled brightly. "And you know the rest!"

The folder she guarded so closely was thick with papers. She had read to me, at most, a page worth of information. What else was in there? It enraged me that she had such easy access to my life, to my story, yet was choosing to give me crumbs.

I wanted to vault over the casket-desk and wrest the papers from her hands. I was larger, younger, and stronger than this sanctimonious bird. I wished I had the courage to grab my file with my information, my details. But I couldn't bring myself to overpower her. Instead, I thanked Nancy with the politeness my parents had taught me and headed to the elevator with the few scraps of information she had doled out.

I still had a thousand questions.

WHAT DO YOU NEED?

I needed to tell my parents what I was doing. I was tired of sneaking into the city for ALMA meetings every month, trying to hide, terrified that I would somehow run into them. I imagined them driving in the city one day and looking out the window, perplexed, saying, "Isn't that Susan?"

I stared at a photo of my parents and grandmother tacked to the wall of the house I rented in Ithaca. They were chest deep in the clear green water of the Atlantic Ocean, leaning on the blue canvas raft that my father had inflated by mouth. He made a ceremony of unwrapping it, testing it for leaks, and patching it with special glue. This raft saw us through years of Miami Beach vacations, from the time I was a toddler and it held me like a floating bed until adulthood. In this photo, the raft was faded to the color of worn jeans. My mother's white plastic bathing cap was strapped under her chin. Both she and my father were tan as walnuts. My grandmother grinned in her ancient, 1930s bathing suit. They were smiling for me, and in their smiles I could see that everything was right in their world.

How could I explain my searching to them? There was only one answer: because I needed to know. I needed to know the answer to the question people constantly asked me. *What are you?* Where are you from? Are you Jewish? Are you Italian? Are you Hawaiian? I knew half of that answer, and the rest dangled uncertainly. I was half-Japanese. And half what? I had no idea.

During a weekend visit home in New Jersey, I rummaged around their house, looking for papers. I snooped. In the metal file cabinet in the basement, I found a single file labeled "Susan's Papers." I found some letters from a lawyer. I pulled out a single page of typed instructions. *5:30am: Baby awakens, is given a bottle, is burped and put back to bed. 9:00am: Baby sleeps until this hour; she is given her vitamins directly from a dropper, bathed and dressed. She is given a bottle at 10:00 and burped.* A scheduled regimen of bottles and burping around the clock. On the back, my mother's careful handwriting, a recipe for formula: evaporated milk, water, and sugar.

According to this paper, I lived in a place with a couch and a carriage, where the "boarding mother" fed me on schedule. Nancy, the social worker, had echoed what it said on the paper, that I enjoyed being propped in a corner of the sofa to watch the activity of "the family." How many people lived in this house? Were there children hovering around my crib, slipping their fingers into my palm to let me squeeze, bobbing a stuffed bear in my face? Would my heart jump if I saw that boarding mother on the street? Would I recognize her smell? My chest ached with the emptiness of not knowing.

I found something else in that folder. A Polaroid photograph, chemically streaked along the bottom, of a small Japanese boy, maybe a year old, sitting in a swing. His hands were resting on the wooden bar. Whoever was pushing him had stopped, perhaps to come around and snap this photo. The boy's legs hung suspended, still. His black hair was cut in rice-bowl style, his eyes large and curious, his mouth opened in a small circle. On the back was his birthdate, 1958, in English characters, and the rest filled with Japanese characters I couldn't decipher. His birthdate was a year before mine. When I saw this, a shudder ran through me. Was this baby offered to them before me? A Japanese boy.

They told me they had asked for a Japanese girl. By 1958 they had already waited ten years when they may have been offered this boy, from Japan, who would have blended into their family seamlessly. They said no. Obviously they said no because he never appeared in the family. Instead, they waited another year until Crystal Breeding called about a girl, but hanbun-hanbun. Yes, they said. We'll take her.

I wondered if they ever regretted not adopting the boy. Where did he end up? Who became his parents? Who was his original family? Was he still in Japan? This man was almost my brother, almost an Ito. Where would I have ended up, had my place as an Ito been taken? It was impossible for me to comprehend.

There were too many questions. They swarmed around me like a million invisible, maddening gnats. I brushed them away, but they just returned. I was choking on questions.

So I wrote them a letter. I told them.

After a week of chewing my nails down to bloody nubs, the phone rang. It was my mother.

"We got your letter."

I couldn't breathe.

"We were wondering. What took ya so long? We've been waiting for this for years." She sounded like a Brooklyn cabby.

"Oh."

"So. Ya need any help?" She was utterly unsentimental. Practical in every way. And they asked their usual question: *What do you need?*

Every time my father went on the road, packed up the car, and turned south toward Virginia, toward North Carolina and Tennessee, he said to me, "Anything I can get you on the road? Anything I can do for you?"

Once on a road trip, we stopped at a Cajun restaurant owned by one of his customers in Atlanta. I loved their special house made salad dressing, made with fresh eggs and cream and cayenne. And for years, whenever he was in Georgia, he bought a glass quart jar of it and packed it in ice in a Styrofoam cooler to bring home to me. He refilled the cooler with fresh ice every night and finally returned home to New Jersey, bearing the glass jar. He made me salad with tomatoes picked out of the backyard garden, tossing in the Cajun house dressing with oversized chopsticks.

"Is there anything you need?" I didn't know if it broke their hearts that I was doing this search, but if it did, they didn't show it. They were soldiers at the ready.

"Well. There is something." I told them what the ALMA search consultant had suggested at the last meeting, about requesting a copy of the adoption record from the county courthouse. This official record of my changing, from the name I received at birth, to the person I became, was a key document. My parents hadn't received it when I was first adopted, but they could pretend that they did.

I gave my mother the January date that I had gotten from Spence-Chapin, when my adoption was finalized in court. "Can you call the courthouse?" I asked. "Just tell them you used to have the paper, but it got lost."

"Sure," she said. "I can do that."

She called the courthouse and lied. She wrote herself a script in her secretarial shorthand and read from it at the kitchen table. "It must have gotten lost when we moved," she said. "We just need a new copy."

A week later, an envelope bearing the seal of the State of New Jersey was in my hands. My name was Mika Noguchi.

A SMALL CRIME

Mika Noguchi. I whispered the unfamiliar name into the cold, silent air. I was alone in the wooden house perched at the edge of Ithaca's Cayuga Lake. Everything outside was white: the sky, the frozen surface of the lake, the snow-covered pines against the shore. My housemates were away. Bitter cold permeated the house, but I was sweating.

The manila envelope held the first clue to my past.

Since it had arrived in the mail a few days prior, I had bent and unbent the metal clasp so many times, it had broken off. I pulled out the two sheets of paper to reread them again.

The plaintiffs, MASAJI ITO, age 42 years, and KIKUKO ITO, age 38 years, have had the child MIKA NOGUCHI in their "constant care" since November 30, 1959.

I had been mysteriously born in New Rochelle, New York, one hundred days prior. I kept reading.

The said child shall upon entry of this judgment be known by the name SUSAN KIYO ITO and that the said child be adopted by Masaji and Kikuko Ito . . . as if the child had been born to them in lawful wedlock.

Mika Noguchi. Who had given me this name? A shadowy figure, likely a woman with black hair, sitting up in a hospital bed, writing those four letters of my temporary name on a form. I imagined a nurse with a white cap carrying it away on a clipboard, where it would be sealed away for decades.

My birth mother's name was absent from the adoption decree. All it said was "the natural parents have surrendered the custody and control of the child."

The next thing I would have to unearth was her name. The search consultant had recommended contacting the hospital to get the records from my birth.

"You'll have to lie a little for this part," he said. My adoptive mother had lied, and successfully.

I was ready.

I dialed the number of New Rochelle Hospital, the only hospital in the town on my birth certificate. I asked for medical records. A woman answered the phone as if she was singing. "Hellooooo, may I help you?"

I started with the truth. "Hello. I was born in your hospital. In 1959." Then, the lie tumbled out. "I'm pregnant now, and my mother—" I hesitated.

"Yes?"

"My mother passed away when I was a child." I prayed that this part of the lie would not turn out to be true. I crossed my fingers behind my back. "I heard she had problems when I was born? And, um, my doctor would like the records from my birth."

"Certainly." A rustling of papers. I couldn't believe she was agreeing, so easily. Just like that. "Tell me again, your date of birth and patient's last name?"

"August 11, 1959." I spelled out the name from the adoption paper. "N-O-G-U-C-H-I."

"And your current obstetrician's name?"

"Oh." I hadn't thought this part through. I grabbed the phone book from the top of the refrigerator and flipped through the flimsy yellow pages. PHYSICIANS. "Just a second. Sorry, it's . . ." OBSTETRICS & GYNECOLOGY. "Dr. Fogel. James Fogel."

"And his address?"

I read the tiny print.

"I'll take care of it right away. And what was your name again, Mrs. . . ."

"Ito. It's Ito." I blurted it out without thinking. Mrs. Ito? That's what my adoptive mother was called. "It's my—married name?" I crossed my fingers.

"Great, Mrs. Ito. You have a good day now!" I imagined the medical records lady with platinum-blonde curls, bubble-gum-pink fingernails, and a bluebird on her shoulder. As soon as I hung up, I realized that without thinking, I had given her the address of this random doctor, a man I had never met. How would I get the records from him?

I waited a week, then called Dr. Fogel's office. I used my birth name. "This is Mika Noguchi Ito. Have my medical records arrived?"

There was a slight hesitation, and then, "Yes. We did receive some records with the name Noguchi." She pronounced it *Naw-gutchy*. "They were so old, though. Black records, on microfiche. We didn't know what to make of them. Are you a current patient here?"

"No, not yet, but I'm pregnant, and . . ."

They told me I could come in for the next available appointment.

Two days later, I dressed in an oversized denim dress. I awkwardly applied pharmacy makeup. Did I look pregnant? In the mirror, I saw a round-cheeked, dark-haired girl with thick eyebrows. I could pass for any age from twelve to twenty-five. I could pass for an olive-skinned European, maybe Hawaiian or Mexican. I couldn't tell if I looked Asian or not. I slipped a braided silver ring with a moon face onto my left hand.

In the parking lot of Finger Lakes Obstetrics, I dawdled in my Toyota hatchback. Here I was, impersonating a pregnant woman.

A married woman. An imaginary woman named Mika Noguchi. A person who never really existed. I had carried that name as a secret even to myself, an anonymous infant left in New Rochelle Hospital.

At the medical receptionist's window, I signed that name in unfamiliar, bogus handwriting. I waited for a piercing alarm that would shriek imposter, fraud, liar, thief. The bored-looking receptionist with white plastic earrings handed me a clipboard. There was a section labeled Family Medical History. I printed in ballpoint pen with an almost violent pressure: UNKNOWN. I scanned the other women in the room, real pregnant women, and wondered how many of them would keep their babies. I strained to imagine the Japanese woman who gave birth to me and wondered if she ever sat in a doctor's office with a fake ring on her finger.

I waited. I waited some more. I watched other women struggle to their feet, their bellies unwieldy. Some had men with them, husbands or partners offering an arm or an elbow for support. My throat tightened with inexplicable emotion. She probably had no support. Or did she? I had so many questions. Was she a college student, like I was? Twenty-seven seemed too old for a typical college student at that time, but that was the story my adoptive mother had told me. Was she alone, carrying me like a basketball under her dress? Did she have anyone to confide in?

Finally, a nurse with a freckled face and red hair called out, "Mike-ah?" I didn't correct her. I assumed that the name was pronounced in the Japanese way, "Mee-ka," but what did I know? She held up a manila folder. It had new orange tabs on the side. "Follow me."

I watched her slip the folder into the wooden box fastened to the exam room door. "Please remove everything, including panties." She patted a blue paper gown. "Keep this open in the front. Doctor will be in, in a minute."

I was alone in the room. I regarded the gleaming stirrups at the end of the table. I had never had a pelvic examination, and I wasn't ready for one now.

Sitting in a straight-backed wooden chair, I tried to imagine the next sequence of events: I would undress. The doctor would enter the room and examine me. I would be naked except for a blue paper gown, opened in the front. I slipped off my clogs.

A box of sterile gloves, similar to a tissue box, sat on the counter. They smelled like latex and powder, and I thought of the rubbery sound they would make when they were snapped onto a pair of hands. I imagined gloved fingers inside me, probing. The tray of instruments—the duck-billed speculum, a bouquet of long-stemmed swabs, sat waiting.

He was going to know. Within minutes, he would realize that I was not pregnant at all. And then what would I do? Would I have to beg, naked and supine, for my blackened, ancient birth files?

I inhaled as deeply as I could. I squeezed my eyes shut and prayed that Dr. Fogel would be a compassionate man. If I was lucky, he'd shake his head at the injustice of sealed birth certificates and inaccessible adoption records. I imagined him chuckling in an avuncular way and handing me the folder. "Of course you're entitled to these!" he'd say.

No. Not likely.

I unfolded the paper gown. I imagined my naked body inside the scooped neck, the open front. Even though I was still fully clothed, I was shivering. Maybe when the doctor came in, he would scoff at me, or laugh. Maybe he would be angry that I lied and wasted his time. He could call the police. Could he? Was this a crime?

I looked at my watch. Three minutes had passed since I came into the room. There was only one thing I could do. Without hesitating, I left the paper gown, half-unfolded in a blue origami shape, on the table and slipped my clogs back on. I stood and opened the door. I lifted the manila folder out of the box next to the door and slid it under my coat, against my chest. I race-walked down the corridor.

I passed the receptionist at her desk. Her earrings dangled like full moons, glowing.

"I forgot something in my car," I said, holding up an index finger. "I'll be back in a minute."

The door to my Toyota was unlocked. I threw the folder on the passenger seat, shoved the key into the ignition, and backed up, making a harsh, violent sound on the gravel. I didn't look back. I pulled into traffic and drove while my birth mother's name waited patiently on the seat beside me. I didn't stop to read it, or to breathe, until I was miles north of Ithaca. I didn't touch the folder, holding the story of my birth, until I was surrounded by forest and snow, until I was certain that any Ithaca police cars with their flashing blue and red lights were far behind me.

WHAT I DID OVER SPRING BREAK

I worked weekends and afternoons at the Old Europe Deli on State Street, on the edge of downtown Ithaca. My boss was a bony, narrow-faced man named Gunter. He taught me how to handle great slabs of meat and cheese and how to use the electric slicer. I learned that some people liked their sandwich meat cut thick and others in slices so thin they were almost transparent. I was afraid of getting my hand stuck in the slicing machine, the blade whining through my thumb.

Most of our customers were older men—townspeople—and grad students from Cornell. While I worked the register and wiped the glass on the deli case, my boss sat at a table in the front window, drinking coffee and playing cards with his friends. The metal bell would clang when customers walked through the front door. Gunter gestured toward me. "Pretty, isn't she? Why don't you ask her to make you a nice sandwich? Meat sliced to order."

One of the regulars was Henry, a short, dark-haired grad student. He had bright black eyes and an insistent voice.

"What are you studying?" he asked me. "Do you have a boyfriend?" I did have a boyfriend, and I said so.

Henry came into Old Europe almost every day and ordered a sandwich with Black Forest ham and dark, grainy mustard. He preferred it sliced thin. He chatted with Gunter and set up camp at one of the tables. For hours, he drank from the same cup of coffee and scribbled on index cards. Although he was getting a master's degree in music, he had a personal obsession with UFOs. He penciled sightings and encounters on these cards and held them together with a rubber band. I yawned as he told me about the clustered areas where aliens were certain to have come close to our species.

"So," he said to me, "you must be obsessed with something. What is it?"

I blurted it out before I could think. "Finding my mother." I told him about stealing my hospital records from the gynecologist's office. I had her name now, which I couldn't stop scribbling and whispering to myself. *Yumiko Noguchi*. She was real. But the New Rochelle phone number from the medical file had long been disconnected. I was at a dead end.

His eyes glistened. "What will you do now?"

I shrugged. "I don't know."

"Bring me what you've got. I'll see what I can do." He leaned on the deli counter and took notes on his little cards while I told him about my search: going to the ALMA meetings, Spence-Chapin, my parents requesting the adoption records. I talked until my mouth was dry. I hadn't realized how much I had needed to share this with someone. My boyfriend had limited patience for my birth family obsession. I wasn't sure if he was jealous of the attention it drew away from him or if, as he said, he was worried about me getting hurt. The rawness of my need made him uncomfortable.

Henry didn't judge my need to know; he fanned it with his questions, with his bright snapping eyes and his insistence. "Tell me more." I told him everything, until it was time to close the deli, and I crunched the door shut against the snow piled up on the sidewalk.

The next day, I brought him my folder of papers: the tiny notes from Spence-Chapin, the copies of blackened microfiche from the hospital, the adoption papers, my altered birth certificate with my adoptive parents' names.

The snow in Ithaca was no longer beautiful. The sides of my Celica were crusted with ice and salt, and freckles of rust had appeared. Everyone spoke incessantly about getting away from winter, about escaping to someplace warm. Someone in physiology class brought in a brochure for a student trip to Bermuda, and we passed it around, sighing with longing. Pink sand and palm trees, a golden sun shining down. And it was affordable. If I worked extra shifts for Gunter at the deli, I could earn enough to go.

I needed to get away. I had become single-minded about my search, and my academic life was slipping away. I was struggling hard in anatomy, in physiology, in the whole mess of my physical therapy program. Instead of reviewing muscles and bone attachments in anatomy, I was reading every book on adoption in the library.

Back during freshman orientation in the physical therapy program, the director had boomed into the microphone: *Look to your right. Look to your left. Two-thirds of you won't graduate.* There was a collective clenching of armrests as everyone vowed, *not me*. But he was right. Some of my closest friends had changed majors, dropped out, or transferred to other colleges. I was hanging on by a thread.

I called the toll-free number for the Bermuda trip. I gave them my name and address. But two weeks later, other girls from my class were excitedly showing the packets they had received in the mail. They had sent in their checks and gotten their tickets and confirmation numbers. They were buying swimsuits by mail order and stocking up on sunscreen.

I hadn't gotten my ticket yet.

I called the travel agency. The woman on the other end insisted that she had sent my packet long ago. The student discount date had passed, and the only packages left were full price, way out of my reach. I was crushed.

I didn't want to spend my spring break in New Jersey. Even though my parents had responded in a supportive way about my search, I was still nervous about seeing them in person. Shadows of guilt and apology lived in my face.

I called my high school friend Gina. We hadn't seen each other since graduation, when we'd separated and headed hundreds of miles apart for college. But she and I had bonded deeply in junior high. We were both only children, which was uncommon back then. She had grown up with her mother and two aunts, a household of women. Gina's parents had separated when she was a baby, and she had never known her father. We wondered together who and where our invisible parents might be.

Gina had fallen in love with Bruce in college and was one of my first friends to get married. It was hard for me to fathom someone my own age as a wife, but they seemed happy. She urged me to come and visit them over spring break. It was snowing where they lived, too, but she made it sound fun.

"Come see us, Susanito!" She always said my name in one unbroken rush. "We'll go cross-country skiing through the zoo."

I missed her. I called the travel agent and booked a flight.

The next day, Henry arrived at Old Europe before my shift. I found him pacing in front of the locked door. While I fumbled with the keys and turned on the lights, he was waving a fan of index cards in front of my face.

"Look, Mika. Look. I did it!"

"Don't call me that. Please. It's not my name. Not anymore." For a while, this new name had fascinated me, then scared me. It was like that other person, Mika Noguchi, was a ghost, living an invisible parallel life. The life I would have had.

"But it's a beautiful name. It fits you. Now—look! Look what I found." He held up cards filled with rows of phone numbers. They were coded by state. Arrows and question marks in colored pencil filled the margins. Four final numbers, circled in red.

"What is this?" I squinted at the marks he had made.

"These are all the people in the Midwest, roughly nineteen

states altogether, because it's not exactly clear what states comprise the Midwest. Anyway, it's all the people, publicly listed in phone directories, with your mother's maiden name. I went through them at the Cornell library." He beamed. I imagined him surrounded by towers of white pages, poring through them with a magnifying glass.

I sat down on one of the rickety chairs. "Where are they?"

The plane ticket was tucked in my purse. The city where Gina lived was the same place where the final Noguchi was listed.

That week, I was the only inhabitant of the lake house. My housemates had fled early for spring break, sun-warmed vacations. I could hear the creaking of ice along Cayuga Lake, frozen branches scratching the roof above my head. Despite my years as a Girl Scout, I had never learned to build a fire. The brick fireplace gaped, exhaling frigid air.

There was one last scribbled phone number on the index card that Henry had handed me. Three numbers had been dead ends: either disconnected, or they had never heard of my birth mother. There was one number left. I picked up the house phone and dragged it into my room, the cord twisting under the door like an umbilicus.

"Gina, I need your help."

"What is it, Susanito? I'm so excited to see you. You're still coming, aren't you?"

"I'm definitely coming." My suitcase was already packed with winter clothes. "But listen." I told her about Henry, his index cards, the list of phone numbers. I told her that the last phone number had the same area code as hers.

"Please, Gina. Would you call her for me? It's a local call for you. It won't cost anything. I just . . . I'm so nervous, I can't do it."

"Sure you can, Susanito. You can do it."

"But I can't." I started crying like a child. It was the final call, and dialing those last numbers would mean one of two things:

either it would mean I had found my birth family, or it meant that my trail would be cold again. The beginning, or the end.

Gina finally took mercy on me. "Okay, Susie. I'll give it a try." She sighed. "Give me the number."

I hugged the phone in my lap as I waited for her to call back. The white princess phone had a long, twisted cord that could snake down the hallways into any of our rooms. I cradled it against my chest, underneath a thick layer of blankets as I curled up on my bed.

It rang so loudly the jangling erupted against my guts. "Hello! Gina?"

"Susie." Her voice was low and tender. "Susie, are you sitting down?"

"I'm *lying* down. Tell me."

"Ye-es." She was almost whispering.

"It's okay. You can tell me. Just tell me!"

"That number I called. It was Yumiko's brother."

"Oh my god." My hands, numb now, almost dropped the phone.

"She lives *here*, Susanito. She lives right here in my town. He gave me her married name, her address, her phone, everything. He gave me everything."

"I don't believe it." I grabbed the plane ticket from my desk. I would be there in three days. "Gina. Tell me every word. Start at the beginning."

She relayed the conversation to me in slow, exquisite detail. The phone had rung three times. I wrote this down on a notepad. *Rang 3x.* Then a man's voice (my uncle!) had answered. They each said hello. Gina said she was looking for someone named Yumiko Noguchi. An old friend, she'd said. The man said, that's my sister, she's not at this number.

Gina said, do you mind? And he said, not at all. "And then he just gave it to me. He said she had a new, married name. She lives with her family."

"Family!" I squawked. My heart was skidding from one side of my chest to the other.

I grabbed the plane ticket and stared at it. She was there. In the city I was traveling to in three days. My mother.

I took a small gulp of air from high in my throat. "Gina. One more favor."

She laughed. "You want me to call her. I know you. Well, I don't think so. This is *your* mother."

"Please."

"Why can't you do it?"

I sat up in my bed. "I'm afraid. I'm afraid I'll die. I'll have a heart attack. I feel like I'm having one right now. Please, Gina, call her and make sure she's the right person. See if she's willing to talk to me or meet me. Please."

A long sigh. "All right, Susie. I'll do it. Because I love you like a sister."

I started crying again. "I love you too."

The next wait was longer. I got out of bed. I paced and fretted, flicking on all the lights in the house. I lit all the candles I could find. I stuffed the fireplace with newspaper balls and some broken-down cartons we'd left on the porch. I sat in front of the hearth with a box of matches and lit little blazes on the grate, glittering roses of fire that lasted no more than a few seconds. The paper and cardboard curled into itself, burned brightly, hissing and whispering, then darkened into a pile of ash. I struck match after match until the phone rang again.

"Susie. I think I need a drink after that."

"What! What happened? What did you say? What did she say?"

"Well. It was her. It's definitely her." There was a low, somber tone to her voice that scared me.

"Oh Jesus."

"I'm going to tell you everything. Just listen." She sounded weirdly harsh and impatient.

I swallowed. Maybe I had asked too much. "I'm listening." I grabbed my notebook and pen, ready to write.

"She answered right away."

"What was her voice like? Was she friendly?"

"Well, it was nice at first. Very cheerful, like, you know. Helll-ooo? Like that. Musical."

"Uh huh. Then what?" I wrote down, *Musical. Cheerful.*

"I asked if she was Yumiko Noguchi. She said yes. I told her my name, and I said I was calling for a friend. Then she got quiet. I think she knew right away. I said, my friend's name *used to be* Mika Noguchi. I told her your birth date. Then I asked, 'Do you know who I'm talking about?' And she said yes."

"She said YES? Just like that?" My face was fever hot. I pressed my cold fingers to my cheeks, and they burned. "Then what? Then what?"

"She asked how I had gotten her number. I said, from her brother. She made a kind of sharp noise like a gasp, and she asked if he knew why I had called. I said no. Then she was quiet."

"So what did you say? What happened then?"

"She said she couldn't talk. She said she had family around." Family. Family??

"Did you tell her I was coming this week?"

"Yeah. I told her." Gina's voice was far off, so small sounding.

"Do you think she'll want to see me?"

"I don't know, Susie. She sounded, um, kind of ticked off."

"Upset? She was upset?" *I've upset my mother.*

"Well, I think it shocked her. The whole thing. You know." That was me, the whole thing.

Of course she was shocked. I was the one waiting for this moment for years, and I was shocked too. I felt as if I'd been electrocuted.

"So then?"

"She asked for my number. She said she'd call me back another time. I gave it to her, and then she hung up. That was it."

I was breathless, panting. "Oh my god, Gina. You talked to my *mother*."

Henry's car pulled up to the curb as I was locking the door to Old Europe, the day before my flight. He climbed out and stared at me with his black eyes. He was wearing a pin on his jacket, a tiny silver alien face. "Are you nervous?" he asked.

"Nervous? I'm going out of my mind. Everyone's away on spring break, and nobody knows what is happening except you and Gina." It suddenly struck me that he had made this happen.

I invited him to my house. He brought a bottle of champagne, and we poured it into mismatched coffee mugs. The bubbles sparked up and hurt the inside of my nose. I made some fried bologna omelets, and we carried them down the rickety steps to the lake on paper plates. It was strangely warm, the first day of March. Maybe spring was coming.

After we ate, I drove the four hours to my parents' home in New Jersey. It was after midnight by the time I pulled into the U-shaped driveway in front of the mint green ranch. The less time at the house, the better, to have to pretend that my life wasn't about to blow apart. The light in my parents' bedroom was glowing yellow, and I knew they were waiting up for me—my father polishing his black work shoes, my mother playing solitaire on the chenille bedspread.

I unlocked the front door. My father appeared suddenly, in his striped bathrobe and rubber zori. "Hey, Sus!" I could tell how happy he was to see me, smiling with all his teeth, moving back and forth from foot to foot. I'd stood in that same spot so many times, waiting for him to come home from his road trips. His job as a traveling salesman kept him on the road for weeks. "Welcome home, Sus! I wish you didn't have to come and go so fast."

I hauled my suitcase up the steps. "It's late," I said. The tears were tight in my throat.

"Mommy's in the ofuro," he said, gesturing toward the little bathroom. I could hear her splashing behind the door.

She emerged a few minutes later, all creamed up, her hair studded in bobby pinned curls. I kissed her warm cheek and yawned. "It's late," I said.

I went into my childhood room and shut the door. I lay in the single bed, surrounded by stuffed animals, my lion and my wombat. Posters of the Eagles and Butch Cassidy and the Sundance Kid on the walls. I promised myself I would tell them everything when I got back.

The next morning, my father climbed the steps from his basement woodworking shop. He was wearing his low-slung blue jeans, sprinkled with sawdust, with a limp beige cardigan. He put his keys in his pocket and changed his shoes, just like Mister Rogers. He took off his canvas sneakers and put on his black leather shoes, shiny and old-fashioned.

I watched him unbutton the worn, pilly sweater and thought of the days I'd stayed home sick from school. On those days, I'd take it from his closet to wear over my pajamas. The sweet, cut-wood smell of it and its limp comfort had embraced me. I suddenly wanted to climb back into my little bed, wearing my father's old sweater. I wanted to crawl into their bed and tell them where I was going. Instead, I flung my suitcases into the trunk of his car, and we drove to the airport.

He parked the car and walked me to the gate, even though I had told him to just drop me off. "It's okay, Sus," he said. "I just want to spend a little time with you." He put his hand on my shoulder and said, "Now you take care skiing. Don't do anything reckless."

"Okay."

"You have a good time. I'm going to stand here till you take off."

I kissed his forehead. In clogs, I was taller than he was. It took everything I had not to unravel. There was a mass of tears wait-ing, pushing at the back of my nose. After I made my way down the accordion-pleated tunnel, through the thick cabin door, they burst out. I sobbed as I pushed my backpack into the overhead bin. I wanted to turn back, to move against the traffic of the other passengers. I wanted to call out, *Daddy, please don't let me leave.* I wanted him to elbow his way through the crowd, pick me up like a little girl and take me home.

I didn't know where I was going, or what was going to hap-pen. I didn't know if it was possible to meet the woman who had made me and to come back the same person.

When I arrived at the airport, Gina greeted me, enthusiastically waving a slip of paper. While I had been suspended in the sky, she had received a phone call from my birth mother. The paper bore Gina's excited scribble: *Holiday Inn—noon—room under the name Noguchi!!!!*

"She called me back this morning. She said she wants to meet you, Susie!" She was married, with a different name, and I carried the name of my adoptive parents. But for a few hours we would meet in an anonymous room reserved under that old name we had both shed.

Gina and Bruce gave me a bus schedule and a map with the hotel location circled. I arrived by bus an hour early and saw an old stone church up the block. Its bulk seemed to promise calm and safety, and without thinking, I walked to the entrance and pushed open the thick wooden doors. I crept into the cavernous sanctuary and huddled in one of the back pews, trembling. It had been years since I'd attended church, and this place was so dif-ferent from our family's Japanese church in New York. But I was on the brink of literally meeting my maker. Waiting these final moments in a church felt somehow fitting.

A pale young man with a conservative haircut and earnest gray eyes approached the pew. "Welcome," he said, and I nodded, wordless. He lowered himself next to me on the worn velvet cushion. "Is there anything you need right now?" he whispered.

I shook my head, and then my eyes welled with tears.

He waited, breathing steadily.

Finally, I stuttered the story out. *I'm meeting my mother. I've never met my mother.*

He listened gravely. "I'll pray with you," he offered.

"Yes. Please." I squeezed my eyes shut and listened to his low, soothing voice. He asked the Lord to bring me courage and calm and an open heart. And love. When he was finished, we both said, "Amen." Then he quietly sat with me for half an hour. The diffuse sun glowed through the stained-glass windows, blurring into rainbows through my frightened tears.

I WOULD MEET YOU AT
THE HOLIDAY INN

"You know, this was all supposed to be confidential." Her voice stung.

I fluttered my hands, not sure how to respond to this woman, my first mother, a mother I had only briefly known and didn't remember at all. "I know. But I want to tell you, the adoption agency really didn't tell me anything. Spence-Chapin." She flinched at the name.

I handed her my adoption papers. "My parents—they got these from the county court." *From this day forward, the child Mika Noguchi shall be known as Susan Kiyo Ito.* One by one, I passed her the blackened microfiche hospital records, charred looking, her name ghostly in white type.

She repeated, "This was all supposed to be secret."

"I went to a support group. For adoptees. They helped me." A muscle in her cheek flinched. I marveled at the color of her lipstick, a sophisticated coral.

She sifted through the documents slowly, with perfect manicured hands. Her fingernails matched her lips. My own fingers twisted against each other, grasping, and I resisted the urge to gnaw at my nails.

She murmured at the doctor's name on the hospital record. "I remember him. He was kind." She seemed to soften. Then she snapped to. "Do your *parents* know you've done this?"

My gut felt punched. "Well, they do know I've been looking, but I didn't tell them we were meeting. Today." I scrambled

59

through the envelope to find a photo of them, waist-deep in the Atlantic Ocean on Miami Beach, their wet, smiling faces.

She gazed at it for a long time before handing it back. "They look—very nice."

"They are."

"When I—when you were born, I wondered if they would be able to find you a Japanese family. I was hoping so."

"They're nisei." Second generation.

She nodded. "Like me." I was heartened by those first small, connective words. She turned her face to the window, at the colorless sky dripping bits of snow. "Were they in camp?"

Camp. I didn't know what she meant at first. I had gone to sleepaway camp from the time I was nine. Camp Tapawingo, on an island in upstate New York, and then Camp Deer Run in the White Mountains of New Hampshire.

Then I understood. "You mean—internment camp."

"Yes."

"No. They were in New York, so they didn't get sent. My father fought in the war, though. He was in the 442nd." I knew she would know those numbers.

"Ah." She nodded and her chin puckered with what looked like a shadow of approval.

"Were you? In camp."

"Yes." Her gaze brushed the ceiling. "I was just a child."

"I'm sorry."

"There's nothing to apologize for." Again, her voice was harsh. I felt stupid. I looked down again at the snapshot in my hands. My guts felt like jelly. I wished I had told my parents. But if I had, they would've worried. They would have fussed and made me buy her a present, *omiyage*. Don't go anywhere empty handed. Even if it's visiting the woman who left you as a baby, you have to bring something. Just a box of omanju, something sweet. They would be circling around the phone now. I couldn't stand thinking about them, worrying about them worrying about me.

She handed the papers back to me. "I admit, I can understand your wanting to do this. But I feel angry about it. I'm sorry. I was promised that this would not happen. I was not expecting it." She folded her hands in her lap. "I never would have gone looking for you. *Never.*"

I nodded. I sat quietly and absorbed the words. Inside my body was a wild howling.

She gestured at the photo of my parents. "I'm concerned about them. Your parents. I wouldn't want them to be hurt."

I chewed the inside of my cheek. "They're fine. Really. They helped me." I took a shaky breath. "I also did this because I wanted to let *you* know. That I'm all right. I thought you might have wondered." *About me. Didn't you wonder about me?*

She inhaled sharply and stared at a fixed point above my head. I turned to see a cheap framed print of a barn in the snow, a broken wheel leaning against the red outer wall. She spoke to the barn, as if I was inside it. "Listen. This happened . . ."

By *this,* she meant me. *I* happened. I was born.

". . . a long time ago. I made a decision, and I had to stick by it, and believe in it, and forget it." Every time she said it, her palm slapped her skirt. "I don't mean to sound cruel, but you never crossed my mind, not in twenty-one years."

I'm twenty, not twenty-one. I couldn't say it out loud. I felt myself evaporating. I imagined myself, trying to cross her mind, the wide barren field of it, invisible.

This was nothing like what I had prepared for. I had tried to prepare for so many potential outcomes: the graveyard mother, the asylum mother, the mother-who-was-really-an-aunt. But I had never tried this out, this particular kind of coldness, a woman who spoke to a barn instead of to my face. I had never crossed her mind.

She didn't look at me. I watched her, though. Her fixation on the painting allowed me the freedom to stare at her. I took in her perfect, chic haircut, an image fit for a magazine. Her spotless black turtleneck, her sand-colored jacket with its clean, elegant lines. A chunky necklace made of rounded pieces of porcelain, held a large

Chinese coin on a length of knotted silk. It looked like something one would buy in an art museum.

I thought of my mother at home. I couldn't help comparing. Her pearl necklace, her wedding rings, the gold brooches my father bought from my uncle's jewelry store. She would never wear an outfit like this. Her wardrobe consisted of plain, squared off skirts, functional buttoned-down blouses, white ankle socks, and loafers.

Finally, my birth mother drew her gaze down from the barn and let it rest on my face.

"I have to be honest. I'm angry. I feel betrayed. I worked so carefully to build a new life for myself, and now . . ." Her hands exploded silently in the air.

And now, I've ruined it. Her new life. I've betrayed her, angered her. My cheeks were wet. I swiped at them with the back of my hand and hugged the manila envelope to my chest, images of the life I had lived with my family. "I'm sorry."

I leaned over and pulled out a red folder that held my fifth-grade autobiography project, titled "It's Only Me." My mother had typed my story and helped me fit the snapshots into the tiny black mounting corners. "Do you want to see this?" I held it out.

"Yes. I love photos." She took the folder and turned the onion-skin pages slowly. They crackled in the silent room. A small smile flickered at the edge of her mouth. She stopped at a photo of me, five years old and serious in a kimono, holding a fan in front of our Christmas tree. "Beautiful," she murmured, and my heart jumped.

She stopped at a photo of me kneeling at the edge of a lake and pointed at the caption. "Camp Tapawingo! Really?"

I nodded. "I went there for two years. It was an island in upstate New York."

"One of my close friends was a counselor there!" She was suddenly animated.

We had something in common. "What was her name?"

Her face slammed shut. "Well, it would have been long before you were there."

"Oh."

She spent an extra moment gazing at one of the first photos my parents had taken of me, wrapped in a blanket in the floor well of their car. This was long before car seats and seat belts. "You just rolled around on the floor, happy as could be," my mother used to say.

I wanted to ask her. I wanted to say, *Do you remember this baby? Did you see me before you left me?* I just watched her as she looked at the four-month-old infant. We breathed together, the hotel room air. The snow continued to fall on the other side of the window. After a long silence, she said, "I brought you in a taxi."

"What?"

"I had to come back, from where I was living. I had to come back to New York when you were ready to leave the hospital. I had to bring you to the adoption agency in person." Her eyes went back to the barn painting.

I held my breath.

"You looked just like this," she murmured. She looked back at the photo, a baby in a car. "They gave me a bottle to take in the taxi." Her lips tightened, and I could see a small quiver in her chin. "You drank it right up."

Time slowed, and I felt my heart booming in my ears. She was talking about a time when we were together, a mother and child in a car. "I was afraid that if you drank it all, you'd want more, and then what?"

I stared at her. And then what. If I had known, if I had only known what was transpiring. That the mother I had not seen or smelled or heard in two and a half months had come back to me. That we would be together for an hour in a car. That she would feed me. And I would fall asleep, lulled by the heat and the movement of the taxi, of her arms, of her lap. I would fall asleep, and when I woke up the car door would open and we would be in a building, I would be moving from her arms into the arms of Crystal Breeding, the social worker, and I wouldn't see her again for twenty years.

We sat, our knees curved toward each other. I thought about the last day we had seen each other, the last time we had touched. So far, on this day, we remained a chair's length apart. We hadn't touched.

I reached into the envelope and drew out some more photographs, formal portraits that had been taken at school. Second grade, my hands folded in front of a picture book, always the same mottled blue-sky background. Later on, the portraits had been modernized, and you could choose between a sky and a smattering of autumn leaves.

She reached out and exclaimed, "Oh, I love school pictures! I find them so touching. Classic. But my children never like the way they turn out." She laughed, as if she had forgotten for a moment who she was talking to. It could be any light conversation with a stranger on a bus.

Wait. My heart sparked in my chest. "My children." She had children. More than one child. More than just me. I leaped. "Do you have any—pictures of them? That I could see?"

I held my breath.

She shrugged. "Well. Nothing recent."

Quickly, I said, "I don't care." Until this moment, I hadn't known I even had half siblings.

She rummaged in her purse and unsnapped a leather wallet. I leaned forward, almost falling out of my chair. How many children? Boys? Girls? My head filled with cold, whirling air.

"Here you go." She slid a small photo out of its plastic sleeve and handed it to me. I cradled it in my palm. A young girl—maybe middle school age? With thick, curly dark hair framing her face, a hanbun-hanbun face. Cheeks like mine, and bushy eyebrows. She wore a red T-shirt with letters embroidered across the chest: MIKA.

I blinked. What? An electric pain scissored through my chest. Why did she have a shirt with my name on it?

Mika. That was MY name. That was my official name. My original name. And here it was, on the body of a girl who looked somewhat like me, but who wasn't me. I started to cry. I tried to be quiet, but I couldn't. I put the photo face down and covered my face with my hands.

I was mortified. I was making a scene. I finally looked up and wiped my face. I saw that she was holding out a tissue. She hadn't said a word. I reached for the tissue and blew my nose and then picked up the photo and looked at it again.

"I'm sorry," I snuffled. "I'm sorry. This was just . . . I didn't expect." I waved at the adoption papers that said, *The child Mika Noguchi shall hereby by known as Susan Kiyo Ito.*

"It's all right." Her voice had softened.

I blinked wetly and touched the little picture. Mika. "How old is she?"

"Seventeen. This picture is old."

I nodded and tried to take it in. I had a seventeen-year-old sister. A sister with my name. "Her name? I mean. I don't understand." I squinted at those four letters emblazoned across her body.

"I know it must be a shock. But it was a name I'd picked. I really liked it. I knew it wasn't a name you would be keeping. So when she was born . . ." She held up her hands and let them fall limply back to her lap.

When she was born, you gave her my name. Because I had evaporated. Because I never crossed your mind.

I swallowed. "What is she like?"

"Oh!" Suddenly my birth mother came to life. She chattered on. Mika is so artistic. She's a free spirit! She's so creative. Here was a proud mother, describing her daughter. I didn't have words for the way that I felt.

"Do you have any—others?"

She pulled another photo from her wallet. A boy, younger, I lightly touched his curly dark hair, his open smile. She told me his name. Kaz.

I looked at both of the photos for a long time, trying to memorize their faces. "Do they—do they know about me?"

"Oh, no." Her face grew suddenly stern. "Nobody knows.

Except, of course, my husband. I did tell him, before we were married. In case it ever came up. I didn't want him to be surprised. But no, they haven't been told."

In case it ever came up.

She stood up, smoothing her skirt. "Would you like to go downstairs? Aren't you hungry?"

Hungry? I felt drained and scooped out. I wasn't sure I would be able to get out of the chair. But, yes, I was hungry.

The elevator was quiet as we descended twelve floors to the ground level. I followed her into the hotel coffee shop with its glass windows open to the snowy street. I could see the stone walls of the church next door, dusted with white. I wanted to shout out to the gray-eyed Christian boy who had prayed with me. Look. Look. Here she is. And I'm still alive.

We slid into opposite sides of a booth and took refuge behind giant laminated menus. This was so strange and so normal, sitting in a restaurant with her. The hotel room upstairs had been such an odd, liminal space, but this was real life. This was being in the world.

A rounded blonde waitress in a gray uniform approached and stood over us, clicking and unclicking her ballpoint pen. "What can I get you ladies?"

I looked at my birth mother. "Yumiko?" I said, and then shrunk back. It was the first time I had spoken her name.

She nodded at the menu with her head, a gesture that said, you go first. Quick. Quickly. Say something. Nothing too messy or smelly. "Um. A club sandwich? And a lemonade." I folded the menu and handed it to her.

"What about you, Mom?" She turned to Yumiko.

I froze, stifling a gasp in my mouth.

Yumiko's voice was stiff. "I'll have the same." The waitress scribbled on her pad and turned back to the kitchen with a slight limp.

I bit my lip. "She said. I mean. Do you think we look—do you think she could *tell*?"

Her eyebrows tilted. "To be honest, I think you resemble me more than Mika does."

"Oh!" I had never heard these words before. That I resembled anyone. That I looked like anyone. I didn't look like my parents or my cousins. I was just me.

"Also, you can call me Yumi. Nobody really calls me Yumiko anymore." I said it silently in my head. *Yumi. You + me.*

I looked at my watch. We were still sitting together, four hours after I had knocked on the room on the twelfth floor. We were still talking, and she hadn't tossed me out into the snow. She had been so angry at first, but here, now, at this diner booth, her eyes had softened. They were crinkling as she talked about Mika. My sister. *Was* she my sister? Because we had slid from the same body? Could she be my sister if she had no idea that I existed? Did her name cancel out my own?

"And you—what do you do?" I dropped the question quietly. Until now, I had been the one providing answers to her questions. I wanted to know so much. I wanted to know everything about her. But every question of mine pierced her anonymity.

She laughed, something I wasn't expecting. "I sell customized Silly Putty!"

"*What*?"

"I'm a manufacturer's representative. That's just a fancy way of saying . . ."

My heart hammered. "I know. That's what my father is!"

"Really." She sat back, her face bemused. "What does he sell?"

I rattled off the list of his dozen companies, mentally going through the ceiling-high cartons in our basement: antique dollhouse furniture, baskets, souvenir ceramics, cloisonne jewelry, knickknacks. It was hard to fathom that she knew this world. I'd never met anyone, outside my father's colleagues, who knew anything about this kind of work.

"Ah. He's in gifts. I specialize in promos—promotional items.

We put a company's logo on cheap giveaways that they can hand out to customers: pens, magnets. We sell a lot of viscoelastic polymer—you know, Silly Putty. It comes in all colors now, even glow in the dark." She seemed genuinely proud.

I giggled into my hands. My birth mother sold Silly Putty.

We finished our lunch. She paid the bill, and I let her. We walked back through the lobby toward the elevators, relaxed and talking easily about small things. I wanted to stop time in this ordinary moment. I was walking with my mother through a roomful of people. This was something that regular daughters did all the time, without thinking. They walked alongside a person whose features theirs echoed. I could feel the swing of our hair, the shape of our faces, our legs of identical length. It was a plain, fleeting miracle of a moment.

As we waited for the elevator doors to open, our gaze drifted through the lobby and landed on a bright neon sign in the opposite corner: Häagen-Dazs. We sighed in unison. "Ice cream!"

Suddenly, we were two women who both wanted ice cream. We race-walked across the lobby, laughing.

"Some people don't believe in eating ice cream when it's snowing, but I think that's nonsense. Don't you?" Yumi's lips twitched. She had suddenly turned sparkly.

"Yes. Definitely yes."

We stood in front of the ice cream counter and perused the offerings. "What do you like?"

I didn't hesitate. "Coffee chip."

Her eyebrows shot up. "That's my favorite flavor!"

I laughed. I didn't want to make too much of a small thing. Liking the same ice cream. Millions of people liked coffee chip, didn't they? But out of the dozens of choices in the glass case, we had zeroed in on the same one simultaneously. Was there a gene for ice cream preference?

She put her hand out when I opened my purse. "I'll get this."

We sat at a little table and licked our cones and shivered from the delicious cold. "And isn't Häagen-Dazs the best brand? The way the chips are so flat. They just melt into the roof of your mouth."

"Yes. Exactly!" Our eyes met over the ice cream. We were in sync. I put my hand on the table to steady myself; I was shaking from bliss. Guitar music and a rough, mystical voice drifted down from the speakers. I sighed. "This music is so nice."

Yumi cocked her head. "Do you know who the musician is?"

I shook my head.

She stood up and approached the counter. "Excuse me. Hello!" A hippie boy with a tangled ponytail asked, "Do you need anything?"

"I'd like to know who is playing this music, please."

He shrugged. "I don't know."

"Would you please check?" She leaned into the glass. I stared. This was something my mother at home would never do. She would eat a restaurant meal that was cold, or too salty, or that was a wrong order. She was the embodiment of the Japanese phrase *shikata ga nai*, meaning "it couldn't be helped." She would just shrug, say "oh well," and then complain about it for days.

The boy ambled back holding a cassette holder. "It's Jimmy Spheeris. *Isle of View.*"

"Pardon me?" Yumi's face turned pink.

"*Isle of View.*" He handed her the plastic box.

"Oh. Oh! Let me write that down." She removed a thin gold pen and notepad from her purse, copied the name from the cassette, and then tore the paper off with a flourish. She handed it to me. "There you go."

I was stunned. "Thank you."

She laughed and then inclined her head toward mine and whispered, "I thought that crazy young man was saying he loved me! *Isle of View!* I love you!"

Back in the hotel room, Yumi kicked off her shoes and removed the pillows from under the bedspread. She propped them against the headboard and stretched out, rubbing her stockinged feet. "This is much more comfortable than those chairs, right?" She gestured toward the other bed.

I lay down gingerly. I couldn't believe how much this woman had changed in the hours since I had first knocked on the door. Was this the same person who had been so angry, so indignant about being discovered? Now, after our ice cream, she looked relaxed and happy. A word bubbled around my heart. Fun. This was fun.

The light was fading outside, and I knew the visit would be ending soon. I wondered if it would be safe to ask the big question I'd been holding all day. I hugged a pillow like a soft shield. I breathed. "I'd like to ask. About my father." I winced, hoping I hadn't destroyed the precious ease we'd been enjoying since the coffee shop.

She nodded slowly. "Of course. Well, it's complicated. I can only tell you a little right now."

"Okay." A little was better than nothing.

She clasped her hands together. "He's a good person. We're still in touch, you know."

I sat up. "You are?" I didn't expect this. I'd heard stories about birth fathers who ditched their pregnant girlfriends or who never even knew they'd produced a child. I thought about the dark-haired man the social worker had described to me.

I wanted to ask, "Is it true that his father ran a funeral home?" but I was afraid it would make her furious if she knew that Spence-Chapin had divulged these details to me.

"Yes." She looked out the window. She spoke each sentence slowly. "He's friendly. Outgoing. He lives in a different state. He's tall. Athletic." Her eyes searched the ceiling, looking for more words.

"Does he have children too?"

"Yes. A few. They're older. Older than you."

"Huh." I blinked. More children, older than me. More siblings. As an only child, I could barely comprehend this thought.

She slid off the bed and stood up suddenly. "Excuse me, I need to use the restroom." I heard water running and she opened the door stiffly. She slid into her shoes. "It's getting late. I need to get back to the family." Oh yes. The family.

"Wait. I need to ask. Did he know? That I was born?"

"Oh, yes." As if it was a given. As if it were obvious.

"Does he know about me, coming here? That we're meeting?"

She took a deep breath. "No, but I will tell him."

"You will? Do you think he'd be willing to meet me too?"

Her palm went up, like a traffic cop. *Stop.* "Not now. But I will let him know." Her eyes slid to the side. "You know, if it wasn't for him, I would have been able to put this all behind me. Completely."

"What do you mean?" I thought she said I had never crossed her mind. *Not once in twenty-one years.*

Her face held a tender little mock-stern expression, like someone who was trying to discipline a child but was too amused. "Well, he kept reminding me. About you. He'd say things like, *She's four years old this year. She's eleven.* He was the one. Who kept track."

I clutched the pillow. He kept track! What?! I wanted to meet him. I wanted to meet this man who never let her forget about me.

"I'd love to meet him. And your husband too. And your children."

A series of storm clouds passed through her expression. "I don't think that would be a good idea." She gathered up her things, tucked the pillows back underneath the bedspread, and then put her coat over her arm. Our time was up.

We descended the elevators and walked through the lobby out to the street. It was dark now, and the snow hadn't stopped. I ducked into the glass bus enclosure to wait for the bus to take me back to Gina's house. The wind blasted tiny flecks of ice against my face. I tried to keep the tears from exploding. I was sure I would never see her again.

She had followed me into the bus stop. I turned to face her. "Thank you. Thank you for getting the room, and for being willing."

"It's all right." She shivered and rubbed her hands together. "Don't you have a warm scarf? Or gloves, even?"

"I forgot them." I put on a polite, cheerful face. "Well, goodbye."

She looked surprised. "Your bus isn't here yet."

"No, but it's coming. You go ahead." *Back to your family.*

She shook her head. "I think I'll wait. I'd like to be sure it really comes. These city buses can be so unreliable." She pushed up her coat sleeve to check her watch and then checked the timetable bolted to the wall. She was acting very motherish.

I blurted out, "I'm sorry. I'm sorry about—I don't know. That things were so hard. That it was such a shock. I know you weren't expecting it."

She opened her mouth. The bus roared up to the sidewalk, a great beast with glowing eyes. It huffed and steamed beside us, and the door squealed open. I turned to her and made my mouth form a smile. "Well. Bye."

"Susan." It was the first time she had spoken my name since she had opened the hotel room door. Her hand rested on my arm. She stepped forward and pulled me into a tight little embrace, her head on my shoulder. I could hear her voice through my hair. "I wouldn't have missed this for anything in the world."

The bus blasted its deep horn, and we jumped apart. I climbed the bus steps sideways, not wanting to take my eyes away from her. She pulled her scarf up to cover her mouth and nose, and her eyes followed me to my seat. The bus swung away from the curb, and she was waving through the whirling flakes, standing in a cone of light under the streetlamp. I rubbed the steam away from the window with the heel of my hand and watched her form shrink smaller and smaller. When the bus turned the corner, she was still there, waving.

PART 2

YOUR MOTHER IS VERY NICE

"She wants to meet you," I told my parents. When I'd told them I'd found my birth mother, they'd been happy for me. I could tell they were pleased she was nisei like they were, that they already felt a connection.

Yumi told me she was traveling to New York for business. Since our first meeting a few months before, we'd become pen pals of a sort. She seemed to be growing more comfortable with the idea of me, and I looked forward to finding sticker-adorned envelopes and packages in my mailbox.

They were eager to know her. My father made a reservation at a sushi place in midtown Manhattan, where we could all meet after church, my mother, father, grandmother, and I.

Growing up in northern New Jersey, I was confused why we commuted an hour to church every week, when our town was dotted with churches within walking distance. But this wasn't just a church. The Japanese American United Church was our community. These people had known my mom and dad—since she was a tough girl playing stickball in Brooklyn, since he roller-skated through the Bronx. Church was an all-day affair that included sermons and hymns in both Japanese and English, followed by a full lunch prepared by the men's, women's, youth, or Japanese-speaking fellowships. This Mother's Day Sunday, it was the men's turn.

George Yuzawa cornered my father in the church stairwell, the gray metal cashbox in his hands. "Masaji! You collecting lunch money today?" My dad enjoyed taking two dollars from everyone, trading their cash for a plastic chip. A chip would buy steaming udon in a cardboard bowl, a banana, and their choice from the cookie tray. Teenagers went from table to table, refilling cups of green tea from swinging brass kettles. That job had held a certain cache when I was younger, playing waitress in the church basement.

My father shook his head. "Not today, George. We're taking Kiku and Obasan out for lunch. Mother's Day, you know." He pointed at the white carnation pinned to his lapel. Everyone wore carnations on Mother's Day—red ones for those with living mothers, white ones for the deceased. Mr. Fujii, a florist, brought them every year. He stood in the vestibule with two boxes of carnations, and a tin container of long pins with fake pearls on the ends.

"Red or white?" he asked. What he really meant was, dead or alive?

I almost said, "Two red, please." For the first time, I had two living mothers.

Mr. Yuzawa said, "Well, have a good time. I'll collect the money today."

He didn't tell George they were meeting my birth mother for the first time.

He turned to me. "Go ahead, Sus, go get Mommy and Nana's coats, and let's take off. I'll fetch the car and wait by the curb." He charged up the steps.

The basement was packed with people, and it took a while to maneuver through the sea of short bodies to get to the coat rack. Part of me was muttering, *Hurry, hurry. Rush so you can see her. The quicker you move the quicker you will see her again.* But part of me was dragging my feet. Part of me wanted to say, *Wait. Let's wait.* I couldn't imagine them all in the same room together. I was afraid to imagine it.

I grabbed my mother's tan trench coat and bunched it up underneath my arm. Why did she have to bring this old coat? Why couldn't she wear something modern, something flattering?

Nobody spoke in the car. My father drove uptown to Edo, a Japanese restaurant where he liked to bring clients. In the window, plastic models of sushi, udon bowls, donburi, and little black cauldrons of shabu-shabu made a colorful display. Yumi was standing outside in a stylish beige trench coat, her black hair lifting a little in the wind.

My heart skittered. "There she is."

Her expression was serious, almost stern, her hands in her pockets. I lowered the car window. "Yumi. Hi."

She turned toward my voice and her face broke open; her smile dazzled. She clipped over and beamed into the car. "Why, hello! Hello! Mrs. Ito! Mr. Ito! Obasan!" They were all bowing, saying hello, hello. I smiled a weird, fake smile as their voices swirled together.

Yumi rushed to take my grandmother's arm and help her out of the car. "Obasan, komban-wah, ah, genki-desu!"

My grandmother's jaw dropped, and her brown eyes went liquid. "Ah! Nihongo!" She speaks Japanese! I thought, *Ten points. Ten big ones.*

My father drove off, headed for a parking garage. The four of us watched the car dissolve into the chaos of city traffic.

"Well," Yumi said, her voice chipper, "it seems they have a table inside all ready for us!" She sounded like a camp counselor.

My mother's brow furrowed. "I hope you haven't been waiting a long time."

"Oh, no. Oh, not at all." Yumi ushered us in, my grandmother first. It was as if she owned the restaurant, as if she were the New Yorker, the host, and not us. Emotions tumbled through me like pinballs. *She's so cool. She's so beautiful. She's so impressive. Is she showing off? Nana likes her! Mom is nervous. Mom is very nervous.* I could tell because my mother was slapping herself in jerky rhythm, responding to some unheard song, slapping her hip through her raincoat, like someone trying to get a horse to gallop.

The hostess, clad in a flowered kimono, showed us to an enclosed booth with thin walls made of shoji paper. I wanted to point out to Yumi, "My father knows how to build shoji screens," but I kept quiet.

My mother jabbed my ribs. "Hey. Remember Gasho?" The Japanese restaurant where I'd waitressed, wearing a similar kimono.

I smiled tightly. I was frozen near the entrance to the little room, staring at the long wooden bench seats with flat indigo pillows. Three pillows on each side. How would we arrange ourselves?

Yumi extended her arm, like Vanna White on *Wheel of Fortune*. "Obasan. You first."

My grandmother clambered awkwardly onto one of the long seats. A pillow slid off the polished wood and fell under the table.

My mother groaned. "Mom, careful! For Pete's sake."

Yumi's voice was smooth, soothing. "It's all right. It's fine. Dai joubu, Obasan." She looked at me. "Susan, you must want to sit next to your grandmother." I nodded, robotic.

"And Mrs. Ito . . ."

"Please. Call me Kiku." My mother's face was shiny from perspiration. She emerged from under the table, holding the cushion. She huffed and tossed it into the booth next to Nana.

"Kiku. Of course. You and Masaji will sit together, right?"

"Sure, sure." My mother slid in opposite me, and then Yumi sat next to me. For the moment, there were three of us on our side of the table, and my mother sat alone. I felt seasick, as if our little boat was about to tip.

The waitress handed out menus and a basket of hot towels. We murmured into the heat.

"Oh, this is my favorite part," sighed Yumi. "What a treat!"

I was glad she was sitting next to me. It made it harder to stare at her. I glanced at her in my periphery, though, her perfect haircut swinging against her chin. She wore a pink suit, soft as flower petals, with a black turtleneck underneath. It was a dramatic background for one of her art-museum necklaces, the centerpiece a ceramic square with squiggles of deep pink and gold, on a chain of heavy beads like berries.

I looked across the table at my mother. Her raincoat was

nearly the same color as Yumi's, but she looked neither glamorous nor stylish. She reminded me of the TV-drama police detective Columbo, rumpled and crooked. I realized that she was the only one still wearing her overcoat; the waitress had taken the others and hung them on hooks.

"Mom," I whispered sharply. "Your coat!" *Minus ten points. Doesn't know how to act in restaurant.*

"Nah, I'm gonna keep it on. I've got a chill." She was being stubborn. She was doing it on purpose. My nostrils flared. *That's great. Look like a slob. Just great.* I buried my face in the menu and decided I would not look at my mother for the remainder of the meal.

My father bustled up to the table, pulling off his coat. "Hi, sorry I took so long."

My mother's eyes squinted. I knew she was about to bark, "What took ya so long?" but then a voice chirped out next to me.

"No problem!" said Yumi.

He eased in next to my mother. "So. What looks good?"

I said I wanted chicken teriyaki. He nodded and looked around the table. My grandmother hadn't opened the menu. She looked inquiringly at my mother, who said, "They have oyaku donburi, Mom, you like that. Or sukiyaki. Long time since you've had that."

It was always like this. My grandmother, in New York since 1920, could still barely read English. She relied on my mother to translate, but it was never a full translation. My mother would skim the entire menu and then offer a few choices. I gritted my teeth. Read her the whole menu, I wanted to shout.

"Yumi? What do you like?" My father glanced at her over his menu.

"Oh! It's so hard to choose. We don't have good sushi where I live, so when I come here, it's such a treat. I don't know. Well, this is one of your favorite spots, right, Masaji? Why don't you just order for me. Whatever you pick will be delicious, I'm sure." She closed the menu with a twinkly smile and handed it to my father.

My father couldn't have been happier. This was his element,

ordering food for people. He loved it. At a table with up to twenty customers or business associates, he'd ask each person what they wanted, down to the salad dressing, side orders, and drinks. Then he'd flawlessly recite it all back to the waiter, pointing at each person with a stubby finger. "The young man in blue will have the filet, done medium rare, with Thousand Island on the salad. His wife, here, wants the snapper. It's fresh today, isn't it?" It was one of his best tricks. *Amaze and astound your friends!* I'd never seen him make a mistake.

He ordered a giant sushi platter to share, which arrived on a beautiful round Imari dish. He pinged its edge with his fingernail and nodded. "Hm. Authentic." Yumi's eyebrow rose.

We unsnapped our chopsticks and reached to the platter for our favorite bites. I watched Yumi dissolve a dab of wasabi in shoyu. "Oh. I can't tell you how special this is. Not since I was little, growing up on the West Coast . . ."

"Oh! You're from out West?" My father asked.

"Originally, yes. But then we were in camp, and after that"— she waved her o-hashi in a swishing movement—"another little town, far from the coast." She put on a bright face. "That was the end of good sushi for us!"

My father put down his chopsticks. "You and your family were in camp?" His face was somber.

"Yes. One of the smaller ones."

"Must have been rough." There was an unfamiliar heaviness in his eyes.

My grandmother clawed at my mother's sleeve. "What? What say?"

My mother answered roughly, "Camp. She was in *war camp.*" Nana grimaced back, her hand over her mouth, shaking her head.

Yumi shrugged. "We were kids. It wasn't so bad. A lot worse for our parents, though. The issei had a rough time."

My father nodded. "A lot of guys in my company, you know, the 442nd, had families in camp. Hard to believe, fighting for the US while their parents are locked up."

I groaned silently. Now my father was going to go off on his war story. *Go for Broke. Not again! Not carrying the hundred-pound radio through Italy!*

I nudged him with my foot. "Dad."

Yumi encouraged him. "You served in the 442nd? Oh my."

"Yeah, over in Italy. It was something over there . . ." Then he started in. The radio. The hardship. Selling the cigarettes my mother sent him overseas. I'd heard it all.

I glanced across the table at my mother, and we shared an eye roll. How many times had we heard this? It was a long time since I'd been mesmerized by Van Johnson and the *Go for Broke* movie. My mother smirked. We tuned out my father's words, his animated gestures, and focused on our food. The only one listening to him was Yumi. Was she just being polite, or was she really interested? She punctuated his stories with "Is that *right?!*" and "Reaa-lly." He was glowing for her, his new audience.

He finally finished the story with a big flourish. "And that was that." He looked around the table. "Oh! Everyone is finished eating except me!" He dove into the cast iron bowl of shabu-shabu, fishing out a limp piece of daikon.

Chewing, he said, "Susan tells us you're in sales as well."

"Yes. I sell promotional items. Mugs, pens, custom Silly Putty."

He sat up, attentive. This was *his* business. They went back and forth, talking about their territories, their merchandise, their lines, the different shows where they represented their wares.

Half an hour passed and none of us—my mother, Nana, or myself—opened our mouths. It was just Dad and Yumi. They were sparkling at each other, waving their chopsticks around. They were like old friends. Maybe they were even flirting. I stole a look at my mother. She was staring dully at the table. She had nothing to add. What would she say? "Oh! I specialize in milk money! I've just learned to operate a Xerox machine. It's a wonderful improvement over those messy old mimeographs."

Finally, the conversation tapered down. The plates were empty but for a few sticky grains of rice.

"That was delicious," Yumi said. "Susan, could you excuse me? I've got to go to the ladies' room." I stood up to let her out.

They all leaned forward, huddling over the table, and said a bunch of complimentary things. My father: "Smart lady. Seems to have a good head on her shoulders." My mother: "Very nice. She seems very nice."

Nana clawed my sleeve with her arthritic hand. "Your mother," she muttered, jerking her chin in the direction of the restrooms. "*Kirei*, neh? Very pretty lady."

My mother! A flush rolled over my skin. I looked across the table. My *mother*—Kiku—was drumming her nails on the table. I didn't respond to my grandmother. But inside I was screaming. *Don't call her that! She's not. Or she was—but she isn't anymore.*

I was confused. Because hadn't I chortled those same words to myself? *My mother! My mother!* Hadn't I been swooning over her too?

I stood abruptly. "I have to go obenjo too."

Yumi and I passed each other in the narrow, steamy hallway that smelled of grilled meat and soy sauce.

She put her hand on my forearm. "Your parents are wonderful. Absolutely wonderful. You are so, so lucky." She beamed her twinkly smile at me and turned back to the dining room. *Your parents.*

I sat in the small windowless restroom, my head in my hands. They liked each other. It all seemed to be going well. It *was* going well, wasn't it? Then why was my stomach burning? Why did I want to snap all the wooden chopsticks with my hands? Why did I want to scream?

My father paid the bill over Yumi's weak protests, and we walked over to Columbus Circle. My father snapped a photograph of the three of us, each wearing trench coats, in front of the stone fountain. I was sandwiched between Yumi and my mother. "Say cheese!" It was a beautiful outing, on a New York spring Mother's Day. The trees were putting out their buds, tenderly, all around Central Park.

We drove Yumi to her hotel. She said she'd retrieve her luggage and wait for the airport limousine.

"Oh, no," my father said. "We won't hear of that. We'll drive you to LaGuardia."

"So much trouble!" she said. But she was smiling.

"Not at all."

She chattered with my father all the way to the airport. My mother and I slouched against the doors in the back seat, my grandmother sandwiched between us.

"My children would never forgive me if I didn't come home for Mother's Day," Yumi said. "They didn't get to do their traditional breakfast in bed today, but they say they have something else planned."

I had never once made my mother breakfast in bed. Mother's Day was something that my father took care of—a nice restaurant meal, a silly greeting card, and a piece of jewelry he'd gotten wholesale from my uncle Yo's jewelry store. I slumped against my grandmother and stared out the window at the gray brick apartment buildings, burnt looking from decades of soot and grime. I felt tired, so tired. Her children. My mother. The whole thing was dizzying.

Your mother. Very pretty lady.

"Well, Yumi, you have a good flight." My father heaved her suitcase out of the trunk. Everyone was smiling except me. They embraced and exchanged niceties. My grandmother bowed, over and over, her shy smile. *You don't need to bow, Nana. She isn't royalty.*

"*So* nice to meet you."

"So nice to meet *you* too."

Then my father cleared his throat, like he was going to make an announcement. "Well, we really do need to thank you, for turning this little girl over to us. We sure do love her." He coughed. My mother nodded, not saying anything.

Bright tears sprang into my eyes. It was the first that anyone had mentioned anything about our odd triangle.

Yumi said, "Oh, no, I have to thank *you*. For taking such good care. She has been very, very lucky."

She turned to me and said it again. "You've been *extremely* lucky."

Lucky. They all looked at me, their faces shiny with pride and maybe a little bit of envy at my tremendous luck. Luck was when your number gets called at the carnival, and you get to walk home with a stuffed bear that is as tall as you. This didn't feel like luck.

Yumi rummaged in her purse and for a second I wondered if she was looking for something to give me, a keepsake. But instead, she pulled out her boarding pass. She was leaving. *Leaving.* She was satisfied that I was with good people, nice Japanese people, nisei like her, who ate sushi and drove a nice car. She was leaving me. To be with *her children.*

She disappeared through the revolving door at the airport, waving and smiling.

"Goodbye" was sitting in my mouth, heavy and thick as a stone. I couldn't swallow it, I couldn't say it. It sat on my tongue, growing denser, larger, until I couldn't breathe. I leaped out of the car and rushed through the spinning doors, crying and gulping. I blinked through thick tears at the crowd, the hundreds of people jostling their bags, but she had disappeared from sight. I crouched behind a column, my face against the cool concrete, and watched my mother and grandmother walk by, calling my name.

"Susan? Susan!" *Where is she?* My grandmother walked slowly down the terminal. *Su-sahn.*

I wept with a grief that made my teeth rattle. I hid from them, turning my body slowly around the column. Finally, I crept out from behind the pillar, my face puffy with shame. They had been sitting patiently in a row of bolted-down plastic chairs. We went to the parking garage, found my father in the car, and drove home in silence.

THE MOUSE ROOM

The strangest job I ever had was in a windowless room filled with hundreds of mice. In the summer after my junior year of college, I moved from Ithaca to the Bronx. Our final year of the physical therapy program, we lived and studied at Albert Einstein College of Medicine. We studied human anatomy, kinesiology, and physiology before our clinical rotations.

Anatomy was a nightmare for me. Picking apart a human cadaver with a scalpel and tweezers was traumatic. I was terrible at memorizing body parts, the names of bony protuberances, and nearly invisible arteries.

In the hospital basement, the bodies lay wrapped in formaldehyde-soaked fabric, then covered in a rubber blanket. We were assigned four to a body. Our corpse had a rose tattoo and only one arm. I decided that he was a sailor and called him Frank.

The anatomy exams consisted of moving through the room of cadavers, their bodies dotted with tiny pins with numbered flags. I clutched a clipboard with a paper numbered one to one hundred. I stared at the little pins piercing a bit of muscle, the fork between two nerves, and couldn't remember if it was the brachioradialis or the pronator. My pencil hovered over the clipboard, trembling. The room reeked of death and formaldehyde. When I left half of my final exam blank, I knew it was over.

I was called into the dean's office. Dr. Grant was owlish and stern behind thick spectacles. "I'm afraid you won't be graduating with the rest of the class," he said. I sank miserably into my chair.

Passing anatomy was the prerequisite for the final classes in the spring semester. I would either have to repeat the whole year or leave the program altogether.

He noted that physical therapy wasn't for everyone. "Maybe you'd be better off elsewhere." I left his office feeling nauseated and climbed the stairs to the roof of the twelve-story apartment building. My guts twisted in shame. I was the only one. The only one who hadn't passed. How would I face my parents with this news? My whole life, all they had asked of me was that I focus on school. They didn't pressure me to get straight As. All I had to do was try my best. But this time, my best wasn't enough. I inched toward the edge of the roof and peered at the tiny cars clogging the Pelham Parkway below. All I had to do was close my eyes and lean over.

I didn't belong here. Maybe I should have gone to art school. Maybe I should have majored in English. Instead, I had squandered thousands of my parents' hard-earned dollars. How many souvenirs and knickknacks had my father had to sell to pay for my education? All I had wanted was for them to be proud of me, the first one in our family to go to college. To learn a profession where I could take care of myself. And here I had failed. I had labored over a set of index cards where I'd painstakingly drawn every muscle and nerve with colored pencils, but these aids had failed to instill their names in my brain.

My birth mother had once studied art. I'd known this but had steered away from the direction in which my genetics had pointed. As I teetered near the edge of the roof, I felt her letter in my pocket. I had been carrying it around for a week. She was coming to New York soon, she said—"perhaps we can get together." I had read it over and over. Her perfect round penmanship. *Perhaps.*

I wasn't going to fling myself off the roof, not when she was coming. It had been almost two years since I'd seen her, when we'd gone out for sushi on Mother's Day. I backed away from the edge of the building and I drove to my parents' house in New Jersey. I told them I had failed.

"It's done," I sobbed. "I'm not going to be a physical therapist. I'm sorry. I'm so sorry." I gulped air, choking. My father came to sit next to me.

"Dai joubu," he said. He patted my back. Dai joubu. It's all right.

I cocooned in my childhood room for a weekend, eating Mallomars and flipping through a stack of old *Seventeen* magazines. My mother came in and said, "Try again. You'll do better next time." My father said, "We can swing an extra year of tuition. Don't worry." It was clear what they wanted. On Monday, I got into my car and drove back to the Bronx.

One student in our class, Joel, was repeating his senior year for the same reason. He had heard about what happened to me. "Sucks, I know," he said.

I nodded.

"There's a good part, though," he said. "You'll have more time. You can get a job. Make some cash." He offered to recommend me to take over his job in a research lab. Something about taking care of mice. He'd managed to pass anatomy his second time around, and he was about to graduate.

In the research wing of the hospital, he introduced me to Dr. Das, the medical director. "Here's your new mouse girl," said Joel.

Dr. Das held out his hand to shake mine. His eyes were kind. "You are a physical therapy student?"

"Yes."

"We have been very pleased with Joel. If he says it is a good idea, you are hired."

Joel gave me a high five. "Fantastic. Let's get suited up." He handed me a paper jumpsuit, blue booties, a hair cap, a surgical mask. He tucked his brown Beatle-style bangs under the elastic. "Gotta be sterile." I stuffed my hair into my cap and followed him through a heavy steel door.

The room was an overwhelming din of smell and noise. Rows

of shelves filled with plastic shoebox-sized bins, each pulsing with mice. Hundreds of them.

Joel picked up a white mouse by its tail, and it swam in the air. "Say hi to your new mom," he said.

I whispered, "I have a new mom too," into my mask. He didn't hear me.

"The white furry ones just breed," Joel went on. "But these—" he cradled a hairless, dusky pink mouse in his gloved palm. "The nude ones are the ones for research. They don't have immune systems."

They were so odd and ugly, with blue veins showing through transparent wrinkly skin.

"You'll do it all," said Joel. He ticked off a list with his rubbery fingers. "Feeding, cleaning, watering, breeding, sexing."

"Sexing?"

"Yeah. When they're born, you can't tell what they are. But eventually, you can see, and you separate them by gender." He picked one up, and we peered at its little rice-sized genitals. He showed me how to draw their meticulous family trees on cards taped to the wall. I would know more about their lineages than my own.

I was grateful to Joel for this distraction. My shame over my anatomy failure subsided, and I got into a routine of new classes and my mouse job. I made a plan for working through my graduation requirements, spread over two years now instead of one.

The date when Yumi said she was going to be in New York arrived. I hadn't heard from her since her letter. I cleaned my studio apartment and went to an Italian deli nearby to buy fancy cheese. I'd learned that she loved cheese, like I did, and chocolate. She called herself a chocoholic. I had mailed her chocolate on her birthday, and her gushingly happy thank-you note gave me goosebumps. I would do anything to please her.

I reread her letter again. *I would like to see you if time permits.* Of course, time would permit!

Feeding newborn mice required a strict protocol and recipe. I sliced crusts from loaves of whole wheat bread. My mother always cut the crusts off for me, too, I murmured. As a child, I had been attracted to the whitest of white foods: steamed rice, triangles of white bread with cream cheese. I ripped the bread into shreds with my gloved hands and poured cans of infant formula over it. The gummy paste was mousey baby food.

Their glass water bottles reminded me of inverted baby bottles. They reminded me of the story Yumi had told me, about feeding me a single bottle while we rode in a taxi from the hospital to the adoption agency. The food, wrapped in foil like miniature burritos, and the bottles, all needed to be sterilized in the giant autoclave.

I paced the hallway while the autoclave rumbled. I wondered if there would be a voice message from my birth mother on my answering machine. I prayed that we would really bond this time and that I wouldn't step on her emotional landmines. Talking about my birth father was off limits. If she mentioned her children, I could listen, but it was unacceptable for me to ask questions. It was an elaborate game of don't ask, don't tell, don't wonder or probe. Just wait and let her call every shot.

I checked the experimental mice for tumors. The nude mice were injected with tumor cells, and soon blisters would appear under their wrinkly skins. The blisters would grow to the size of peas, then blueberries, and soon cherry-sized lumps. The tumors needed to be coaxed as big as possible without actually killing the mice. If I waited too long, I'd find a decomposing body in the bedding, which was useless. But if I brought a mouse up to the lab too soon, the tumor wouldn't be optimal, and the mouse would die in the unsterile environment. The difference between "too late" and "too soon" could be a matter of hours.

Just as I was perusing Tumor Row, Dr. Das let himself in. He was also swathed in sterile clothing from head to toe. "Hello, Miss Susan." His brown eyes were warm and smiling over his mask. "How are your little charges doing?"

I lowered my eyes. "I think it's going well." But I was nervous.

Maybe he would suggest I'd be better off elsewhere, like the dean had.

"Let's take a look." He strolled from shelf to shelf, his hands behind his back like a general inspecting the troops. He bent down and pulled out random bins, peering inside, and making small sounds with his tongue. *Tsk tsk tsk.*

"What is your current inventory?"

I scanned the index cards on the wall. *W* for mice with white fur, *N* for nudes, *B* for babies who were yet to be sexed. I scribbled numbers on a pad. "One hundred five white furred males, seventy furred females, sixty-eight nude males, eighty-five nude females. Forty-nine babies, unclassified."

He nodded. "You know the furred males are not of use." Of use.

"I know." I swallowed dryly under my mask.

Dr. Das put his rubbery hand on my arm. "I think it is time to reduce the numbers. Can you manage this?"

"Definitely, Dr. Das." I didn't want to seem like a wimp.

"Good." He stacked three bins underneath his arm. The mice inside had grape-sized tumors. "These are perfect, Miss Susan. I will take them upstairs now. Good job."

"Thank you, Doctor."

I waited for him to leave, then I bolted across the courtyard to my building. My apartment was still immaculate. The answering machine's digital message counter showed a big red zero. I sat on the couch and panted. I told myself it was still early. She probably wanted to rest and then she would call. We would both be happy to see each other. This time it wouldn't be an unwelcome shock. *I would like to see you if time permits.*

I didn't know the name of her hotel. If I did, I could just leave a casual message at the front desk. I could leave my phone number. What if she didn't have my number?

The phone rang. "Hello!" My heart jumped.

"Sue! Hey!" It was Laraine, a medical student who lived on my floor. She wanted to know if I was free for racquetball. I demurred and quickly hung up.

I fussed with the apartment. I wiped the shelves with lemon oil, fluffed the sofa pillows, and arranged the expensive cheese on a plate. My kinesiology textbook sat accusingly on the table. If I wasn't careful, I would end up failing this class as well, and there was no recourse for that. I sighed, took out a yellow highlighter, and tried to concentrate. When it was dark, I started nibbling at the cheese, and before long there was nothing left but a smeared wrapper and a few cracker crumbs. When the clock clicked over to midnight, I had to admit to myself she wasn't going to call that night.

The next day, I went to class and tried to focus. I absorbed nothing. I rushed home and the green button was blinking. One message. I punched the play button.

"Susan. This is Mommy. Just calling to say hello. Nana and I have a bit of a head cold this week . . ." I hit erase. Wrong mother. Where was Yumi? Maybe she wasn't going to call at all. Maybe she would spend the week in New York and I would never see her. My skin prickled with rejection.

I stomped into the mouse room. Why was I taking care of them as if they were infants? They were rodents. There was an entire profession dedicated to exterminating them. Their shrill voices shrieked a nightmarish chorus. I started coughing and realized I had forgotten to put on my mask. "Good!" I yelled. "Get germs! See if I care!"

Then I found three dead mice, bloody tumors splitting through their purple skin. I scooped the carcasses into an inside-out rubber glove, like a knotted-up bundle of dog waste. I tossed it into the incinerator and the fiery mouth swallowed them with a roar.

Three days passed. My apartment degenerated into a pit of dirty laundry and unwashed dishes. The irises I had bought faded and shrank, bowing their rotten heads. There were just two days left before Yumi would be flying out of New York.

I had to face the truth. She did not want to see me.

Meanwhile, the furry male mouse population was out of control. They were climbing over each other, fighting over the mouse chow, chewing through the black rubber stoppers of the water bottles. I prayed that Dr. Das wouldn't make a surprise visit and see how I was failing at this as well. I knew I had to decrease the numbers, as Dr. Das had so euphemistically put it, but I couldn't face it.

Impulsively, I grabbed two by the tails and said, "You're coming home with me." I tucked their bin under my arm and carried them to my apartment. I fed them crumbs of leftover cheese. They scrabbled around, their magenta eyes bright.

The phone did not ring. She clearly wasn't going to call. The two white mice, whom I'd named Snow and Flake, were nocturnal. All night, they cried and jumped around their bin. I put a pillow over my head and moaned. Everything was a disaster.

In the morning, I took the bin outside. I knelt on the grimy, unsterile sidewalk and tipped it on its side. Their naked little feet touched the earth for the first time. Snow and Flake cowered against each other, trembling in the chaos of the Bronx.

"GO!" I shouted. They shot under a wire fence and disappeared, two flashes of white against the ground.

When I got back to the apartment, I saw the blinking green light.

Yumi's voice rang out, bright and cheery.

"Suuu-san? It's Yumi. I'm at the Plaza Hotel. I'd love to get together!"

I stared at the machine. I pushed the rewind button and listened over and over, her voice squealing as it wound backward. There was no apology. Just this bright voice, like a twinkling light. Forget it, I thought. Go home. Just forget it.

But after half an hour, I picked up the phone and dialed the number. She picked up after the first ring.

"Suuu-san!" She sounded happy. She sounded as if she had been sitting right by the phone, hoping it would be me. She asked if I wanted to come to the Plaza. Then I hung up the phone and rushed to the subway.

The Plaza Hotel! Robert Redford and Barbra Streisand at the

Plaza in *The Way We Were* had made me swoon. My father pointed it out whenever we drove past.

"Two hundred bucks a night," my father had told me, shaking his head. He stayed in motels most of the year, so they had to be cheap. He chose Motel 6, or if he was feeling extra splurgy, maybe Travelodge. He plugged his little electrical coil into a mug to boil water for instant ramen. Then he washed it out and boiled another cup for Sanka and a single cookie.

I tapped on the door of Yumi's room. The door cracked open half an inch, and I could only see her eye. "Susan! Quick, come in!" She pulled the door open so I could scurry in.

"I got involved in a phone call, and then rushed to take a shower. I didn't think you'd get here so fast!" She shook her wet black hair like a dog. Her body was wrapped in a thick white towel. I stared at her legs. They were my legs. It was the first time I had seen their shape on another human being. Muscular, with sturdy thighs and a familiar curve of calf. Her ankles were my ankles, her feet as wide and flat as my own.

My legs were the only parts of my body that I really liked. People often mistook me for a runner or swimmer, when in fact I was utterly unathletic.

I pointed. "I recognize those legs."

Her eyebrows arched and then she laughed and went into the bathroom. I heard the blow dryer through the door. I walked around the room and stole glances at her things. A copy of *The Road Less Traveled* sat on the bedside table. My stomach jumped. I was reading that book, too, underlining passages with a pen. Here it was on her nightstand. My adoptive mother would never read a psychology or self-help book.

I loved that she had a little tower of books next to her bed. My own parents were not readers, although they nurtured my love of books. They kept a subscription to Reader's Digest Condensed Books, which arrived once a month. I was the only one who actually read them.

I drew aside the heavy drapes to look at Central Park below.

The light had faded to blue-gray, and a border of glimmering streetlamps circled the dark patch of trees. A few horse-drawn carriages with swinging lanterns passed the hotel. How often I had gazed up, wondering about what sort of people stayed in these rooms.

"How rude of me to make you wait!" Her face was pink and glowing, fresh from the steamy bathroom. She rubbed creamy lotion over her skin. It smelled like milk.

"It's all right," I said. "It was a busy week." Then I realized she was speaking about the last few minutes, and not the previous several days. I pressed my lips together.

"So!" She exclaimed. "Are you hungry? I'm starving." She picked up a leather menu. Would you like to go out? Or . . . ?"

I shrugged. "Whatever you . . ."

"Room service is fun. Especially when somebody else is paying, right? Thank you, expense account!" She bounced on the bed.

I stared. I had never seen her like this, so playful. It was nothing like our first meeting at the Holiday Inn, when she had been so tense and angry about being found.

She flipped through the menu. "Mmmm. Hot fudge sundae. Doesn't that sound delicious?" Without waiting for a response, she picked up the phone. "Pick something, Susan. Whatever you want. Hello! Room service? This is Room 612. We'd like two hot fudge sundaes, and I guess we'd better get something sensible too." She looked at me and waved the menu.

I stabbed my finger randomly. "Shrimp cocktail. Perfect. And a pot of tea. Black tea. And . . . ?" She looked at me quizzically. I shook my head and mouthed *water*. "A pitcher of ice water! With sliced lemon! Please!" She hung up gaily.

I sat on the edge of the bed. I fiddled with the zipper on my coat, pulling it up and down.

Yumi plumped up pillows behind her back and leaned into the headboard. "So, Susan. Take off your coat. Relax. Tell me everything. Tell me what you're up to these days. How is school? How is that strange job of yours, with the rats? Are you seeing anybody? Are you in love?"

I gaped. This woman was not acting like a mother. At least not like my mother. My adoptive mother had never in my life asked me if I was in love. She tried to deny the existence of my boyfriends. She was impatient with my romances, reminding me that she had not had time for love until she was well into her twenties. She had met my father at church. And here was my birth mother, leaning forward like one of my girlfriends, wanting all the juicy details.

"Well. My boyfriend from college? He went to veterinary school. In Texas. So we're kind of . . . long-distance. I love him, but I've met a few guys here. Medical students, you know."

"Ooh!" She rubbed her hands together.

I blushed. "But none of them are really . . ." I lifted my hands. "I don't know."

"Ah." Her face grew serious. "You don't want to stop seeing him. But he's far away, and these others are all around."

I stopped abruptly. "Yes."

She leaned over and took an emery board from a drawer. It made a little sawing noise across her nails. Her lips were pursed in a thoughtful frown. "These things are complicated. You're so young. Too young to settle down, but you're not a teenager either."

I was speechless. I had never spoken with an older adult about any of my relationships. Never been taken seriously. Never been spoken to seriously.

She nodded soberly. All the gaiety had faded. Suddenly I wanted to talk and never stop.

The food arrived on a cart with a crisp white tablecloth. I giggled. It reminded me of the cart I used to roll the mouse food into the autoclave. Each dish was covered by a silver dome, which the waiter removed with a flourish. The ice in my water tinkled as he poured it into a stemmed glass. Two hot fudge sundaes in giant goblets were piled with whipped cream. She signed the bill and grabbed a long-handled spoon. "Dessert first, right? We don't want it to melt."

Who was this woman? Was she going to be my buddy? My girlfriend? Was she my mother? Some other sort of mother I'd never imagined?

We plunged our spoons into the ice cream. She licked the fudge from her lips. "I just love chocolate."

I just love *you*, I said silently. The week of waiting, the agony of the answering machine, all dissolved. We talked until two in the morning, until there was nothing left on the tray but crumbs and melted ice cream droplets. I talked until my throat was hoarse. I told her all the stories my mother never wanted to hear, never approved of. She listened with her eyes closed, her head rolling slowly across the pillow. Finally, our voices sank into whispers. She gestured at the opposite bed and when I lay down, she pulled the bedspread over my shoulders.

"Oyasumi-nasai," I mumbled. It was the goodnight endearment I never failed to exchange with my parents.

She gasped. "It's been a long time since I've heard that." I didn't know what she meant: if she didn't say it with her children or if it had been a long time since she'd used it with her own parents. She sighed and softly repeated it back. "Oyasumi-nasai."

The next morning, she looked at me the way a person regarded a regrettable one-night stand. She wouldn't meet my eyes. There was no talk of calling room service. We wouldn't be eating French toast in bed, giggling like the night before. She dressed in the bathroom and emerged in an elegant suit. I watched as she tucked her belongings into her suitcase. The heavy zipper made a violent sound as she closed it. Then she glanced at her watch and said, "I'm going to call a cab. I hate being rushed and worrying about missing my flight."

I scrambled into my clothes and washed my mouth out underneath the bathroom faucet. I didn't have a toothbrush. I pressed a hot washcloth against my face and slipped a tiny bottle of fancy shampoo into my pocket.

"Well," I said. "This was so nice. It was nice, last night." Didn't she think it was nice too? Hadn't she had fun? She had laughed so much. The room service tray was a wreck of dirty dishes, melted ice cream, and shrimp tails.

She turned and smiled, but it was a mouth-only smile, a smile with perfect lipstick. "Yes. It was very nice. Thank you for coming all the way from the Bronx." Her eyes said, *time to get out*. She opened the door.

I stumbled into the hallway, feeling slapped. The elevator sank so fast it made my knees collapse. I walked through the opulent lobby, as surreal as a movie set. I felt like an extra, a person who moved through the room without a name.

I climbed out of the subway station at Pelham Parkway and went straight to the mouse room. The vacuum seal of the door opened with a whooshing sound. I grabbed a plastic bin and began pulling out the furred males by their tails. They swam in the air, their bright eyes wild. Like they knew where I was taking them.

When I first started the job, I had pleaded with Dr. Das to consider donating the extras to a pet shop, but he said no. Something about their immune systems, hospital policy, and red tape. This was the only way.

Soon the bin was crawling with dozens of quivering white mice. I carried them down the hallway to the death room. I'd only been there once before, with Joel. I dumped the writhing ball of mice into a clear plexiglass box and fastened the lid with clamps.

I thought about my birth mother, getting into a taxi in front of the Plaza Hotel. By now she would be on the plane, fastening her seatbelt. She would fly over patchwork fields and land in her home city. Her children would meet her there, my siblings who knew nothing about me. She wouldn't say much about her trip to New York, although she might bring them a miniature Statue of

Liberty keychain or a snow globe with the Empire State Building. She might say lightly, "I ate pretzels and hotdogs from a cart on the sidewalk." But she would never say, "I saw your sister. We sat up in bed eating hot fudge sundaes."

I attached a slim black rubber tube from the box of mice to a green metal tank of hydrogen monoxide. After a deep breath, I twisted the spigot clockwise until the dial reached one hundred percent. It hissed and I watched the mice lose their minds. They jumped and scrambled and flew through the box like giant white popcorn kernels. I closed my eyes and counted to ten, then twenty. I kept counting until a minute passed and then I twisted the handle to zero.

The mice were nearly still. They lay in a heap, twitching, huddled on the bottom of the box. Their pink eyes, still open, had turned bright blue, as pure blue as crayons. I scooped up their warm little bodies into a paper sack and carried them to the incinerator. I flung them into the fire and then retched in a trash bin.

I felt proud and grim and terrible. I had sacrificed them to the higher goal of science, to help humans who suffered with liver cancer. I dragged myself back to the apartment. The answering machine was blinking with a green number one. It might be my boyfriend, calling long distance. Or one of the medical students. Was it from my mother in New Jersey, reporting back on her tomato plants in the backyard garden? Or my father on the highway in Tennessee, his car filled with black sample cases? Maybe it was my next-door neighbor Laraine, asking if I wanted to play racquetball. I knew almost certainly that it was not my birth mother. She was back in her own land, back in the place she called home, and I had no idea how long it would be before she dialed my number again.

TOTALED

For a few years, my birth mother and I were almost friends. After my college graduation, I drove cross-country to California, miraculously passed the physical therapy state board examination and got a job as a pediatric therapist. During that time, she had business trips that brought her to San Francisco semi-regularly.

We had sleepovers in my studio apartment near the ocean. She slept in an oversized T-shirt on a giant overstuffed pink couch I'd dubbed "the hippo." It took my breath away to wake up and see her lying a few feet away, unguarded, her hair tousled. She accompanied me to aerobic dance classes and impressively kept up with everyone. We giggled and shopped and ate good food. We went to a favorite nearby Mexican breakfast spot or stayed home to have toast with jam in my miniature kitchen.

It was the best of times.

I had accepted the fact that I had half siblings who didn't know I existed, one who shared my original name. I suppressed the desire to ask questions about my birth father. It was just her and me, being easy together in a place where nobody knew her.

At times she still acted cagily: not giving me her hotel or flight information, waiting several days before contacting me. And it hurt. It made me acutely aware of the power she held.

While working at my first hospital job in California, I met a dimpled doctor in the elevator. He was sweet and excelled at eye contact. One day, he passed me his phone number on an index card. I invited him to my little apartment and served him a bowl of vibrant green Moosewood spinach soup with crusty bread. I'd been waiting days to hear from Yumi, and her protracted silence was upsetting. John, the doctor, comforted me on the hippo couch.

I taught myself patience with Yumi. Above all, I wanted this relationship with her. I knew that eventually I'd hear her voice on the phone. Sometimes she called, and sometimes she didn't. I moved from one San Francisco neighborhood to another, from the studio to a shared flat with roommates. I jumped from hospital work to pediatric physical therapy.

"Suuu—saaaaan?" Her voice was bright, like sunshine.

I didn't hesitate. "Why, hey! Hello. When did you get in?"

"Oh, sometime yesterday." Perfectly vague. "I'm sorry I didn't call last night. We had a business dinner, and I got in late. I didn't want to bother you." A blue flare of anger rose up in my chest, but I extinguished it quickly. *You could have called any time.* I bit my tongue.

She said she would take a taxi to my house at five o'clock, that she didn't want to bother me with driving all the way to her hotel. Wherever that was.

"It's not a bother. Really."

She insisted. I gave in.

When I got home from work, she was sitting neatly on my front stoop. As always, her impeccable style humbled me. Could she teach me to dress like this? Black pants, elegant leather flats, a flowing gold wool jacket. I mostly wore chino pants and polo shirts for work, L.L. Bean casual.

She stood up and handed me a shopping bag with a ribbon on the handles. "Just a little something." I dug into the tissue paper for a little box of chocolates. A bouquet of tulips. A T-shirt printed with the logo for Powdermilk Biscuits.

"They're the fictional sponsor for a radio show called *A Prairie*

Home Companion. Have you heard of it?" I hadn't, but I loved biscuits. My father had been a partner-owner of a highway gift shop and café in North Carolina that featured southern biscuits. I loved them with sausage patties or dribbled honey.

She had brought me gifts! I was giddy. The shirt was too big, but I immediately put it on over my shorts, fingering the hem.

"Come see my new place." The long window in my front door was covered by a life-sized poster of Albert Einstein on a bicycle, his hair flying, his feet out. Our neighbors had put up posters of Charlie Chaplin and Clark Gable, and once, our front doors had been featured in a newspaper article about San Francisco neighborhoods.

"This is wonderful!" she said. She followed me up to the third floor and reached into her bag for a camera. "Sit by the window! I want a picture." She snapped a photo of me wearing my new shirt.

My housemate Tom passed by the living room and waved. "Wow, Powdermilk Biscuits!" he said. "*A Prairie Home Companion!*" He fist-pumped in the air and they both cheered. He mouthed at me, "Your mom's so cool!"

"Dinner?" she said. "How about Mamounia?" It was a Moroccan restaurant near my first San Francisco apartment, out near the ocean. We had discovered it during a prior visit and loved sitting on cushions on the floor, eating with our hands. It was not the kind of place I would ever take my parents. They veered toward the familiar and comfortable: Japanese for sushi or Italian for spaghetti and meatballs. They'd never tasted Indian or Thai food or eaten anything with their fingers other than french fries. Mamounia would make them uncomfortable. My father would try to be a good sport, but my mother would be looking toward the door, searching for an escape.

"Take me to McDonald's, please," she'd say, and she wouldn't be kidding.

Yumi loved culinary adventure. So we drove out to Mamounia, where the staff wore pointed gold slippers, and we lowered ourselves onto embroidered floor cushions. The servers poured warm rosewater from an ornate silver kettle onto our hands.

"What is this beautiful thing called?" she asked. She was so inquisitive and not shy. She'd chat up anyone. My adoptive mother would never think to ask such a thing.

The server answered, "It's called a tass."

Yumi nodded, repeating it softly. Tass. I suddenly wanted to blurt out, "And what is my birth father called?" But a question like that would ruin our dinner, our beautiful meal in this elegant place.

We shared a communal round table next to two men. They smiled as we held out our hands to be washed. "Feels so good, doesn't it?" said one of them.

"It's absolutely wonderful!" exclaimed Yumi.

The conversation bubbled along, mostly carried by Yumi and exuberant Patrick. He and Richie were celebrating an anniversary. We raised a toast with our water glasses.

"Have you ever had brains? Our favorite!"

I blanched, but she was game. "I've never had it, but I'll try." She dipped her fork into their plate. "Mmmm. It IS good."

I needed to show her that I was willing to try too. I wanted her to be proud of me.

I scooped up a morsel the size of a bean and swallowed it whole. It was soft, flavored like tomatoes and olives. Everyone applauded. "Good girl! You did it!"

After this little hazing ritual, we became fine friends. We passed our plates back and forth—chicken and couscous, vegetables, lamb and prunes.

"So . . ." Patrick pointed at me with a chicken bone. "You live here . . . where?"

"Over in Cole Valley."

"And your mom? Does she live around here too?"

My spine stiffened. *Oh, no. Oh, no.* Here was the end of our good time, our evening out, our girlfriend laughs. I looked at him with panic in my eyes.

He persisted, winking at Yumi. "You *are* her mom, right? Or maybe you are sisters? I mean, you look just like each other."

I stared down at the couscous and began counting them, one tiny yellow grain at a time. Then I heard her voice. It was light, almost lilting.

"Oh, I live a long way from here." Her voice was warm and relaxed. So she hadn't exactly said yes. But she hadn't denied it, either. I lifted my eyes. She and Patrick were consulting the dessert menu, laughing.

Then I understood. Here in this gilded, tasseled tent a few blocks from the Pacific Ocean, she was free. She could openly be my mother with these two men. They were not going to judge her.

After dinner, we walked around my new neighborhood. I could feel her relaxed next to me, her pleasure in gazing through the window of the hardware store. "I just love those salt and pepper shakers!" she said, pointing to a ceramic mouse and cheese. I told myself to remember them for her birthday.

We walked and talked. She squealed out loud when she saw something that delighted her. I wanted to slip my hand through the crook of her arm. I wanted to skip with her on the sidewalk. Instead, I allowed myself to steal glances at her calm, happy face.

When it was time for her to go back to her hotel, I pleaded with her to let me drive her.

"Oh, no," she said. Her voice was light as breeze. "I've already made friends with my taxi driver. He'll be here at exactly ten." And as if she had snapped her magic fingers inside her pocket, the yellow car pulled up, right outside my house.

"Maybe we can get together again before you leave?" I asked hopefully. I so wanted more of these nights, more of these easy, golden times together.

"I'll call when my meetings are over," she said, and slipped into the back seat. She pulled the door shut and waved gaily through the window. The taxi chugged away, to its secret destination over the hill.

The next morning, I didn't have time for breakfast. I ran to the corner store and grabbed a pint of orange juice and a sweet roll to eat in the car.

I paused to cross the sea of traffic on Upper Market Street. Two lanes zipped by in either direction. I unscrewed the top to the orange juice. A mustached man in a pickup truck idled on Market, waiting to turn in my direction. He saw me peering around and gestured with his palm: *come on*. I nodded thanks and hit the accelerator, trusting him.

The impact was deafening. Metal and glass exploding. The passenger door collapsed inward and nicked me in the right elbow. Orange juice flew everywhere. It splattered on the windshield, soaking into my pants. The car ticked and hummed, smoke rising from the crumpled hood like a cigarette, a tiny column rising into the sky.

My head was foggy. What had happened? Another car, a silver SUV, barreling down Market Street, had broadsided me. The driver leaped out of his car, yelling. "What's the matter with you? Didn't you see?"

No. I didn't see. To be honest, I hadn't even looked. I had crossed on the advice of that other guy in the pickup, the guy who had waved his hand like that, who had said without words, *it's okay, just go, just go*. And so I had gone. Without looking.

My car was totaled. The wheels hung off like a loose tooth from a thin metal membrane. Pools of liquid, bright neon yellow, puddled on the street. I sat down on the curb, dizzy. A few people, pedestrians or neighbors, came out and murmured. *You okay? You okay?* I had no words to answer.

The police arrived, it seemed, within minutes. I crawled into the carcass of my car and wrenched open the glove box, pulling out my papers. I wrote down my insurance details for the other driver and he disappeared, muttering. The cop asked me, "Where do you live, hon?" and I waved up the hill. Up there. Just a few blocks.

A tow truck appeared. "Where do you want me to take it?" It was useless, really. Just scrap now. I gave him my address, and he dragged my car, my little tan and white baby, back to a spot in front of my building.

I sat on the front stoop and sobbed. This was the car my father had found for me when I was a junior in Ithaca, living far off campus on Taughannock Boulevard. I was so proud of this little used Toyota Celica. I had driven it cross-country from New Jersey to California. I had just finished my monthly payments. I had loved this car like it was my child.

I called work and told them I wasn't coming in. I sat in the empty apartment, numb. The hours ticked by. It was almost dark when the phone rang.

It was Yumi. "Susan? Are you up for another dinner?"

My voice felt hollow. "Hi. I was in an accident . . . my car . . ." I started hyperventilating.

"I'll be right there." It seemed as if she appeared in minutes, in the same yellow taxi trundling up the hill. She came through the door with a brown paper sack. Fruit, soup, crackers, chocolate. She bustled around my kitchen as if she owned it, not asking where anything was. I sat on the living room sofa, my arms wrapped around my knees. She brought the soup, cream of tomato, in a blue bowl on a tray. Three little chocolates on a paper napkin. Where did she find a tray?

I ate my soup tucked into the couch cushions like a little girl. When I was finished, she put the tray on the coffee table.

"I'm sorry this wasn't much of a fun visit," I said.

She made a *pfff* dismissive noise.

I gazed through the window at my crumpled car. "My daddy got me that car," I murmured. It made me sick to look at it, the wounded metal, the fluids pooling on the street, running down the hill in rivulets. I felt filled with grief in a way that I didn't understand.

She curled up next to me on the sofa. She wrapped her arms around me and smoothed my hair.

"It's okay," she said, and her voice was soft as cotton. "You're not hurt. It's so good you weren't hurt."

I leaned my cheek onto her shoulder. She smelled good and clean and like a mother. The tears rolled down my face, and I let myself sob. She rocked me back and forth, back and forth. She stroked my cheek and patted my hair. "It's all right," she murmured, over and over. I never wanted the night to end. I thought, *If I could have had this before, I would have driven myself into oncoming traffic years ago.*

LUCKY

A bright purple flier stapled to a utility pole on Mission Street caught my eye: *The Name You Never Got*. A silhouette of a pregnant woman with her hand on her belly. I stepped closer and gasped at the subtitle: *A Woman Searching for the Daughter She Gave Up for Adoption*. It was an ad for a one-woman show—about adoption? By a birth mother? Incredible.

I tore off a paper tab and tucked it in my pocket. I was twenty-five, and it had been five years since I had found and met Yumi. She was deeply, vehemently private, and the thought of her performing our story on stage was unfathomable. I had to see this show.

I reserved two tickets. Then, impulsively, I called a guy I had met on a health workers' delegation to Nicaragua. I'd gotten deeply involved in Central American politics and had gone part-time at my physical therapy job so I could also work as a paid organizer for the Committee for Health Rights in Central America.

David was an emergency room doctor, a guy with good politics and kind eyes. And I needed to go to this play with someone who could revive me if I had a heart attack.

David was upbeat. "Sounds great. Unfortunately, I'm on call. But wait. Maybe my roommate can go. Hold on." Then a clunk.

His roommate? I had never even met his roommate. I heard a brief, muffled conversation and then, "Susan? Here's Paul."

I swallowed. "Um, hi, so I have this extra ticket to this thing. And uh, David said maybe you'd want to go . . ."

It was awkward. Why hadn't David just said no thanks, so I could ask somebody else? But suddenly I was on the phone with someone named Paul, and Paul said yes, and we had plans to meet near the theater.

I think David knew. He must have. That the show, a hilarious but heartbreaking one-woman performance by a woman who had, indeed, given her daughter up for adoption and then found her as a teenager, would blow my mind. That I would sit in the dark hyperventilating quietly. That I would be struggling to hold it together, blinking furiously, not saying anything because if I said something, I would lose it completely. David must have known that Paul would also be sitting there beside me, motionless, as well—that everyone else in the theater would have gotten up, leaving crumpled coffee cups and the purple programs scattered under the seats. And that we'd be the last ones in the place, too overwhelmed to move or say anything. Paul would speak first.

He cleared his throat and glanced over. "How'd you like it?"

I stammered, "It—it had quite an effect on me." I kept rolling and unrolling the purple program.

"Me too," he said.

"Really?"

"Yeah."

"Well. It hit me in a kind of personal way." It felt awkward and embarrassing to be sitting on a volcano of emotion on a first "date." It wasn't even a date. But I didn't know him and didn't think it would be cool to spill my entire adoption story to someone I had just met a few hours before.

"It hit me in a personal way too," he said quietly. I looked at him. Paul was a wiry guy, a law student, he'd said, with a paintbrush mustache and green eyes the color of a beer bottle. Nice eyes. His eyelashes were wet.

I took a breath. "Wait. Are you adopted too? Because that's why I . . ."

"No."

His eyes were sad and serious. "Do you want to get something to eat?"

I followed him out of the empty theater. Ronda, the performer, was in the lobby, talking to lingering audience members. I shook her hand and thanked her. "That was so, so moving," I said. "I'm adopted, and . . ."

My throat closed up. She squeezed my hand. I thanked her again, and then Paul and I walked to a coffee shop. We talked until we were the last ones inside.

As it turned out, Paul wasn't adopted. He was a birth father. His ex-girlfriend had gotten pregnant. She hadn't wanted an abortion. He was Catholic and didn't really want one either.

They'd gone to Lamaze classes, he told me. He had cradled his daughter's slippery body after her birth. They signed the adoption papers that afternoon, and he never saw the baby again. Their relationship dissolved soon afterward.

I couldn't stop staring at him. A birth father, alive and real. A birth father who *cared*. He thought about his daughter every day. I thought about what Yumi had told me about my birth father. *He kept track of how old you were. He was the only reason I thought of you.*

Paul told me he had put his deceased mother's wedding ring in an envelope and given it to the social worker, along with a letter for his child, dense with love and regret.

I fell in love with him, instantly and hard. Were we suited for each other? I didn't care.

We each lived in shared flats with roommates at either end of San Francisco's Mission District. I shuttled between two part-time jobs: as a health activist for Central America and as a pediatric physical therapist. Paul had just graduated from law school. Each of our schedules were packed, with little time to share.

We didn't intertwine our lives. I didn't meet his friends, other than David, and he didn't meet mine. We spent occasional nights together in each other's rooms, then dove into our days.

One cold night, I walked the mile to his house and arrived shivering. I wrapped myself in a quilt, warming my hands in the glow of the space heater in his room.

"I'll make you something special," he offered. In the tiny kitchen with the curling linoleum floor, he sharpened a knife, juggled tomatoes, and grated a hill of white cheese. He sliced sesame millet bread, spread it with soft butter, and fixed me the best grilled cheese and tomato sandwich of my life. At three in the morning, I woke up to the light of his desk lamp as he studied for the bar exam.

I felt so tenderly toward him, but something made us hold each other at arms' length. Even though we lived in the same city, we wrote each other thick, handwritten letters filled with odd angst. Why couldn't we get closer? We cared for each other, but there was a sadness that enveloped us.

Fall arrived. I was homesick for East Coast seasons, the leaves and the crisp air. "Come east with me," I said, and he agreed.

We went upstate to stay with my old friend Ken Shiotani. I'd stayed in Ken's tiny Greenwich Village apartment years before when I had snuck into the city for ALMA adoption meetings. Now, Ken and his wife, Susan, lived in a white farmhouse in the country, practicing public law. Pumpkins lined their front porch railing, and the shedding trees in the yard were bursting into gold and red. In the mirror in their guest bathroom, I noticed that my sweater was tight. I wondered if it had shrunk in the laundry or if I was gaining weight. Too many grilled cheese and tomato sandwiches.

Paul and I drove our rental car to Ithaca, and I showed him my favorite places. We hiked to the plunging Taughannock Falls, down the street from the lake house where I lived when I had searched for Yumi.

I cried at the sight of the colorful leaves. I hadn't seen foliage like that since before I had moved to California. Breathtaking orange and red leaves stuck to car windshields. They mounded up into soft blazing piles. It rained, and I cried more, the colors even more brilliant and wet. They flew off branches in the gusty wind.

I wanted to save them, to catch the bits of color in my black rain-coat. I knew they would be gone soon.

Back in California, I found myself still crying without warning. My breasts felt huge and overly sensitive. I started to wonder if there was something wrong with me.

Then a whisper of possibility floated into my mind. I picked up the telephone book, flipping the thin yellow pages, and dialed the first number on the page labeled "Clinics." *Unplanned pregnancy? We do same-day tests.* I spoke with a woman with a warm, con-cerned voice, who told me to come in the same day. "Bring some clean urine," she said.

I called him. "Paul?" I could barely eke out the words. He answered, in a quiet voice, that he'd pick me up right away.

We drove out toward the beach, and the address led us to a small white door in the basement of a nondescript church. A hand-lettered sign read: Crisis Pregnancy Center. I had no sense of who these people were. It *was* a crisis, that was clear. A woman in a beige polyester pantsuit and an uneven white-blonde perm opened the door.

"Hi? We talked on the phone?" I gave her my mayonnaise jar, sloshing with warm urine, in a brown paper bag.

"It'll be about an hour," she said and then she disappeared down a dank smelling hallway. Above our heads, we heard faint plonking piano music and small running feet battering the floor-boards; we were underneath the church's daycare center.

Paul and I sat side by side on a vinyl couch, chewing our cuti-cles, blindly turning the pages of *People* magazine. Half an hour passed, and then another. Finally, the woman called us into a room with no windows. We followed her in and sat in two metal chairs.

"Congratulations," she said from behind an ugly, dented desk. "You're pregnant."

The world became very quiet, and I could almost feel the little ball of cells, popping and dividing inside me. I envisioned a tiny seahorse, swimming in an upside-down pear. The woman began talking rapidly about baby clothes, donated diapers, and financial assistance. She fanned several pamphlets and brochures across the desk. Food stamps. Did we look poor? I was a health professional.

She chewed at her lipstick. "I can see that you're young. But there's plenty of help out there for you." I knew I looked young. The week before, I'd been stopped by a teacher in the hallway of the middle school where I worked, who demanded I show a hall pass.

We didn't say anything. Paul had his palm pressed over his eyes.

I looked down at the floor. I swallowed.

The woman's eyes narrowed. "You're not considering . . . abortion, are you?"

"I . . . don't know."

She leaned in close, and I could smell her medicinal mouthwash. "Are you at all familiar with abortion procedure?"

"Not really."

"Well, I'll tell you. The most common method is by *suction*," she said, her nostrils flaring. "The baby, *your* baby, would be sucked out by a machine that is *fifteen times more powerful* than your household vacuum cleaner!" She turned away, as if she couldn't stand the look of me, and reached into a file cabinet. "I could show you pictures. That would change your mind."

I stood up. "That's okay. We'll think about it."

Paul's face was like a gray stone. He took my hand, and we edged toward the door.

The woman waved her hand, as if she could tell we were a lost cause, and said acidly, "The majority of relationships don't survive an abortion," she said acidly. "That's a *fact*."

We thanked her and walked to the slate-colored ocean a few blocks away. This stretch of beach at the end of the city was not beautiful. The pale sand was littered with cigarette butts and shards of broken glass.

Pregnant. We walked along the water for miles, not talking, just staring out at the foaming sea, clenching each other's fingers. I could barely look at him. The damp air salted my face.

I was his second pregnant girlfriend.

I shook my head. I didn't want to admit that there was something amazing about it, that my body could do this incredible thing. Through the pockets of my jeans, I pressed on my belly, trying to feel something. The embryo probably wasn't even the size of a bean. Its days were numbered, I knew, and I swore to feel everything I could until it was gone.

Paul and I didn't talk about options. Without much discussion, we understood that we wouldn't be parents together. Our relationship was fragile. We had taken a camping trip to Joshua Tree and had pitched a little tent in the desert. We'd gone to New York. We'd once danced on the sidewalk in Japantown, the music floating over us from a karaoke bar. But that wasn't enough to build a family on.

During the next three days, I paid attention to every detail of my body. The queasiness in my gut thrilled me. I nibbled on wheat crackers with reverence. My breasts ballooned even more, so weighty that when I was alone in the apartment, I carried them cupped in my hands.

I kept my hand on my belly under my stretchy sweatpants. I followed each twinge with my finger. I was fascinated by every symptom that I had read about or seen in movies. Here was morning sickness! Here was frequent urination! It all thrilled me.

I called Yumi. She would understand. She had been an alarmed, unmarried pregnant girl herself, twenty-five years ago.

Her voice was bright when she recognized my voice. "Su-san! How *are* you?"

Something crumpled inside me. The words came out brokenly. "Not so good."

I heard her breath catch over the phone. She inhaled and then let it out. "What is it? What's the matter?"

"I'm pregnant."

"Ohh." The vowel sound she made was filled with empathy, pain, recognition. It was exactly the sound I needed to hear. *Thank you*, I said silently.

"What will you do?" Her voice was solemn and soft.

"I've got an appointment. On Monday." I didn't say the word out loud.

"Ah. Well, that's probably for the best, isn't it?" She knew that Paul and I weren't anticipating a future together. I'd confided in her about the uncertain nature of our relationship.

I sighed. "I'm sure it is. But it's still . . . hard."

"Of course. It must be very hard." Tenderness coursed through the receiver, and I closed my eyes. It was as if her palm was on my forehead, stroking it.

"You're lucky that you have this option."

"Yes."

"It's what I would have done, if it had been available to me." And then she stopped short.

I closed my eyes and held onto the doorframe, the coiled cord from the telephone twisting around my body. *If it had been available to her.*

"Susan?"

I smiled into the receiver. "I'm fine." A strange laugh rose from my throat. "It's kind of silly, isn't it? If I didn't have my life to begin with, there's really nothing to miss, is there?"

She tried to smooth over her own words. "Is there anything you need? Can I do anything for you?"

Come to me, I wanted to say. *Come be with me and hold my hand.* But I couldn't choke the words out. To hear her say no would have been unbearable.

"No," I said. "I'm sure it will all be fine."

She sent flowers and, later, a get-well card and a package of herbal tea.

I didn't speak to my parents that week. Normally we spoke every weekend, when my grandmother was at their house, so that I could talk to them all together. But I couldn't bear the thought of talking to them. If my father asked me in his jolly voice, "Moshi-moshi, Sus. How you doing?" I knew I'd cry. I'd cry, and I wouldn't be able to stop.

My parents had never had the "sex talk," or any talk, with me. I'd learned about reproduction from a book about raising Keeshond dogs. The chapter on mating, with graphic description, had horrified my ten-year-old mind. I read it to my neighbor, Janie. We'd shrieked and laughed in disgust.

"But . . . *humans* don't mate like that, do they?" We demanded an answer from her father, who turned tomato red. "Susan, honey, I think you'd better go home and ask your parents." He ushered me to the door.

As I walked the two blocks back to my house, I knew I wouldn't be asking them. I knew they'd never offer to explain. Human reproduction was a strange, foreign concept that had nothing to do with our family. I'd appeared magically in an agency office, swaddled in a pink blanket, and they'd brought me home. That's where babies came from.

The night before my appointment at the women's health center, Paul came over with a bouquet of irises. I arranged them in a blue vase and lit candles on either side. Sitting on floor pillows, we held hands and stared at the flickering light.

Paul said quietly, his eyes glittering green, "Please understand. It's not the right time, for you to be here. We're not the right people for you. Not right now." He gave me a slight nod.

My voice came out steadier than I had expected. "Tomorrow, we're going to let you go. We don't want to hurt you. Please understand. So we're asking you, if you can, to leave tonight."

I didn't want to give up my little clump of pulsing cells. Paul wrapped his long arms around me while I sobbed into his shirt.

I blinked wetly at the smoking candle flame. "I love you," I whispered. "We love you." We curled up like spoons on the bed. The candle burned all night, and we slept like a little family.

In the morning, we went to the women's health center and waited on a velvet lavender couch, a stack of *Ms.* magazines on the table. Paul was the only man in the waiting room.

"You okay?" he mouthed.

"I'm okay," I nodded. "Really."

I heard someone call my name. I stood up and followed a curly-haired woman in purple corduroy pants. She led me into a small bright room and gave me a Valium and a paper cup of orange juice. Later, over the next few decades, I would spot this woman at farmers markets or in bookstores. She didn't recognize me. But I would never forget her face.

She showed me small steel instruments on a tray and photos of a machine, and I closed my eyes, thinking of the vacuum cleaner warning from the church woman. Then there were forms to sign and a check to write. I went back to the lavender couch to wait some more.

When I heard my name again, Paul stood up with me, and we walked into an even smaller room. I gulped at the narrow table and the stirrups, covered by a pair of colorful oven mitts. I undressed and put on the gown they gave me, then lay down and looked up at the ceiling. There was a large poster tacked overhead: a forest with autumn leaves, bright orange and red, and a narrow foot path winding through the trees. I fixed my eyes on the path and told myself, *You're going for a walk. Just walk through the leaves. It's autumn. It's your favorite time of year. Ithaca.*

The door opened, and three women in white came in: the gynecologist, her assistant, and a sweet-looking freckled girl with a long carrot-colored braid. "I'm here to hold your hand," she said, looking at me and then at Paul. "If you need it." I nodded; she took my left hand.

The doctor patted my knee and eased my feet into the padded

stirrups. Her hair was short and spiky, a dark rusty red. The assistant's was like rippled cardamom.

I laughed weakly. "You're all redheads."

Paul took my right hand. His eyes were steady and sad. It was hard to look at his face.

"First we'll open things up." I felt the metal dilators, narrow to thick. When the whirring sound began, I looked up at the forest on the ceiling. A mad swirl of crimson and ochre. The center of me was on fire. I flew down the narrow path through the foliage, the leaves dropping from my hands.

I WOULD MEET YOU
IN A HOSPITAL

My birth mother's voice pulsed through the phone, thin as thread. "Susan?"

I recognized it immediately, but it was an insect voice, tiny and reduced. "Yumi. What is it?"

"I'm in . . . the hospital." It sounded as if it took her last bit of strength to say the words.

I sat on the floor, the phone cord trailing after me from the kitchen. "What hospital? What's happened?"

She gave me the name of the hospital, which I frantically scribbled down. She explained, haltingly, that it was supposed to be a routine surgery, a hysterectomy because of enlarged fibroids on her uterus. I flinched when she said *uterus*. She described it as a misshapen, unnecessary organ. That uterus had been my home. I'd left my fingerprints on the inside of that womb; I'd kicked against its walls. And now it had been cut away, our only point of contact. The surgery had not gone smoothly; immediately afterward, she'd developed a burning fever. "It's just like when . . . I had you."

I'd remembered that from the microfiche records from New Rochelle Hospital. They had mentioned septicemia. Infection. Now she was scheduled for another operation, to somehow fix the problem.

"How long do you think . . . how long will you be there?" I was worried.

I could barely hear her. Either her voice was growing fainter, or she was losing her grip on the phone. "I don't know. Have to go now." A fumbling, as she struggled to put the phone back on the bedside table. It crashed, metallic in my ear, the receiver banging on the metal bed railing. Then a click and silence.

I sat motionless for a good while. Then I scrambled to the yellow pages. What would she say or do if I just showed up? She could turn me away. But what if she was really sick? What if she was about to die?

It scared me to imagine her, a previously healthy person having to endure two major surgeries in one week. I took out my new credit card and read it over the phone. It was way more expensive than a normal flight, but I didn't care.

I took a taxi from the airport. It was a weightless, strange feeling: to walk out of the little tunnel alone. Nobody waiting to greet me. I stood alone and waited for my suitcase and then went to stand by the curb. A half dozen taxis crept along the sidewalk, and then it was my turn. An older man with a grizzled beard, a stiff brush of gray hair, stopped. "Where you going?"

I bit my lip and recited the name of the hospital. He didn't ask why I was going to a hospital. He turned the volume to high and sang nasally to country music. I was happy to be released from conversation. The tragic-happy music carried me to the hospital's nonemergency entrance.

I'd done it. I'd flown more than a thousand miles, without notice, to see a woman who was possibly either too ill or unwilling to see me. Had I totally lost my mind? But the litany wouldn't stop. *She's my mother.* I could possibly be coming to tell her goodbye. It can't be that bad, I told myself. But maybe it was.

I pulled my luggage to the information desk and gave Yumi's name to the white-haired volunteer. She was on the sixth floor, surgical ward. Was I a relative? I swallowed. I thought of what she would want. "No," I said. "I'm a friend."

"Well, visiting hours for non-family members are not until 6 p.m." I looked at my watch. It was only three in the afternoon. I knew my place as non-family.

I went into the hospital gift shop and bought magazines. Then I descended to the basement cafeteria. I sat and read *People, Time, Glamour*. After two hours, I went back to the information desk and asked to use the in-house phone. "Certainly, dear." She dialed the room number and handed the receiver to me.

I swayed a little, my head light, as the line chirred. Then her voice, small. "Hel-lo?"

"Yumi." I took a deep breath. "It's Susan."

I could hear her effort. "*Su*-san." An invisible smile. She sounded—almost glad?

"Yumi. I have to tell you something."

Silence.

"I'm here. I'm downstairs in the lobby." The white-haired volunteer lady raised an eyebrow.

"Oh, Susan." A breathy sigh. "You didn't have to do that."

"Well." I shifted from foot to foot. Was she going to tell me to leave?

Another pause and then: "Come up. But I have to warn you. I look *terrible*."

She wasn't wearing any lipstick, and her mouth was as pale as the rest of her face. They hadn't let her wash her hair in days. But she didn't look so bad. It was strange to see her in a hospital gown, with its snowflake pattern on blue fabric. She looked small, lying under a waffle weave blanket.

I'd never seen my adoptive mother in bed either. Mothers just didn't seem to sleep. She often dozed off lying on the living room floor, watching a late-night television show, but she always went to bed after I did and awoke way before me. I'd rarely seen her wearing pajamas.

And Yumi was always so perfectly put together, her wardrobe

impeccable. I felt badly for her and her sad little gown. Her eyes were closed when I entered her room. The rolling wheels of my suitcase rumbled against the linoleum. Before I could say anything, Yumi's eyes snapped open and she smiled, a trembly, vulnerable smile. She reached out her hand. "Susan."

I didn't know what to do. We hadn't really ever held hands before. I extended my own hand, and we kind of shook, in a weak, awkward way. She let her arm drop heavily back onto the blanket.

"I told you I don't look great."

I shrugged. "You look fine. Really."

She peered over the edge of the bed at my suitcase. "Where are you staying?"

"Gina's. Of course." I saw her lips ready to move.

She nodded, and her eyes fluttered closed. She even seemed to sleep for the briefest moment. Then she shook herself awake. "Did you have a good . . . trip? To Mexico?"

She'd remembered that I'd spent the last few months in a Spanish immersion program in Cuernavaca. "Oh, it was great. Look, I brought you some things." I struggled to lift my suitcase onto the radiator ledge and unzip it. I brought out a striped woven blanket and unfolded it onto her lap.

"Beautiful," she murmured, her fingers twisting in the fringe. "Such bright colors."

"And here are things for making chocolate: the raw stuff, and a special pitcher, and the official wooden chocolate-mixer." I twirled it between my hands, and the wooden rings rattled against each other. "Bate, bate, cho-co-la-te." I sang the Mexican children's chocolate song.

"Mm. I can't wait. You know . . . I love chocolate."

"I know."

She was so subdued. It was frightening, and it was exhilarating. This person who had always intimidated me now seemed vulnerable as a baby rabbit. She looked up at me with soft, affectionate eyes. "You're so nice to do this."

I looked out the window. "Well. Those things, they reminded me of you." I could feel our relationship turning. Maybe this would be a new phase of closeness. If she lived.

A nurse came in with a plastic basket. "Vitals time." She wrapped a glass thermometer in a thin plastic sheath. Yumi opened her mouth obediently and took it under her tongue. The nurse held her wrist and counted with her watch and then pulled the thermometer out. "Still a little high there."

Yumi smiled wanly. "I'm trying to think cool thoughts."

"That's it. Think snow! Ice! Igloos!" The nurse pumped the gray cuff around Yumi's arm and read her blood pressure. "Hmph." She scribbled something on a little card and turned on her squeaky white shoe. "Don't you go and get her too excited now."

I sat down on the vinyl chair next to Yumi's bed. "I should probably go soon."

Yumi shook her head. "Susan. Look out the window."

What? I peered through the white plastic blinds. There wasn't much out there: a few stores, a gas station, a row of nondescript houses.

"Can you see the JCPenney?"

I saw the neon sign on the adjacent building. "Sure. Would you like me to get you something?" Anything.

Yumi licked her lips. The dry tip of her tongue traveled painfully around her mouth. "I want you to go down to that store. Come back in an hour."

"An hour? But . . ."

She circled my wrist with her fingers. There was something fierce and urgent in her grip. "Mika is coming to see me soon. I'm going to tell her about you."

I gasped. "Mika? Now? Are you sure?" This was not what I had expected, not in a hundred years. I wasn't ready. It was all upside down.

She pulled at my wrist. "What time is it?"

"It's six thirty."

"Then go. Now. Go, go, so you don't run into her in the elevator."

I ran. I clambered down the stairwells, six flights, until I reached the ground. I burst out on the sidewalk and searched for the JCPenney sign.

It was not a modern store; it had probably stood unchanged since the sixties. There were uneven metal shelves heaped with cheap, useless items. I wandered, stunned, through aisles of men's and boys' packaged underwear and socks. I browsed wallets and coffee pots and pastel-colored Tupperware sets. In the center of the store stood an old-fashioned candy counter, with a cotton-candy machine whirring pink sugar and a bin with hot salted peanuts. Jars of candy corn and jellybeans stood in rows along the top of a glass counter. I bought a quarter pound of candy corn and quarter pound of peanuts and spent the rest of the hour alternating between each paper bag: a bite of salty, a bite of sweet. When both bags were empty, I crumpled them up, stuffed them in my pocket, and headed to the exit. The hospital loomed above the JCPenney parking lot. The sky was deepening into a dusky gray blue around it. I counted up six stories and stared at the bright square of what might be Yumi's window. Mika was in there. She was receiving news that I was her sister.

I thought of leaving. I thought of calling Gina and saying, *I'm here, please come get me.* But I didn't. I waited until 7:29, and then I rode the elevator back to the sixth floor. I nodded at the nurse who had taken Yumi's temperature earlier; she had dark blonde hair cut into a frizzy perm. She was writing in a patient's chart. She swung her head toward Yumi's door. "Go ahead, but then the other one will have to leave."

The other one. Other daughter. Did she know?

The door was closed. I tapped on it with just one knuckle, softly. There was no answer. Then again, a real rapping on the wood. I heard voices, a voice. I couldn't understand what they were saying; it wasn't "come in," but it wasn't "go away" either. I pushed the door open.

Mika was sitting in the vinyl chair. She stared at me. She was wearing an embroidered blouse the color of rubies, a scarf draped around her shoulders. I couldn't begin to fathom what her expression said.

Yumi shifted in the bed. "Susan," she said. "This is Mika." I nodded. My tongue felt like cotton.

"Mika?" she said. "Here's Susan." She lifted her hand off the bedspread and let it fall. "I'm tired."

Mika stood up. Some of her bracelets jingled, making a little music. "You should sleep."

Yumi pointed at a leather bag on the bedside table. "Mika, take some money from my wallet. Girls. Have some dinner."

Girls!

Mika and I stole quick glances at each other. Have some dinner? I opened my mouth, but I really had no idea what to say. The script was gone. The story was flying out of control.

Mika pulled a twenty from a black leather wallet and rummaged in the bottom of Yumi's purse. "Mom, do you have any lipstick? I look like I'm dead."

"I'm sure there's something in there."

Mika took out a gold tube and went into the small bathroom. I could hear her murmuring to herself. She came out and handed me the lipstick. "Want some?"

I hesitated. I never wore lipstick. Did I look dead too? It felt like such an intimate thing, wearing the same color, passing the same tube of pigment over each of our mouths: mother, daughter, daughter. But I couldn't. I had no idea how to. I was sure I would look like a clown. "No, thanks, I'm fine."

She shrugged and tossed it back into the bag. "Okay. Is there someplace good around here? I don't know this neighborhood."

I stood helplessly. Yumi's voice was down to a whisper. "I think there's a Chinese place—around the corner."

Mika nodded. "Fine." She looked over at my suitcase. "That's yours?"

"Yes." I grabbed the handle awkwardly. "Well."

An enormous sigh came from the bed. Yumi looked as if she

were barely holding onto consciousness. "Have fun, girls." And then she exhaled, and her head slumped onto the pillow.

I followed Mika onto the elevator. We both reached for the "L" button, pulling back when our hands collided. Our eyes studied the blinking light, passing from number to number. Six. Five. Four. Finally, she spoke. "Well. This is not what I expected."

It was hard to not feel apologetic. I clenched the handle of my suitcase, bumping along behind me. "I had no idea she was going to do that just now."

"You didn't?" She looked sideways at me.

"No. She just told me, all of a sudden, to go down to the JCPenney and wait. And when I got back, you were there."

"But how did you get here? Why were you here, at the hospital?" She gestured at my suitcase.

"She called me. The day before yesterday. She said she was in the hospital, and I got worried. She sounded so . . . sick." Mika stopped walking. I took a few steps, and then I stopped too. We stood on the sidewalk, two women and a suitcase, and people flowed around us as if we were boulders in a river. She was realizing that she was not the only daughter. That she was not the oldest child. That someone else cared about that woman in her sixth-floor hospital bed. I spread my hands out, as if I were holding an invisible bowl. *Please don't hate me*, I wanted to say. Her eyes were dark and hard with shock.

We were standing in front of a restaurant with a gold-lettered sign. Dragon Palace. A carved, snaky dragon with fake ruby eyes curled over the door. I studied the menu taped inside the window. "Do you think this is the place?"

Mika opened the door. "It's fine. Whatever."

We slipped into opposite sides of a red vinyl booth. Mika stretched out, leaning her back against the wall and extending her legs across the seat.

She sighed and picked up a menu. "I love booths," she said. "I think all restaurants should only have booths. Chairs are so small.

Uncomfortable." She shuddered, looking at the diners sitting at round tables.

I nodded. "Right. Booths are the best." It was a bridge, a small one. We sank into the mundane task of choosing food. One of her eyebrows rose. "This place is pretty cheap. We can get a lot for twenty bucks."

I patted my purse. "I have money too." I tried to focus on the menu. "Really, I'll eat anything." A waiter came and stood over us, a pencil hovering over his pad. Mika pointed at half a dozen items—spring rolls, spicy eggplant, something in black bean sauce. I nodded. I wanted to let her lead, to let her feel like she had control over something during this surreal, out-of-control evening.

Mika leaned forward and put her hands flat on the table. "How did this all happen? How did you and Yumi get together?" I was surprised to hear that she didn't say "my mother" or "Mom."

"It's hard to know where to begin."

"Where did you grow up? Who adopted you? How did you find Yumi? When? Just start anywhere!" Her voice was urgent. Her eyes had lost their hard, shocked expression and were now bright with curiosity.

"Well, I grew up in New Jersey. My parents were both nisei too." I described the green house on Summit Street, our little town of Park Ridge. The Japanese relatives and the un-Japanese community. Going to New York for Japanese church. The constant question people asked me. *What are you?*

She snapped her chopsticks apart and a splinter flew across the table. "Yes, I get that question too. But wait a minute. What *are* you? I mean, who's your biological father?"

I laughed my snorty laugh. "That's the million-dollar question."

"What do you mean?"

"I've known Yumi for five years now, and still she hasn't answered that question."

"Whoa." She nodded then, a slow and thoughtful nod. She looked me straight in the eyes. "Well, that's Yumi for you."

"What do *you* mean?"

"She's like that. If she doesn't want to talk about something, she's not going to talk about it."

"Like what?"

She held a piece of bright purple eggplant between her chopsticks. "Like . . . you know she was in the camps, right? The internment camps?"

"Yes."

"She doesn't want talk about it. She just says that it wasn't all that bad. If I ask questions, she changes the subject." The eggplant fell back onto the plate.

The dishes were cleared away, and we snapped open our fortune cookies. Mine read: *Your life will improve after meeting an influential stranger.*

She held up the little slip of fortune. "I can't believe she won't tell you who your father is. Well, I actually *can* believe it, but . . ." she shook her head.

"She said it's definitely not *your* father." I'd met her husband, Ed, before, and he'd been friendly to me. "That would make things so much simpler."

"What has she told you? Anything?"

I thought back to the day we met at the Holiday Inn. "That he lives in a different state, he's friendly and athletic, and he has three kids. You might even know him! A family friend." I didn't add, *And that he thinks about me.*

Her brows knitted together. "Family friend. Three kids. There was a guy, maybe it was him, but he died."

"Died?" My stomach plummeted. "What was his name?"

She told me. Ted Tuckerman. I scribbled it onto the back of the fortune.

It was only a wild guess, a stab in the dark, but I hadn't considered the possibility that he could be dead. Maybe that was why Yumi said we'd never meet. The last time I'd ventured a question about him, over a year before, Yumi had said briskly, "You won't meet him, and I can't tell you why. Maybe one day I'll tell you why it's impossible."

I tried not to dwell on the shock and sadness that my birth father was dead. I wanted to ask more questions, but it was all too much to take in: a gravely ill birth mother, a newly informed sister, and a possibly dead birth father, all in one day.

After dinner, Mika and I walked to a park. There was an outdoor concert, with people scattered across the lawn on blankets and folding chairs. A jazz band played into the warm indigo sky, and strings of tiny white lights glittered in the trees. We stopped at a rolling cart where a man sold paper cones of flavored ice. We grinned at the vendor and looked at our reflections, blurred and dancing, in the metal door of the freezer. As we walked away, she turned to me. "Do you think that guy could tell we were sisters?"

She had recognized me as kin. We held our palms up, measured the wide expanse from thumb to finger.

"What big hands you have." Her voice was mischievous, wolfy. "Just like mine!"

We started laughing, twirling to the music, skipping along the park's gravel path. I wanted to tell everyone, to run from blanket to blanket, whoop and scream at all the people sitting in the grass. *We're sisters.*

LONG-LOST DAUGHTER

"There's someone I want you to meet," my birth mother told me over the phone. I was shocked. She never wanted me to meet anyone. But there was a man named Barry, a longtime friend of hers. He was going to be in California the same time she was. They had plans to visit old friends of his, Meryl and Peter Lake, and she invited me to join them for dinner at their home in the Santa Cruz mountains.

I had to ask. "Is Barry my . . . ?"

"Your father? No. But he has known about you for a long time."

The Lakes' house was deep in a redwood grove, dwarfed in the shadows of calm, towering trees. It felt more cabin than house, with rough shingles, a lumpy stone chimney, and a gnarled deck. I pulled into the long driveway.

A woman with a silvery chin-length bob and a mossy green sweater stepped onto the deck.

"Is this her? Oh, she's here!" She waved down at me with a grand sweep of her arm: half yoga, half interpretive dance. *Welcome*, it said. We know who you are, and you are welcome.

I lifted my pink bakery box of cookies off the passenger seat. Never go empty handed, my mother had taught me. Don't forget the omiyage.

Yumi bounded out the door and called my name. "Suuusan!" I barely recognized her, tanned and earthy looking in a red T-shirt and khaki hiking shorts covered in pockets. Her muscular legs sprouted from nubby woolen socks and hiking boots. I had

129

never seen her dressed like this, with this kind of energy. I remembered that Meryl was a leader of women's backpacking trips. Yumi had been transformed by their time near Lake Tahoe. Her perfect, sculpted hair was almost messy looking under a canvas bucket hat. Its brim was woven with a garland of twisty branches and live moss.

Meryl's arms were outstretched. "So *you're* the long-lost daughter!" She enfolded me in her arms, and I smelled lemon and wood smoke. Then she stepped back and held me at arm's length. "I'm Meryl. Welcome! We are so very glad you're here. We've heard all about you."

I was stunned. I glanced over her shoulder at Yumi. Did Meryl really say the word *daughter* out loud?

Yumi either didn't notice or didn't care. She put her arm around me for a second, a half hug. "Did you have any trouble finding us? This place really is in the middle of the woods, isn't it?"

Before I could answer, she took the box from my hands. "You didn't need to bring anything."

I mouthed, "Omiyage," and she smiled. "Of course."

I followed her and Meryl through the house—glowing wooden floors, brightly painted walls, and handmade fabric. A loom with dangling strands of green and gold threads stood in the corner. It was beautiful, as if it grew organically out of the redwood forest.

Meryl's husband Peter looked like a trim, fit Santa Claus in hiking boots and jeans. He clinked a sweating bottle of beer with another bearded, balding man with rimless glasses. Yumi steered me by the elbow. "Susan," she said. "This is Barry."

I wasn't sure if I should shake his hand, hug him, or just wave, lamely, from a few feet away. I shrugged, with a weak smile.

"Well. It's been a long time," he said. He looked me up and down. His gaze moved from Yumi to me and back again, and his eyes reddened at the edges.

"The last time I saw you, you were . . ." He scanned the picnic table. "You were the size of that loaf of bread."

Yumi followed his gaze, and we all stared at the sourdough, swaddled in a checkered napkin.

"Barry was the only one who saw you in the hospital when you were born," she said. "I was advised not to. Not until later. Much later." I remembered the story of our taxi ride together, from the hospital to the adoption agency, the bottle she fed me.

She'd flown from her midwestern town to visit Barry and his wife in New Rochelle that August in 1959. She was seven months pregnant, but they didn't realize it. *I wore very loose clothes and a very tight girdle.* One day during her visit, she'd walked to a nearby park.

Her water had broken as she sat on a bench, reading a paperback. Amniotic fluid flowed through the slats and puddled underneath on the ground. Then the pains began.

A police officer in an indigo uniform leaned against his car, listening to the buzz and crackle of his radio. She called out to him. "Excuse me."

He didn't hear. Then, "Help." A little louder. "Help, please."

He turned and saw her. Doubled over on the park bench. He hurried over. "I need to go. To the hospital, please."

He drove her to the hospital in the back of the police car. In spite of the pain, she didn't make a sound, but she was leaking. Leaking through her dress onto the upholstery of his car. She took a pad and pen from her purse and wrote down Barry's phone number.

"Please," she said. "Call my friends. Tell them I'm at the hospital."

He took the slip of paper in his white-gloved hand.

"Tell them I had an appendicitis attack." Her eyes were glassy with pain.

She entered New Rochelle Hospital in a wheelchair. Soon it was clear to the emergency room physician what was happening.

Her gurney was wheeled to the maternity floor, where a black rubber mask over her nose and mouth put her into twilight sleep. It was common then, to let women sleep through labor. *Please,* she said, before the sparkling darkness overcame her, *please don't tell my friends.*

And shortly after midnight, I was born.

Somebody told. Somebody—a nurse, the hospital operator, a random staff person—told Barry and his wife, as they hurried to her. They were stunned that I was a baby and not an appendix.

When Yumi woke, they were at her bedside, with bewildered expressions and a vase of yellow roses. *We had no idea,* they said.

I know, she said.

You only looked a little bit plumper than we'd remembered, said Barry's wife.

I'm sorry, she said. *I'm sorry to burden you with this knowledge.*

It's all right, they said. And then: *We saw her. We couldn't help it, once we knew. We had to look. Just a peek through the glass.*

Yumi didn't look up. She didn't meet their eyes. But her hands, open on the blanket, twitched a little as if to say, *Tell me.*

She's beautiful, said Barry's wife. *So tiny. So very tiny.* Her voice caught. *No bigger than a loaf of bread, all bundled up in that pink blanket.*

I'm glad you saw her, Yumi said. *But I'm not going to.*

What will happen? asked Barry's wife. Her eyes were bright with tears.

She'll stay here, my birth mother said. *I'll go back home, and she'll stay here.*

Meryl poured me a glass of wine, deep gold and smelling of fruit. I drank it down quickly, and it was refilled right away.

Yumi also drank. I stared at her, her strong tanned legs exactly like mine. Her laughter floated up to the trees. It was like a dream, being in this redwood forest with her, somehow free of secrets.

"You look so alike!" Meryl exclaimed. "Let me take a picture."

Yumi tilted her head toward mine. She rested her arm on my shoulder and we lifted our glasses. The sun shone through the illuminated globes of liquid. *What a beautiful mother and daughter,* said Meryl. Her camera shutter clicked.

Meryl and Peter's grown son, with a ponytail of hay-colored hair, had caught the evening's dinner. He crouched over a red plastic cooler and dug through a pile of chipped ice with his hands. He lifted out several hefty, silvery salmon, and everyone applauded.

"Right under the Golden Gate Bridge," he said. "They practically leap into the boat, they're swimming so thick."

He laid them out on newspaper and expertly cleaned them until they were nothing but slabs of deep orange flesh. He wrapped them in blankets of tin foil and laid them on a grill over mesquite and branches of rosemary.

I missed my father with a deep and sudden pang. *He would love this,* I thought, *people catching fish and bringing them home for dinner.* I remembered the way he would take Cap Rudy's midnight boat out from Miami Beach, where we spent every hot, thunderstorm summer. My mother would let me stand on the hotel patio in my pajamas and count the lights on the horizon before I went to bed. "Third light on the right is our boat," my father told us, and I scanned the dark water for the blinking signal. "He'll bring us some good red snapper," my mother said, and in the morning there would be filets wrapped in newspaper in the refrigerator. My mother would steam a pot of rice in the electric cooker, and my father would slice the red flesh into delicate strips. That was my favorite breakfast: the freshest sashimi, melting in our mouths, drizzled with soy sauce in bowls of hot white rice. When I lifted the fish into my mouth with snap-apart wooden chopsticks, a sense of pride always washed through me: my father had pulled this fish from the sea.

He would have loved this party, these people. I imagined him kneeling on the cedar deck with the young ponytailed guy. He would have offered to scale and clean them.

I asked, "How do you get to go on one of those boats, under the bridge?" I wanted to bring my father the next time he came to California. He handed me a business card with the name of a fishing-boat operation, and I slipped it into my wallet.

I sat next to Yumi all evening. We drank golden wine and ate the buttery salmon. My box of cookies was passed around. My birth mother's face was transformed by the rosy sunlight that paused over the deck before the chilly dusk set in. It was soft and happy and relaxed. There were no secrets to keep from these people; the truth of who I was sat plainly at the table. It was the happiest day we had ever spent together.

I stopped for a quick dinner before my calligraphy class at a corner café called the Edible Complex. Standing in line by the cashier was John, the dimpled doctor I'd dated briefly when I'd first moved to California. We had drifted apart, and I hadn't seen him for four years. I wondered if I should say anything. He was still so handsome.

He looked surprised when I said hello, but then he put his tray down on my table. We talked and talked and learned that in the four-year gap, we'd both gotten involved in Central American solidarity organizations. He'd spent time doing medical relief work in El Salvador, and I'd been in Nicaragua. In the coming weeks, he'd call me late at night to say, "Listen to this," and read me passages from Rilke or MLK. His voice on the phone soon became my favorite sound. He was the only person I knew who had as many books—in shelves as well as stacked on the floor—as I did.

The next week, I invited John to dinner with Yumi and Barry in my studio apartment on Pine Street. I loved this place. On the edge of San Francisco's Japantown, it was one of a dozen studios within a grand Victorian mansion. Two small rooms with floor to ceiling glass windows, a closet-sized bathroom, and a little porch no bigger than a rowboat. It was charming and quirky and all mine.

I wanted Yumi to meet John; I had a feeling that he was special, more special than anyone I'd been with in years. Maybe even serious. I wanted to show them both off to each other. I was still giddy from feeling so openly shared at Meryl and Peter's house.

I made a salad and the same green, fragrant Moosewood spinach soup that I'd prepared for John on our very first date, years before. Yumi and Barry brought a fruit tart. We crowded together for wine on my tiny deck, under the plum tree that had started dropping sweet, swollen fruit. Yumi gathered them into a bowl and helped me wash them. "This is so wonderful," she said. "Fruit right outside your door!"

John and Barry sat on the sofa and exchanged conversation about their work and where they grew up. Yumi acted as sous chef in my miniature kitchen. *He seems very nice,* she whispered, and I blushed. I really liked him. She sliced some cheese and baguette, and the men's voices drifted over in a rumble from the sofa.

I thought I heard someone say, "I disagree." The men were shaking their heads and looking at us. John said, "I think she has the right to know." I realized with a shock that they were talking about Yumi and me.

"I think she has the right to her privacy," Barry said. His head inclined toward Yumi.

I froze. I glanced at Yumi. Her cheerful banter had quieted, and her face was expressionless. I wrestled the cork from the wine bottle, and it crumbled. A few little fragments floated down and settled in the wine. The soup was boiling over, burping huge bubbles of green onto the stovetop.

I carried bowls to the table and the four of us ate quietly, spoons clinking against porcelain. I turned up the cassette player and let Vivaldi wash over us. We talked about the fog coming in from the ocean, the weather report, and about how terrible Reagan was as a president. We maintained a polite conversation.

When dinner was over, Barry and Yumi didn't linger. They left quickly, after a polite, murmured thanks. Yumi's flight was early the next morning.

Of course, I said, *of course.* I nodded and smiled.

They shut the door behind them, and I watched them descend the steps through the wall of glass. Yumi turned to wave one more time. Her frozen smile met mine.

"What did you think?" I asked John while he helped me wash the dishes. I expected him to say what everyone did: She's beautiful. She's charming. She's amazing.

"She was nice."

I bristled. "Is that all?"

"I mean, this thing about not telling you about your father. I don't know if that's right."

I held a sponge in midair. I agreed with him, of course. But I was angry that he'd articulated what I was trying so hard not to see.

I blasted hot water over my hands and then wiped them fiercely with a towel. "Listen. I'm really tired. Maybe I'd better call it a night too."

His eyes were perplexed. "But I thought . . ." he glanced toward my bedroom.

"Maybe some other time." I stared at the floor while he gathered up his coat, his little pile of books. Things he had wanted to read to me. I let him softly out the door.

"I'm sorry." I listened to his footsteps in the alleyway fade away.

Two years later, John and I married in a forest-themed church in San Francisco, followed by a reception at Greens, a vegetarian restaurant overlooking the bay. My parents and grandmother shone with happiness. To my surprise, Yumi and Mika came, and for a few days we coexisted as a kind of extended family. I adapted a kind of don't-ask-don't-tell policy. I knew that I wouldn't be introducing them as my birth family, and she realized that many of my friends probably knew. Using the contact from Yumi's friends, I arranged a salmon-fishing expedition under the Golden Gate bridge the day before the wedding.

Going out on a salmon-fishing boat instead of a wedding rehearsal dinner felt perfect. We wouldn't be sitting stiffly around a long banquet table, with people barely able to hear each other. Our family would spend the day out in the sunshine, on the ocean, doing something essential, just as ancient families had done—hunting, fishing, for the wedding feast.

Yumi caught the biggest fish. That night, we feasted together like a family in our A-frame cabin in the Oakland Hills. My grandmother prepared multiple pots of rice. The house smelled deliciously of the familiar teriyaki marinade my mother used to cook everything: hotdogs, steak, fish.

I was worried I would stumble through our first wedding dance, so I asked my parents to demonstrate for us. "Nah," said my mother, wiping her hands on a dish towel. Yumi and my father waltzed through the living room to a folksy Kate Wolf song, and I learned to dance without stepping on John's toes.

We blended together, that evening before the wedding, like kin. My two mothers chatted side by side on the brown velvet sofa while my father marveled at the amount of salmon that was still left over. "Plenty of good nokori, huh, obasan?" he said to my grandmother. They would feast on salmon for days while John and I were on our honeymoon in Banff.

I leaned on the wooden banister of our bedroom loft and listened to the voices of my family murmuring, a soft mixture of Japanese and English drifting up to the peaked cedar roof.

JUST A BEE STING

John was attending a medical conference in Washington, DC, and I planned to meet up with him for the last few days. In the shuttle van, I buckled up and fell asleep immediately. The driver shook me awake at the airport. I felt drugged, my head buzzing with a strange heaviness. I staggered onto the plane and dozed again.

"I think I'm sick," I told John when he picked me up at Dulles. "I feel woozy."

His eyebrow arched. "Do you think you could be pregnant?" We had stopped using birth control only recently. We had thought it might take months, maybe even a year. Not so soon as this.

I flipped through the yellow pages, searching for a clinic open on a weekend. I avoided anything hinting at the word "crisis." While John sat in a darkened auditorium learning about diseased livers, I climbed into a taxi and headed to the Georgetown Women's Center. This was years before drugstore pregnancy tests would become available.

A technician drew a tube of blood from my arm and told me to call back in three hours. I wandered the streets of a city I didn't know, glancing at my watch, the tiny second hand jerking through space.

My blood sat in the glass tube. Half of the blood was coded with my birth mother's DNA. Half of it was blood of my invisible birth father, whose name Yumi still wouldn't reveal. Blood of so many unknown relatives. And now this blood would tell me if I was carrying another family member.

When I called, the woman on the phone exclaimed, "Congratulations!" just as the church woman had at the crisis pregnancy clinic, years before. She altered women's lives with one word: *Yes. No.* I stared at the telephone, affixed to the wall outside a bookstore. I went in and bought a book about pregnancy. I ran my finger along the due-date chart, counting months. *Early January.*

We were happy. I grew and grew. Back in California, I walked along the grassy trails of Sea Ranch, through the wild wind, my energy bursting. I wore John's jeans to accommodate my five-month pregnant belly.

In the summer, we traveled to the beach in North Carolina with his brother's family. Nags Head, where I had almost drowned in the undertow as a teenager. I swelled in the humidity like a sponge, my breasts enormous, my face squishing with fluid.

"Look at me," I said to John, frowning in the mirror. "I don't look like me."

"Honey, you look wonderful." He cradled my puffy face.

John flew directly from our family vacation to El Salvador, heading a medical delegation to the war zone of Guazapa. My father-in-law disapproved, saying out loud that he thought John was abandoning me in my delicate state. I didn't feel abandoned, though; I was proud of the medical solidarity work we were doing. While he was interviewing field doctors in El Salvador, I spent a day loading a container full of wheelchairs, crutches, and medicine bound for Nicaragua. By evening, I noticed I couldn't lace my sneakers. My feet were swollen like small footballs.

When I picked John up at San Francisco airport, I asked him, "Don't you think I look fat?"

"You're pregnant, sweetheart," he replied. "That's how you're supposed to look."

I eased myself onto the scale. I'd gained thirteen pounds since he'd left for El Salvador the week before. I pulled out my dog-eared copy of *What to Expect When You're Expecting*. In a red-printed column, it said: *Call the doctor if you gain more than three pounds in one week. If your face or hands or feet are swollen. If. If. If.* . . . I checked them all off. I called my obstetrician, Lisa, and whispered, "I think something is wrong."

Lisa's voice was calm. "Swelling is pretty common," she said, "but it would be a good idea to get a blood-pressure check. Can John do that?"

We stopped by his office before going to dinner. We planned to eat, see a movie, and then browse a bookstore—our favorite date. In the exam room, I held out my arm. I was impatient to get to our favorite Mediterranean restaurant. My mouth had been dreaming of spanakopita all day.

I heard the Velcro tearing open on the cuff, felt its smooth blue band wrapping around my arm. I swung my feet and smiled at John, the stethoscope around his neck. I loved this small gesture of him taking care of me. The cuff tightened, and I felt the pounding of my heart echoing up and down my fingers, through my elbow.

"Lie down," he said quietly.

The numbers were wrong. He measured it again, his eyes serious as he watched the mercury climb. He shook his head. "What's Lisa's number?"

His voice was serious on the phone as he talked to her. He turned and told me to pee into a cup. "She wants me to do a dipstick for protein."

I sat on the toilet while he searched his office for protein strips. I handed him a paper cup of gold liquid, cloudy and dense. He dipped the strip into my urine. It changed color immediately, from white to powdery blue to indigo.

"Hm," he said, frowning. "You've definitely got protein in there."

"What does that mean?"

He was on the phone to Lisa again. "She says we need to get to the hospital." We walked across the street and took the elevator to the maternity floor. They were waiting for me. The nurses hurried off my clothes and shoes and wrapped another blood pressure cuff around my arm. The shades were pulled down to darken the room. They moved with serious urgency.

Suddenly, I had a new doctor. Lisa, obstetrician of the normal, was off my case, and I was assigned a special neonatologist. Dr. Weiss was bald, with thick glasses, clogs, and a soft voice.

A squirt of blue gel on my belly for the fetal monitor, the galloping sound of hoofbeats, the baby riding a wild pony inside me. What a relief it was to hear that sound, although I didn't need a monitor; I could feel the baby punching my liver.

There was a name for what I had. Preeclampsia. Well, preeclampsia was better than eclampsia, and as long as it was *pre-*, then they could stop it, couldn't they? And what was eclampsia, anyway? An explosion of blood pressure, a flood of protein poisoning the blood, kidney failure, the vessels in spasm, a stroke, seizures, blindness, death. But I didn't have any of those things, not yet. I had *pre*eclampsia. It felt safe, and I was calm.

They slipped a needle into my wrist and hung a bag of magnesium sulfate. To prevent seizures, they said. "You may feel a little hot." As the drug slipped into my bloodstream, I felt a flash of electricity inside my mouth. My tongue was baking. My scalp prickled, burning, and I threw up onto the sheets. It felt like I was being microwaved from the inside.

I was wheeled down to radiology. We saw pictures of the baby onscreen, waving, treading water. A real child, not a pony or a fish.

The X-ray tech, a woman with curly brown hair and a red Coca-Cola T-shirt, pressed the wand deep into my belly. She asked, "Do you want to know the sex?"

"Yes!"

"There you go." She pressed harder and then pointed. A flash between the legs, like a finger. A boy. I nearly leapt off the gurney.

"John! Did you see? A boy! It's going to be Samuel!" Sahm-*well*, the Spanish pronunciation, named after our beloved host father in Nicaragua.

He looked away.

The neonatologist stood next to my bed. He recited numbers slowly. "This baby needs at least two more weeks for viability. He's already too small, way too small. But you . . ." He looked at me sadly. "You probably can't survive two weeks without having a stroke, seizures, worse."

"What are the chances that we could both make it? Me and the baby."

"Less than ten percent. Maybe less than five percent." The space between his fingers shrunk into nothing.

I was toxemic, poisoned by my own pregnancy. The only cure, he said, was to not be pregnant anymore. The baby needed two more weeks, just fourteen days.

I looked at John hopefully. "It's not that long. I can wait. It will be all right."

"Honey. Your blood pressure is through the roof. Your kidneys are shutting down. You could have a stroke."

I smiled at him. I said that having a stroke at twenty-nine would not be such a big deal. I was young. I was a physical therapist. I knew about rehab. I could rehabilitate my*self*. I could walk with a cane. Lots of people did it. I had a bizarre image of leaning on the baby's carriage, supporting myself the way some people use a walker.

He spent the night on a cot next to my bed. "I can't lose this baby," I said.

I lay in the bed and counted days. If I could just make it to October.

The next day, they took a sample of my amniotic fluid. This revealed that his lungs weren't developed enough. That he was "nonviable." That even though he was twenty-two weeks by cal-endar, he was only eighteen weeks by size. Nonviable.

I lay with my hands on my belly, feeling Samuelito's limbs

turning this way and that. There was nothing inside me that could even imagine saying goodbye.

"I don't know what to do," I sobbed.

John held my hand. "It's so hard." He paused. "I don't know either, honey."

"Is there anything we can do?" I was desperate.

He looked at me gently. "I wish they had a different recommendation. But I trust Lisa. And the neonatologist. I did some research too. It just . . . it's not looking good."

They were recommending termination of the pregnancy, as soon as possible.

The next morning, I called my parents. "We're in trouble," I said. My mother started crying. She was alone in the house. "I've got to find Daddy." He was on the road, traveling somewhere—where? North Carolina, Kentucky, Tennessee? On the road meant invisible, unreachable, gone. He only called home, long-distance, once a week.

"I'll come out tomorrow," my mother insisted.

"There's no reason," I told her. "It's all going to be over."

Then I called my birth mother. She didn't cry. Her voice was smooth as water. "I've known other women who've had the same thing, and it's turned out fine."

"It won't be fine. It's too early, way too early." I was not like the others. Most preeclampsia cases happen much closer to full term, and they are resolved by emergency C-sections.

She continued. "I'm sure everything will be *fine.*" Her voice was flat, gentle. She didn't offer to fly out to California. I wondered about the stroke. If I really had one, would that bring her to my bedside? I caught a glimmer of understanding of what it meant to be a parent. And seeing for the first time that as much as I longed for it, this was not what she was. Not to me.

The next day brought more magnesium sulfate, the cuff that inflated every five minutes, the fetal monitor booming through the room. No change in status for either me or Samuelito.

I signed papers of consent, my hand moving numbly across the paper. My mind screamed, I do *not* consent, I do *not*, I do not.

In the evening, the special doctor entered with a tray and a syringe. He was followed by a nurse with mournful eyes.

"It's just going to be a bee sting," he said.

And it was: a small tingle with quick pricking bubbles under my navel. A glass tube like a thin straw went in and out with a barely audible pop. It was fast. I said silently, *I love you, I love you, you must be hearing this, please hear me.* And then a Band-Aid was unwrapped, with its plastic smell of childhood, and spread onto my belly.

"All done," he said. *All done.*

My child was inside, swallowing the fizzy drink. It bubbled against his tiny tongue, a deadly soda pop.

It was a drug to stop his heart. To lay him down to sleep, so he wouldn't feel what would happen the next day, the terrible thing, the D and E. *Dilation and Evacuation* was its official name. They told me I would sleep through it.

Evacuees were what Japanese Americans like my birth mother were called when they were ripped from their homes, tagged like animals, flung into the desert. Evacuated, exiled, thrown away.

I lay on my side, pinching the pillowcase. I wondered if he was startled by the drug's taste, if it was bitter, or strange, or just different from the salt water he was used to. I prayed that it wouldn't hurt. That it would be fast.

John sat next to the bed and held one hand as I pressed the other against my belly. I looked over his shoulder into the dark slice of night between the heavy curtains. Samuel—my Samuelito—jumped against my hand once. He leaped through the space into the darkness and then was gone.

That was my first experience of being a mother. I went home gushing fluid, peeing and sweating the quarts of liquid my body hadn't been able to release. I wept oceans.

My parents called me several times a day. "Is there anything you need? Can we come? What can we do for you?" I imagined them wringing their hands, pacing, feeling helpless.

"Nothing," I said dully. *I need my baby.*

A week passed before I called my birth mother again. Her voice was bright.

"Oh!" she said, surprised when I told her what had happened.

She said, "When I didn't hear back from you, I assumed everything *must* have turned out all right." *Seven days,* I thought. Seven days and you never called, not once, to see how I was. How *we* were.

"Well, it didn't turn out all right," I said. My throat was rough. Her first grandchild was gone, and she never picked up the phone. It had been easier for her to support me through my first abortion.

"Well," she said, "I'm sorry. You're so young, though . . ."

"I have to go." I hung up before she could say it.

Is that what she told herself, at twenty-seven, when she had birthed me and then let me go? Did she just set her vision to the future, to the other children she would eventually have? Was it really that easy?

There weren't many choices for my birth mother when she was pregnant with me, unmarried, in 1959, in that small town. She could have used a knitting needle or rat poison and tried to end it herself. She might have run away to an anonymous town where nobody knew her and passed herself off as a widow with a child. But that would have meant tearing herself away from her family, her community, and everything she knew. Instead, she bought a girdle. She ate like a bird. She did what she could do to ensure that I would be as small as possible.

After I was born, early and small, she signed the papers for my adoption.

Her choices had narrowed long before the day she found out she was pregnant with me, though. They started shrinking when

Japan attacked Pearl Harbor. When our country went to war with a country whose people looked like her family. Her family had no choice when their West Coast business was shuttered, and they had to pack their lives into a single trunk. They were forced to show their allegiance by moving into a barbed-wire compound in the high, dusty desert. She was ten years old.

They had no other option when the war ended, and they were offered a place to live in a tiny, all-white town in the Midwest. Her family would become a charitable, benevolent experiment: she was befriended, but untouchable. She was too Other for that.

After losing Samuel, I was terrified by how my body had betrayed me. John and I talked about pursuing adoption instead; it seemed better than running the gauntlet of another pregnancy. My heart felt solidarity with a prospective adopted child. I would be able to say to them, "I know how you feel." I would help them stay in touch with their birth relatives; I would fight for their records. John and I attended an informational meeting, gathered letters of support from our friends, and initiated a home-study.

Our attempts at contraception were half-hearted, though, and six months later I was pregnant again. While on a plane to a health delegation in Nicaragua, I felt the familiar swelling in my hands and feet. I sought out the clinic in the Mexico City airport during a layover and wept when my blood pressure was, once again, dangerously high.

I was put on a plane back home and spent the next six months on bedrest. Mollie was born a month early, small but healthy. Four years later, Emma made a surprise entrance while I was in graduate school. These daughters filled our life, but I would never forget that son, our small cowboy, and the way he galloped through me.

Part of me believed that I had failed a crucial test of motherhood, the law that says your child comes before you, even if it means death. I had put myself first when it came to Samuel. Sometimes I could not bear what that felt like. But I looked at my girls, and I knew that they would not exist if I had made other choices. If I had stayed with that Paul and never had that first abortion. If I had refused to give up on Samuel's chances. If my birth mother had taken a coat hanger to me instead of hiding me under a girdle. If she had stolen away with me and pretended to be a widow in a new town. If she and my birth father had made a life together. If, if, if.

There are lifetimes of *ifs* to consider. But in the end, my birth mother and I made the choices we did.

I could not condemn her or myself for what we had each decided for ourselves, years ago. Had we chosen wrongly? Selfishly? There was no answer to those questions. My life had been steeped in the tea of reproductive choice since the moment of my own conception. All I could do was wish us peace for the choices that we'd made.

DAIRY QUEEN

The summer after I met my half sister, Mika, she graduated from college. She was leaving the following week to live abroad for a year. Her family planned a celebration and going-away party.

"Sooozin?" Her voice on the phone. "Want to come to my graduation party? My father makes incredible homemade pizzas."

"Really?" It was the first invitation I'd ever received from a blood relative. "Yes!"

There were some terms to agree to. I would not mention in public my status as sister-of-the-graduate. I winced.

"Listen," Mika said. "Yumi made me promise not to tell anyone."

My throat tightened. Maybe I shouldn't go after all.

She continued. "I told my friends about you, of course. They think it's great." It was a relief to know I wasn't hidden in someone else's closet.

"So they know. I know they know. They know that I know. And the only person who doesn't know . . ."

She laughed.

Mika was the guardian of Yumi's secrets. Mika teetered in the middle, wanting to be true to both of us, unable to appease either one. She carried a huge burden, torn between her mother and me, her secret sister.

Unable to resist the invitation, I bought a plane ticket. Mika was busy with final exams and graduation events, so I slept at Yumi and Bob's house, a yellow house in a modest neighborhood.

Bob, with his thick glasses and bristly mustache, greeted me kindly and offered me a mug of mint tea. He seemed surprisingly relaxed about my presence. If *he* didn't mind, why did I have to be such a secret?

Yumi showed me to a tiny guest room with a foldout sofa bed. She opened a cabinet and removed a puffy, cloud-like futon comforter. "I only take this out for special guests." Special. I thought about the miniature cross-stitched pillow ornament she'd sent me one Christmas: YOU ARE SPECIAL, it said in miniscule Xs. She'd pulled a needle through the fabric herself, with blood-red thread.

I barely slept. Above an old television set, a gallery of family photos gazed down at me: Mika and Kaz as infants, through elementary school, in high school. Sepia portraits of Japanese people in kimonos. My ancestors. I strained to memorize their faces. I considered asking if I could have a copy of one, but this was something I could not ask. I'd hold these images in my head, and that was all.

The room grew lighter. I watched the rectangle of window turn from indigo to icy blue. Then Yumi appeared in the doorway, in a flannel robe. White pajama bottoms and her pedicured feet were visible beneath the hem. "Would you like to shower?" she asked. She offered me a stack of creamy towels, and I followed her down the hallway and through her bedroom.

The bed was neatly made and piled with embroidered pillows. I thought about my parents' room, the surfaces stacked high with cluttered magazines, random knickknacks, and dusty cosmetics from decades past. I could write my name in the dust that covered the furniture. As I passed Yumi's immaculate bureau, I gasped at the sight of my own face in a small gold frame. It was a portrait I'd sent her from my own graduation. It sat propped between photos of her other children. I was stunned to see it there, in this intimate space.

"Here you go. There should be plenty of hot water." She smiled brightly and shut the bathroom door with a soft click. I undressed and stepped into the shower stall. As the warm water fell around me, I began shaking. I held the melting bar of soap and inhaled the scent of her shampoo. Suddenly, I was weeping uncontrollably. I was naked in my birth mother's house. Salt water and lather mixed on my face; my body was slippery, surrounded by steam.

I sat next to Yumi and Bob at the graduation. Yumi wore enormous Jackie Onassis sunglasses and a pink suit. I held a gift for Mika on my knees: a small, snappy point-and-shoot camera for her post-graduation adventures. In the sea of anonymous parents and friends, I blended in. We clapped and cheered when Mika crossed the stage for her diploma.

I tried to be helpful for the party. I tore open packages of paper plates and gold paper napkins. Bob made an impressive assortment of homemade pizzas. A chocolate truffle cake with Mika's name in icing was flanked by champagne and plastic flutes. I connected the stems and lined them up in parallel rows.

Mika's friends trickled in, carrying flowers and wine. Yumi greeted them all exuberantly.

"Helloooooo! Thank you so much for coming!" I tried to be inconspicuous. I stood awkwardly against a wall in my velvet dress, holding a plastic champagne flute.

I wandered through the party picking up abandoned plates and used plastic cups. Some guests were watching me with sidelong glances. A tall guy with black-framed glasses raised an eyebrow when our eyes met. He looked at me and then looked across the room at Mika. He nodded almost imperceptibly. They *did* know. They were checking me out.

Yumi bustled cheerfully around the crowd, pouring champagne, chatting with everyone. Music from the boom box shook the hardwood floors as she danced with Bob, stomping her shoes, looking beautiful.

I had never seen my adoptive mother dance or host a party.

"Nah," she'd say. "Not for me." She had never hosted a dinner party in my life, other than family holiday gatherings. Sometimes, my father invited the neighbors over for New Year's Day, and he made a tempura feast in an electric skillet in the dining room. But for the most part, he was on the road, and she was allergic to socializing.

After the party, I realized that I had still not set eyes on my half brother, Kaz. He was living at home then, working in a local park. He hadn't appeared at Mika's graduation or the party. He slipped in and out of the house, climbing the stairs to his room, and shutting the door. I heard his footsteps as I lay awake in the television nook. He slept late, stayed out late, and disappeared for long stretches.

When I asked Mika about his absence from the graduation events, she shrugged. "Kaz does his own thing."

I studied his picture in the hallway—his dark hair and thick eyebrows. Was his nose the same shape as mine? His mouth? I wished I was brave enough to knock on his door and say, "I have a secret to tell you."

The night before I flew back to California, Mika was out with her friends. Yumi and I sat kitty-corner at the kitchen table with mugs of tea. I perused various photos I had sent her over the previous years. They were clinging to the door of her refrigerator—backpacking trips, coffee picking in Nicaragua—arranged within a huge patchwork of other people, Christmas card photos, school pictures, postcards from travelers. I pointed at an image of myself. "Doesn't Kaz wonder who I am?"

Yumi shook her head and shrugged. "He's never asked."

The summer air surrounded us, thick and humid. Yumi fanned at her face with a section from the newspaper. "It's warm. A good night for Dairy Queen, don't you think?"

I sat up. "Dairy Queen! I miss those. We had one in Park Ridge."

"There's one just a few blocks away. Let's go!" She gestured toward the back door. We passed through her neighborhood and cut through a long asphalt lot with weeds growing through the cracks. Was it a short cut? Or was it a way of being invisible from the street, where a neighbor might see us walking together? I was excited to visit a Dairy Queen—what my parents used to call "DQ." I loved the swirly cones dipped upside down in chocolate that hardened into a solid little curl like a pig's tail, delicate and exquisite in my mouth. The purple frozen Mr. Misty that hurt the inside of my nose. I loved that Yumi was also a fan of DQ, and I loved walking there with her. I felt like we were friends, stepping through the weeds on a summer day.

The sticky hot air clung to our skin. At DQ, we ordered cones dipped in chocolate and began walking back, licking melted dribbles from our wrists. I counted down to the question I'd been holding all week. "When do you think . . . do you think . . . you'll ever tell him? Kaz?"

She licked her soft vanilla cone. "I don't want to tell him unless you're here in person."

I stopped and stood still. "I'm here now."

"Exactly. Tonight, or tomorrow morning, then. What do you think?"

"Of course. Of course I want you to."

We wound our way back through the neighborhood. Yumi waved at a man mowing his lawn, to a woman getting out of a minivan. A sliver of light was spreading, and I felt giddy. Next, maybe she would begin introducing me to her neighbors, her friends, maybe even her siblings. Maybe I was beginning to emerge from the closet.

I helped her chop vegetables for dinner that night, trembling, jumpy. I was going to have a brother. Maybe we would go for a ride in his noisy car.

Mika was in the garage, sorting through bins of clothes, packing for her trip.

Kaz blasted through the kitchen door at half past seven. I heard him clump up the stairs to his room; then he clattered down a minute later, jacket in hand. I took in the shape of his face, his thick wild hair, one dimple in his cheek. "I'm going out with Dan." He stopped then and nodded at me. "S'cuse me."

I stared at my birth mother. *Now,* I thought. Tell him not to go. Tell him it's important. Tell him I'm leaving in the morning. Tell him he has to stay and hear this.

Yumi didn't look up from the cutting board. She said, calmly, "Kaz, this is Susan. She came for Mika's graduation." Then she turned and called out through the garage door. "Mika! Come in here."

Adrenaline blasted through my body. It was happening. She was going to tell him.

Mika appeared, balancing a stack of cardboard cartons below her chin. Her hair was tied up in a bandana. A sheen of sweat glowed on her cheeks.

Yumi wiped her hands, slowly, on a dish towel. "Mika, do you have that nice camera that Susan gave you?"

"Ye—es." Her brows knitted together. "Why?"

"I just thought it would be nice . . . to take a picture." Mika raised an eyebrow at me.

Kaz was moving toward the door. "See ya later."

"Kaz, wait." Yumi sidestepped and actually blocked him.

"*What?*" He scowled.

"I want Mika to take a picture. With her new camera. With *Susan.* And with you too."

He stood for a moment, an expression of confusion. Mika looked at me. I looked at her. She smiled a tiny smile. "Come on, Kaz," she said. "Let's just do it." She knew that I would die for this sibling picture. She rummaged in her bag. "Here. Here's the camera."

Yumi clapped. "Wonderful! Let's take it in the living room."

We filed into the pretty room with its Asian antiques, the red cabinet, the clean and elegant furniture. Yumi pointed like a director. "The three of you. On the couch."

We sat down, knee to knee. Kaz did not seem curious why this portrait session was happening. Yumi peered through the viewfinder. "One, two, three. Cheese!"

We cheesed. Then another one, this time standing up in front of the mantel. Then one with me and Mika. She handed the camera to Kaz. "Just girls!" The three of us smiled, and the shutter clicked and advanced. Whirr.

"Okay now, I've gotta go." Kaz picked up his jacket with a thumb. He headed toward the door again. I almost grabbed his arm. I almost screamed. But I didn't. Yumi said something to him about driving carefully, about drinking, and he nodded. He paused for a second before letting the screen door slam. He looked me in the eyes and held up his palm. "Nice to meet you."

"Yeah. You too." My voice was shrunken and dry.

He was gone.

I looked up at Yumi. She went back to the cutting board, the knife making a rhythmic chopping sound on the wood. The smell of garlic curled around her in sharp tendrils. I stared at the back of her head, the perfect black shape of her hair. She was talking in her bright, chipper voice. His friends were probably waiting in the car; it was not the right time. *Oh well.*

I WOULD MEET YOU
AT A WEDDING

When our daughter Mollie was nine months old, plump and cheeky with spiky black hair, I opened my mailbox to find a heavy cream envelope with my name on it. I had been cordially invited to the wedding of my half brother, Kaz. He had a bride, Barbara, and a three-month-old baby, Wendy. I traced the gold script with my finger.

I called Yumi. "You told him!" It had been five years since she had told Mika who I was.

"No."

"He must know! Why else would he have invited me?"

"He thinks you're a friend of Mika's."

"Wait. He's not inviting ALL of Mika's friends, is he?"

"No."

A long silence. She asked, slowly, "Are you going to come?"

"I wouldn't miss it for the world." I paused. "But if I come, I think you should tell him . . . about me."

"I think so too." Her voice was heavy with resignation.

She did tell him, mere days before his wedding. That he had a sister. That I was not simply a friend of Mika's, and that I would be coming to the wedding—with my own baby, his niece.

Kaz called me right away.

"Hiya, Sis!" His voice was friendly.

I said, "Did you know? I can't believe you didn't know."

"I had no idea," he said. "But you know what? I'm glad. Welcome to the family!" It was the first time I had heard those words.

Mika picked me and Mollie up at the airport and drove us to Yumi's house. John was working overtime in his solo medical practice, so he stayed home. Everyone was bustling with wedding preparations. I'd packed one of my good dresses, but when I tried it on, it didn't fit. Breastfeeding had ballooned my chest, and the zipper wouldn't close.

Mika rustled around in Yumi's closet. "Try this on."

"I can't wear her dress." I glanced over my shoulder.

"Yes, you can. It will look good." She called out, "Mom! You don't mind if Susan wears one of your dresses, do you?" I didn't hear the muffled reply.

I slipped the soft turquoise dress over my head. Its loose sleeves and long skirt draped easily around my body. Yumi and I were the same size. Mika said, "It's perfect. You'll be comfortable, and you look great."

Mollie wore a ruffled jumpsuit printed with huge roses. She was a social, affable baby, smiling with her two teeth at anyone nearby.

The ceremony was brief and to the point. A row of bridesmaids glimmered in gold satin next to the bride, who had cascading red hair and a long, rippling train. My brother wore a spiffy tuxedo. Their baby, Wendy, had fluffy blonde hair and green eyes like her mother, but they were shaped like Kaz's.

After the vows and the kiss, the married couple walked down the aisle with Wendy in Kaz's arms. I waited in the receiving line, jiggling Mollie. Kaz smiled, and we lifted up the cousin-babies to gaze at each other. Mollie pawed the air. Kaz introduced me to his bride. "This is my other sister. Susan." Barbara greeted me with an air kiss and glanced over my shoulder at her new mother-in-law.

At the reception, Yumi and Bob and Mika sat at the family table. I found the little card with my name on it and made my way to table 11. It was filled with people who were decades older than me. I had been assigned to a table with Yumi's oldest friends. Was this a test of my ability to keep her secret? I longed to quiz them, to tell them when I had been born. August 1959. Where were you then? Do you know what Yumi was doing that summer, on that trip to the hospital in New York? She wasn't getting her appendix out.

Instead, I focused on the baby and made small talk. A pleasant woman with deep dimples asked, "How do you know the family?"

I was used to smiling faintly and mumbling something about being a "friend of the family." I said something about my father being in the same business as Yumi. But a devil perched on my shoulder, stabbing my cheek with a tiny pitchfork, hissing, *say something*. But no. I was going to behave. I wouldn't betray her, not at her son's wedding.

I picked at the chicken and rice pilaf, looking at the family table on the other side of the room. I fed Mollie morsels of food. When the dancing began, I was relieved to stand and jostle her in my arms.

Yumi and Bob did their traditional parents-of-the-groom dance, and then they traded with the parents-of-the-bride. I remembered how Yumi had waltzed with my father in our living room, the night before my own wedding. After a few trips around the dance floor, Yumi sidled off the parquet tiles. With flushed cheeks, she approached us and held out her arms for Mollie. Mine were aching from hours of carrying her. The baby relaxed in Yumi's embrace.

A woman in a glittery green dress let out a little shriek nearby. "Oh, she's *adorable*! Look at those cheeks! Look at that precious hair!"

Yumi shifted Mollie from one arm to another. She smiled vaguely and walked away, jiggling to the music.

The woman persisted. "Is this baby Wendy? Your granddaughter is just *beautiful*."

Yumi turned. She deposited Mollie back into my arms, a smooth slam dunk. I held her. I inhaled her hair—a little sweet from her shampoo and a little savory from the chicken on her ear.

"This is not my granddaughter," Yumi said.

The room swayed. The dancing went into slow motion. The disco ball shot out tiny shards of light.

Yumi's words were garbled. "This is my houseguest's child." As if to soften things, she added, "She IS beautiful!"

I suddenly remembered an Easter sermon I'd heard about Jesus being denied three times. Peter, his friend and disciple, said it over and over when questioned. *I do not know this man.* The words had cut through my heart. As I held my daughter, the weight of Yumi's denial suddenly felt unbearable. I swallowed hard and walked backward, holding her body against me like a pillowy shield. I made my way blindly into the ladies' room, its air cloying and heavy. I locked the two of us into a metal stall and sat, fully clothed, on the toilet. I bent over Mollie's head and sobbed, feeling that a final, irrevocable crack had just opened.

This is not my granddaughter.

She had denied being my mother dozens of times. I'd gotten used to it. Each time I had flinched but told myself that it didn't matter.

Now it mattered. I swore that Mollie was not going to be an invisible grandchild. I would not have her lie to conceal Yumi's shame, two generations removed. My birth mother had gotten pregnant in 1958, and I would be damned if my daughter would pay the price into the next century. I cried until Mollie's hair was soaked and matted. She pushed against me, anxious to leave the toilet stall. I stood up, smoothed the wrinkles from the turquoise dress, and carried her back to the reception. She fell asleep on my shoulder as the dancing died down and the last guests went home.

At the end of the night, I buckled Mollie into the back seat of Bob and Yumi's car. We drove back to the house without speaking. The next morning Mollie and I flew home to California. We would never be back.

ORIGAMI

Mika and I sat together on a school bus, trundling north toward the Oregon border. I was thirty-two, and she was in her late twenties. I'd left Mollie, now a toddler, with John so that the two of us could attend the Tule Lake pilgrimage, a historic educational weekend to learn more about the Japanese American incarceration experience. The old yellow school bus was rustic, with rough seating and no air conditioning, to more closely resemble the experience of those who had been kept captive. Yumi had spent her childhood in one of these camps, and this pilgrimage, decades later, was a place for the two of us to get a glimpse of her experience. Both of us were hungry for these crumbs of our history.

The parents who raised me had not been subject to incarceration. Although almost eighty percent of the Japanese American population on the US mainland was forcibly removed from their homes, those Japanese Americans in northeastern cities—like my adoptive parents who had grown up in New York—were renters who owned no land. Unlike the West Coast Japanese who owned valuable agricultural and business assets, they had been mostly left alone. I had learned from my parents that prominent Japanese American community leaders—our church minister, their family physician, businessmen—had been picked up the day of the attack on Pearl Harbor and incarcerated on Ellis Island for anywhere from weeks to years.

"They dragged Reverend Akamatsu right out of church in handcuffs," my mother would say, grimacing at the memory.

"Doc Iwamoto too," added my father. The Japanese American community was left vulnerable with the removal of their bilingual physician.

For those families forced into the camps, with only a few days to pack and sell their land and belongings at a fraction of their worth, they had almost nothing to return to after the war.

Although my father had fought in the all-Japanese 442nd World War II regiment, I didn't understand what incarceration camps were until I was in college and read *Journey to Topaz*. By then they seemed far away and long ago. I had heard hushed references to "camp" from my parents and congregants of our Japanese American church, but the significance of the word eluded me. I didn't realize that my own beloved godmother had spent years in the Tule Lake camp. She had grown up in California and moved to New York after being released. I hadn't realized any of this.

Fifty years later, hundreds of us "pilgrims" to Tule Lake National Monument—site of the former Tule Lake camp—slept on rough cots in a nearby elementary school gym. We stood in line for bathrooms and meals, knowing that even though it was rustic, it was still much more comfortable than what the issei and nisei had endured. We had the luxury of bathroom stalls, not public latrines in a filthy row. We were fed food without bugs or decay, food that didn't sicken us.

The pilgrimage was a four-day intensive education into a piece of history that had remained a mystery to us, even from those whose families had been deeply impacted.

We met a writer, Hiroshi Kashiwagi, lauded as the poet laureate of Tule Lake. I told him that I was exploring creative writing, and he gifted me a broadside of his poem, "The Haircut." The pilgrimage was a combination of intergenerational community building, family reunion, and educational forum. It was there that I learned about the No-No Boys, who had answered "no" on the government questionnaire that asked about loyalty to the United States, even as their families lived in barracks behind barbed wire.

Mika opted to go on a hike to nearby Castle Rock. I hesitantly took a seat in the dining hall near a group of older women and smiled at the ones who looked up from their task to nod at me. Their conversation, in Japanese, floated around me like tiny letters in alphabet soup—familiar, comforting, but not totally comprehensible. I caught words here and there and recognized some that my grandmother and parents had once spoken. When I had heard them say *kodomo*, child, I knew they were talking about me.

The long table bloomed with folded paper birds of all colors: royal purple, light gray, a shimmering gold one. The women were deep in their work, weaving an origami wreath of a thousand cranes for the upcoming memorial service, honoring the souls who had died at the camp.

I spread a square of sky-blue paper flat on the table and then folded it in half. So far, it seemed easy. I tried to follow the women's movements, but their hands were swift. I wanted to make a perfect crane: tsuru, flying from my palm. Fold again and then flip that side of the triangle under. Oh, no. Now what? I was lost. The women around me kept creasing, folding, spreading, their fingers moving with easy grace. My thumbs were huge, thick, in the way of these paper wings trying to unfold.

I hesitated. "Wait—can you show me that last part again?" A woman with a black pageboy cut flipped the paper from triangle to kite to—how did she do that?

My heart fluttered, beating in confusion. I retraced my steps, turned the paper upside down, and then in reverse. I wanted to crumple the paper into a blue ball, an origami rock.

I unfolded the paper with damp, shaking fingers. I persevered. Ganbatte. Don't give up. That was what the incarcerees whispered to each other behind barbed wire. I told myself, *I'm going to make this crane.* Why hadn't my parents taught me how to do this? I was going to pull the skill to do this out of my blood, make it flow into my fingers.

But what if I couldn't? It would only prove the thing that I feared most. That I wasn't really Japanese. That I was an imposter. A fake, a watered-down, inauthentic Kmart version of the real thing. I wondered if Mika wrestled with this. If she ever felt like she was not Japanese enough. Did it feel differently for her, growing up with a Japanese mother and a white father? Was there less pressure? I wondered what it had been like for her to have mirrors of each side of her heritage.

I stopped, unfolded everything, smoothed the paper out on the table, took a deep breath, and started again.

Maybe it was my paternal genes that made this impossible. I thought of the ways my unknown birth father marked my body. The furry dark hair that blanketed my arms and legs. Asian people didn't have to deal with this. I wished I had the smooth gold skin of my nisei parents, the way they tanned like caramels under the sun. My skin reddened into a dusky burnt color. My face erupted into freckles. My huge feet were so indelicate. My dark brownish hair curled when I wished it would be silky, inky black. I blamed him and his ancestors for all the parts of me that make me conspicuously un-Japanese.

Strangers challenged me—guessing all kinds of nationalities and ethnicities. My pencil hovered over forms that said to check one for ethnicity. One? I marked ASIAN, defiantly, then felt guilty. It was a lie. A half lie, anyway.

I was ready to give up. Hundreds of origami birds piled up into a brilliant mountain of color, spiky wings and beaks poking out like hatching newborns. What difference would it make if I didn't contribute one? There were plenty enough for the memorial service.

I looked down again at the failed sculpture in my hands. There were so many folds in the blue paper, the color was starting to wear away at the creases. My would-be crane, still an awkward triangle, was scarred with white lines. I folded it again and again, until finally something squat and deformed emerged. I shoved it into my pocket and got up from the table when I noticed the little obasan sitting next to me. Her graying head, with its round rice-bowl haircut, barely reached my shoulder.

Her knotty, bent fingers were working a piece of pale butter-yellow paper. The folds she made were awkward, her eyes huge with concentration behind her thick spectacles. She didn't seem to be having much more success than me.

Finally, she placed her lopsided product on the table and sighed. "This no tsuru," she muttered. "Look more like sick chicken."

I took my crane out of my pocket and sat it down next to hers. They made a sort of clumsy, humble symmetry. Obasan looked at me with a hint of a smile behind her round glasses. She reached for my sleeve, swayed a little bit, and I helped her to her feet. She and I walked slowly to the kitchen. It was time for tea.

UNDERTOW

I'd heard the term before, and it always made me feel claustrophobic: the *sandwich generation*, women who were squashed like a layer of peanut butter between the needs of their kids and their aging parents. I'd think, shuddering, I'm lucky *I'm* not in that category. My parents were both fit, active, and happily employed, even into their seventies. My father was still driving through the South as a traveling salesman, and my mother still worked at the same elementary school I'd attended as a child.

I had two children now, Mollie, almost four years old, and newborn Emma. My parents came to visit, and as always, they wanted to know how they could help. They had no interest in wine country, or Fisherman's Wharf, or driving down the crookedest street in the world.

My father, fresh off the plane, rolled up his sleeves and asked, "Where's my list?" We told him about the leaky bathroom faucet, the hole in the roof, the new light fixture we wanted to install, and he trundled off to Ace Hardware, humming. He was never so happy as when he had something to fix. My mother sat next to him like a surgeon's assistant, handing him tools out of the plastic orange toolbox. When they weren't spackling or hammering or wrestling with something under the sink, they cooked dinner and helped with dishes and laundry. In other words, they took care of me.

I wasn't ready for the tables to turn. During his visit, my father was confidently climbing a twelve-foot ladder, changing light fixtures in our high A-framed ceiling. A few days after they returned to New Jersey, I received a phone call that he'd been diagnosed with an abdominal aneurysm. I knew what those things were. When I was studying to become a physical therapist, I had observed an aneurysm surgery. The surgeon lifted the liver, the spleen, the stomach, and pointing them out to me one by one, piled them neatly onto the patient's chest. He repaired the swollen, ballooned-out aorta and then stuffed the organs back in.

My mind spun as I imagined my dad spread open in that way. "I'm coming out. I'll be there tomorrow," I said into the phone.

Then I looked around. Mollie was leaping back and forth between the sofa and the coffee table. "Look at me! I'm flying!" Emma beamed one of her first beatific smiles. How could I leave them? How could I take them? There was a roulette wheel ticking, and I knew my father's number could be coming up.

The thought of flying cross-country, changing planes, and then visiting the hospital with a squirming three-month-old and an active four-year-old made me anxious. I decided to leave Mollie with John, and I'd take the baby. The night before I left, I stayed up late, typing instructions: "LUNCH: Use blue Pet Shop lunch box, she won't carry the pink one anymore. Make sandwich with peanut butter only, *no jelly*. One small granny smith apple. One juice box. Buy Juicy-Juice, it's 100% juice. She'll try to talk you into the fizzy stuff that's 5% juice but hold strong."

I went through the bath routine, the story routine, the Play-Doh rules, and the library book schedule. He already did half of these things anyway and did so quite competently, without a road map, but I felt compelled to write it down.

I wondered if Mollie would be scarred from this. I worried that she'd feel abandoned. One day, she'd be telling her therapist, "That time my mother took my baby sister to New York and *left me behind* . . ."

Emma and I, toting diaper bag, bottles, infant carrier, blankets, rattles, chew toys, and Zweiback, flew three thousand miles without event. We both slept, with me dreaming of being six years old in a blue bathing suit, floating in the salty Atlantic Ocean, in my father's arms.

My father's surgery, which was supposed to be a six-hour ordeal, stretched into an excruciating fourteen and a half hours. There were terrible complications, too-fragile arteries, a mass of frail tissue to painstakingly stitch together. In the morning, the nurses paused before letting us see him. "You won't recognize him," they warned. When we entered the intensive care unit, it was hard not to scream. His sweet head was swollen like a pumpkin, a freaky jack-o-lantern. Millions of tubes, the beeping monitors. Yet I did recognize him. Somewhere inside that nightmare was my daddy. I saw his funny forehead birthmark, shaped like a lima bean. I recognized those hairy legs, his weird toenails. He was in there.

My mother and I took turns pacing the halls with Emma and sitting next to Dad in the intensive care unit, stroking his fat fingers. I sat on the floor in the visitors' lounge, nursing Emma in my lap, crying onto her bald head.

Yumi happened to be in New York on business. She came and stood in the hallway outside my father's hospital room, paying her respects, and we had tea in the hospital cafeteria. I introduced her to Emma, and she cuddled her new granddaughter while I ate bland food I could barely taste.

The fleshy bean-shaped birthmark was my landmark during the two weeks of his coma and of my whispering into the swollen curve of his ear, "Daddy. It's Susan. Right here." I touched it lightly with my finger, until one day he blinked and woke up.

There was such joy witnessing that first blink. His fingers squeezed mine weakly. The tubes were removed, one by one. Over time, he slowly returned to us.

One day at the hospital, my mother collapsed heavily onto the vinyl waiting-room sofa, which whistled under her weight. She grabbed a limp copy of *Field & Stream*. "Go in. He's got something to tell you."

"What?" I twitched my eyebrows.

"How should I know?" She sighed and shrugged. "He wouldn't tell me."

I tiptoed into the room. "Hey, Daddy." I picked up his hand, careful of the clear pretzel of tubing.

"Hello, Sus. How's my rascal?"

We made hospital small talk: his first taste of Jell-O, the new neurologist, the man in the next bed over who had moaned all night and then expired at dawn. The sound of his voice brought me to tears. I had thought I'd never hear it again.

"What did you want to tell me?"

"Well, Rascal." He picked at the bedcover. "You get a lot of time to think when you're lying around. It got me thinking about things I wanted to say and never did. First thing I want to say, you know already. You know the story. That day we brought you home, when we got you, was the happiest day of my life."

"Aw, Dad." It was true. I'd heard it a million times. Crystal Breeding. The pink blanket. How they had asked for a Japanese baby for more than ten years before I came to them. The waiting list that dragged on and on, and finally I arrived, a half-and-half girl, instead.

"There's another thing."

I looked up. His thick eyebrows quivered. He was struggling. "I need to ask your forgiveness." His voice croaked.

I was perplexed. My father was the last person who would have any reason to ask my forgiveness. My mind spun with wild possibilities. I clutched the chrome bed railing.

"Tell me," I whispered.

He winced. "Remember the summer we went to North Carolina, the beach at Kitty Hawk?"

I nodded. *And what?* I tried to remember. I was fifteen years old. I had bought a kite to fly over the dunes. We climbed hundreds of stairs inside a lighthouse with spiraling black and white stripes. There had been sailors.

The beach below the kite-flying dunes was covered with fine hot sand and flat, tight waves that hit the shore and pulled back like lengths of rope. I wandered in up to my waist and then dropped down to my knees, watching my brown hands turn pale under the water. My father took a running dive from the shore and started sidestroking a parallel line to the beach. My mother had taught him to swim after they were married, in the choppy waters of the Long Island Sound.

I just wanted to float, to be carried along by the salt water. I turned on my back and drifted, my hands making jellyfish motions along my hips. Water filled my ears, and the world disappeared.

I rocked up and down on the waves, my eyes shut against the glaring sun. Beneath my lids, I could see its orange starburst shape. I hummed and fluttered my hands and feet, perhaps even dozing off.

A long time passed before I thought about my burning face, my lips getting salty and swollen. I splashed myself into a vertical position and squinted at the shore. I heard a tiny imitation of my mother's voice. She was standing at the edge of the surf, a tiny stick person with waving arms.

Damn. I'd floated a long way out. I stretched out and began swimming, breathing hard, pushing back walls of water with my palms. I swam for a long time and then raised my head, my legs treading like an underwater bicycle.

My mother was a dot on the shore, my grandmother beside her. The water around me was cold, much colder than in the shallows. It felt deeper than any other water I'd been in. I imagined the sea going down for miles, nothing below me but endless dark and the glowing forms of skeletal fish. Suddenly a bubble of panic rose from my gut. *I'm going to drown. I'm never going to be able to swim back. I will die in this water.* I started screaming, running on nothing, stumbling in the water, my arms fighting the waves as I panicked and flailed: "Mommm! Help!" My voice floated on the surface of the water, then evaporated into nothing.

My legs were burning, heavy, exhausted. I was going to die. I began sobbing, my tears making hot tracks on my shivering skin. *Stop*, I growled at myself. *Stop it*. I forced myself to breathe slowly, to resume the slow bicycle treading. I tried to meditate as I floated. I was too afraid. I waved my wrinkled fingers, reaching high above the surface. Soon I would try the dead man's float. But how would anyone see me if I was flat on the water?

A dark head like a seal bobbed up from the surface, just yards away. A shark! A stingray! I whimpered. Then I saw black eyes and the gasping hole of his mouth. "Sus!" It was my father.

I paddled toward him, sniffling with relief. "Daddy!"

I flung myself against him, his wet brown shoulders.

He panted, treading water. "Undertow very rough. Abunai." Dangerous.

I tightened my arms around his neck, a heavy human necklace. "You're here."

But he was sinking, a gurgling thrash under the water. "Susan, let go!"

"Daddy, please help me, I can't swim that far!" My legs were running again, my breath stabbing my ribs.

"Sus, I'm not strong enough."

My eyes were blind, full of tears and the sting of salt. "We'll both drown!"

He shut his eyes, and I heard a little sob. "I'll get help for you. You float. Don't get too tired. *Don't try to swim*."

"Daddy. Don't go!" My voice rose to a shriek.

"Sus. I love you. *Please*. It's the only way." He leaned in, put his wet lips against my cheek, and flung himself through the water, away from me.

"Daddy!" I lay my face in the water. It felt like it was melting into the sea. I cried and coughed, and then I was overcome with tiredness. I floated like a jellyfish, my eyes closed.

I was alone.

Eventually, they came. I heard a "Hey!" and then an odd sight: what looked like a long line of inflated white paper dolls, hinged together at the hands. Sailors. Dozens of them. Their line began on sand and extended, hand in hand, deep into the ocean where I floated. They wore white bellbottomed trousers and little white caps. The last one, the end of the line, galloped toward me through the water. He reached out an enormous dripping hand, and I grabbed it.

They pulled me into shore, a limp Raggedy Ann, a watery kite flown by sailor dolls. When I finally felt the grit beneath my knees I stumbled to my feet and blinked at them, the crowd of them white and dripping. They shouted some sort of male victory noise for catching me alive. I was their enormous, flailing fish with tangled, seaweedy hair and a burnt nose. My embarrassment caught up with me, and suddenly I wished that I *had* been swept out to sea.

My mother grabbed me harshly and threw a towel around me. "Susan. Never go out so deep again."

I tried to explain. "I didn't know. I was just floating."

"Baka! Can't you get it through your thick skull, you almost died?" She didn't know whether to cry, hug me, or slap me. I looked over her shoulder at my father. He was slumped on the bamboo mat, staring out at the ocean. His face was the color of ash.

"Do you remember the trouble you got into? Out there in the water?" my father asked from his ICU bed.

"Yeah. I remember those sailors. I was so embarrassed . . ."

His mouth crumpled. "I realized that I might die here without asking you to forgive me . . ." He stared down at the blanket, at the knobby hills of his legs.

"For what?"

His voice rasped. "For leaving you out there like that."

"Dad, it was the only way. You went to get help." I smiled. "It's *me* who should apologize for almost strangling you in the water." I tried to make a joke.

He covered his eyes with his hand. "Not a week goes by when I don't hear your voice. *Daddy, don't leave me here.* Some days . . .

I just can't live with myself." His fingers trembled, wet. "When you were that little baby, Sus, I made a promise that I would never leave you. A promise." His voice was thick and gritty. "You were so small, and you'd already had enough of that. Of being left."

I thought about the long search for my birth mother, how I struggled to find her, like swimming against the tide through the darkest water. How it had felt like a long, slow drowning. I reached out a finger and caught a drop of brine from his chin. "More than forgiven."

My father endured two weeks of being in a coma, more reconstructive surgery, and six more months of hospitalization before he saw the light of day. He emerged from the hospital a paraplegic and was barely able to sit up for more than a few seconds at a time.

Emma and I flew back and forth two more times during those months, and at Christmas, we brought Mollie along as well. Every day, we drove from my parents' house to the hospital, with diapers, juice, crackers, crayons, books, Barbie, the Barbie horse, and extra batteries. Mollie set up base with her crayons at the foot of Papa's hospital bed and hung out with unprecedented patience. He inched his way back slowly and was finally transferred to a long-term rehabilitation center.

I swung back and forth between acting out as a regressing daughter and the grown-up in charge (I took all phone calls from the doctors and translated their strange, coded language into messages for my parents). When I left New York, I fretted and left my mother the same kind of detailed instruction sheet I'd been leaving John. "Call about permanent wheelchair with adjustable leg rests. Rub Daddy's back with Vaseline Intensive Care. Make sure he eats enough protein: two cans of Ensure a day, plus meat."

After years of living independently on opposite coasts, three thousand miles between us was way too much. My father called with his physical therapy progress. He had stood on his own for the first time since before his surgery.

"I held onto the red chair in the living room . . . just five seconds or so, but I was *really doing it*! This therapist is something else." For a second, I was jealous and wished I could have been his physical therapist, helping him to his feet, letting him balance on my shoulder.

Emma, eleven months old with a head of fluffy dark-blonde hair, was doing the same in California. She pulled herself upright at the coffee table, then lifted her hands in victory. *One, two, three, four, five.*

GUEST ROOM

When Mollie was five and Emma had just turned one, I received an unexpected phone call from Yumi.

"Do you have room for a visitor?" she asked. She had stayed with me multiple times during my single years, but she hadn't visited since I'd been married or had children. It turned out that she had a brother whom I'd never heard about. Who, as it turned out, lived not far from me. Except he had just died. I had emotional whiplash from learning about a nearby uncle and his death all in one phone call.

She was flying in for the funeral. I didn't hesitate at the opportunity to host her, for her to get to know my children—her grandchildren. I knew that our time together was limited and unpredictable.

She played peek-a-boo with Emma, who was wearing a peace sign onesie. She shared a recipe for homemade Play-Doh, which delighted Mollie. A kindergarten graduate, Mollie was starting to put together the puzzle of my dual mothers, earlier than I ever had.

"So Nana isn't your real mommy?" Where had she heard that term?

"She is. But I wasn't born from her body." Mollie squinted at me. I tried to articulate the distinction between an adoptive mother and a birth mother. I explained that Yumi, who had just appeared in our living room, was my birth mother.

"So who is your birth father?" She couldn't be more direct than that. I could barely control the snort. "Beats me, kid," I muttered under my breath.

"Does *she* know?" Mollie pointed to where Yumi was stacking blocks for Emma.

"Mmmm. Yes. I think so."

"Why don't you ask her?"

I was sweating. My daughter was now a thinking, analytical being, and she instantly articulated the obvious.

"Um. I think she really doesn't want to say."

"But why?"

Why, indeed.

We were in the car, Yumi in the passenger seat and Mollie in the car seat behind her. I was driving Yumi on an errand, to pick up something she needed for her brother's funeral—pantyhose or something. As we wound our way through the hills into town, I heard a thumping.

Mollie was rhythmically kicking the back of Yumi's seat.

"I wish. I wish. I wish." *Kick. Kick. Kick.*

"Moll, stop. Please."

The thumping continued. "I wish she would say. I wish she would tell."

I clenched the steering wheel.

"I wish she would say. Who. Your. Father. Is."

I turned up the radio and searched for the Disney station. Anything to stop this. I didn't dare glance at my birth mother, who felt like she had turned to stone beside me. I shot a STOP expression back at Mollie, who raised her two hands in the universal gesture of "who knows?"

All week, Yumi was picked up at our house by relatives, most often her nephew. My cousin. She introduced him to me out on the driveway.

"This is Susan. She's a friend of the family." He waved nonchalantly. "Nice to meet you."

It took all my will to resist shouting, "I'm your cousin! She's my mother!"

I had lied for over a decade to preserve our relationship. But the pretense was evaporating. It wasn't going to stretch into the next generation, and we both knew it. My children wouldn't be calling her a "friend of the family."

I had left behind my physical therapy career and recently completed a master's degree in creative writing. My final thesis, titled "Filling In the Blanks," was an attempt to answer, through my imagination, all the questions that still haunted me. During the week that Yumi was at our house, I had scheduled an overnight writing retreat in a mountain cabin with three of my MFA cohort friends. At first, I considered cancelling, but Yumi insisted that I keep my plans.

"We'll all do just fine here, won't we?" she said, stacking and knocking over block towers with Mollie. She said she would be delighted to help John take care of the girls.

I hesitated. But I had been looking forward to this writing getaway for months. And I was moved by the idea of my birth mother nurturing my daughters.

John was an enormous supporter of my writing. "Go," he said, holding Emma. "It will be good for you."

As it turned out, Yumi was a warm, engaged grandmother. She cooked up hearty meals and spent lots of "floor time" playing with them both.

The girls barely registered my absence. Emma took her first steps that week, straight into Yumi's outstretched arms. But it would be the last time my children would ever see her.

SEPARATION

A pizza restaurant was an unlikely spot for finding a sense of belonging. But there it was, a circular wooden booth with an unsavory sticky table, a dented tray of bubbly pizza, and six Asian-ish faces. Someone had told me about a group of Asian adoptees, a few of them biracial like me, others from Korea or China. Often with other adopted people, I'd felt isolated, the lonely unicorn of my experience. I'd known Asian Americans. I knew some biracial people. And I knew adopted people. But until that night, I had never met anyone else who was all three.

One woman, born in Japan to a Japanese woman and an American father, twirled a tiny glass vial, no bigger than an almond, on a thin gold chain around her neck. "When I found my birth mother," she said, "she was wearing this. It contains a few drops of amniotic fluid that she'd saved from my birth."

I gasped out loud. A green cloud of envy saturated my body. Amniotic fluid? In a necklace? "Wow."

Another woman laughed. "We're not all so lucky." She chewed a breadstick. "I'll never find my birth mother. I was abandoned in China. No papers, no trail, no nothing."

There were unique details to each person's experience, but our shared vocabulary of longing bound us together. When it was my turn, I described the sixteen-year roller coaster of reunion. The constant flux of connection, disconnection, rejection, denial with Yumi. Six heads leaned in to listen across the table. I felt at home.

One of the group members, Mark, was also biracial and Asian.

I felt a special affinity with him, a painter. We alternated meeting in the pizza place with meeting at his house. It was a true artist's lair, filled with things like baskets of antique light bulbs, color and texture everywhere. I loved being with this little niche group of Asian adopted people. It was a place to bring my insecurities about my birth mother and the vexing question of what to do about finding my birth father. For more than fifteen years I had been waiting. Patiently. Hoping that she would finally share his name, finally allow us to meet. Her words about his *wanting to know me* reverberated in my mind. He was out there, getting older every year. He was out there, maybe wondering where I was.

One day, a year or so after joining the group, I received devastating news. Mark had ended his life. I was shaken. Sickened. I paced and wept for days. I questioned my own grief, telling myself, you didn't know him that well, you haven't seen him in months. But I was devastated. If Mark was a mirror of me, then for the first time in years I was able to see my own pain. I had been desperately holding on to the pretense that everything was all right, and now I was shattered.

I wrote a letter to my birth mother. I felt an urgent need to cut through the fog of forced politeness in our relationship. I was terrified that if I didn't break my complacency, I might follow Mark down the same road. That if I continued to hold so much unspoken emotion inside me, I, too, could implode.

I had been too afraid of her anger and potential rejection to ask again about my birth father after our first meeting. Whenever I even brought up the subject, the air surrounding her turned icy. Her twinkles dimmed, and she withdrew. I told myself to be patient, to be good. If I was good enough, she would understand that I could be trusted with this knowledge. In the letter, I wrote that I was still very interested in knowing who my birth father was. She'd said he had thought of me throughout my life. Was this man still alive? Could I meet him?

I typed out the name that Mika had casually mentioned during our first meeting. Was it him? Was Ted Tuckerman my father? *I know he passed away,* I wrote, *but I'd still like to know.* I put the letter in the mail, my stomach in knots.

Yumi didn't respond to my letter. Months passed and I spiraled into despair. Finally, I received a typewritten letter. Her anger radiated from the page. She was furious that I would "besmirch" the name of her friend. She would not answer my question, and she never wanted to hear from me again.

I was shattered.

My adoption anthology, *A Ghost at Heart's Edge,* which I'd been working on for years, was published that winter. Along with a poet friend, I'd compiled a collection of poetry and stories on the theme of adoption, including the lyrics to Joni Mitchell's poignant song, "Little Green." I was obsessed with adoption stories, from Moses to Superman. I believed they were among some of the most powerful and resonant narratives in literature.

My coeditor, Tina, and I organized a small book tour in the dead of winter. Several of the anthology's contributors happened to live in the same city as my birth family. My heart ached to know that I would be flying into that familiar airport, and that Yumi wouldn't be meeting me.

I had emailed my half sister, Mika, about the book tour, telling her that I'd be at a local bookstore and that I hoped to see her. I hadn't heard from her in months, after years of visiting, writing to each other, and exchanging little care packages in the mail.

When we checked in for the bookstore event, the bookseller said, "Susan Ito! You've got mail!" She drew out an envelope with my name on it, in my sister's familiar swooping script. My heart jumped. Mika.

I don't know what I was expecting. Congratulations? An invitation to dinner or drinks? What I wasn't expecting was a terse, one-paragraph letter of farewell. Her note said that what I had done was unforgivable and that not only was she not coming to the reading, she never wanted to hear from me again.

They were both done with me. Kaz, with whom I'd had only sporadic contact, vanished as well.

I slipped into depression. If the person who had given birth to me didn't want anything to do with me, should I even be alive? Annual milestones we normally celebrated slipped by. I was used to hearing Yumi's chipper voice on the phone, the round bubbles of her script on an envelope. I sent her a card on Mother's Day and then on her birthday, without response. My children's birthdays drifted past.

One night, while I was driving, I had to force myself away from the bright line of traffic moving toward me. The biggest semis were like magnets. Just the smallest rotation of my hands on the wheel could pull me into a collision. I imagined an explosion of metal and glass and then silence. And then my friend Mark's voice, telling me I was home.

I dreamed about Yumi. In one dream, she was lying in a hospital bed, her face turned away from me. "I don't know you," she said into her pillow. Mark was standing on the opposite side of the bed. "You can't talk to my sister like that," he said, and he reached for my hand over the sheets.

In another dream, she and I sat in a café, laughing and eating chocolate pastries. Her fingers waved stickily. Laughter scooped dimples into her face; she was happy to be there.

"I thought you were—mad at me," I stammered, and she laughed. "Mad? Why would I be mad?" I woke up happy, relief spreading through my skin, until I realized it had only been true in my sleep.

I was wooed by heights. Hiking with my family, we traversed a mountain trail no more than a foot wide. I was vertiginous, my right palm leaking nervous handprints onto the rock wall. If I sneezed, if I lost my balance, I would tumble hundreds of feet below to the iron-stained creek water like blood. I was so tempted to let go.

That summer, a friend of mine got married in upstate New York. Afterward, I rented a car and drove to Ithaca, homesick. I drove to the deep gorges of Upper Treman Park. My boots crunched on the trail. Bits of shale crumbled in my fingers, and I held them in my pocket, sharp like arrowheads. Their edges bit into my skin. I welcomed the bursts of pain. Even in the hot, humid summer, it felt cool between those walls, wet and shadowy.

The steps mounted and curved around gorges where the water rushed, foamy white and deep green below. It was silent in the gorge except for the distant whispering that grew to a roar, water thundering over rock. Lucifer Falls.

I stepped up onto the low stone ledge at the overlook point. The water churned and foamed below. The noise was deafening.

All I needed to do was lean over. All I had to do was incline my body a few more degrees, and gravity would take me. I remembered then that there would be no note. Pen and paper were in the rental car. I squatted at the edge of the ledge, sobbing. My husband, my children, my parents. I couldn't. I stumbled back to my car and decided to live.

LIKE A HEARTBEAT

For years after my fragile sixteen-year relationship with my birth mother dissolved, I carried my despair inside. I managed to get through the chores of life—child raising, teaching, errands—but I was broken inside. Then one day, I saw a notice for Japanese taiko drumming. A spark fluttered between my ribs. I was interested. Interested in something for the first time in a long time.

I drove out to an enormous barn, a hulking structure in the tawny hills. It was framed by dusky pink light and meadows thick with the dark shapes of cattle. People hauled giant drums and wooden stands from vehicles. In the barn, others fastened rubber tires onto folding chairs. I shyly made my way inside.

The sensei, a small, auburn-haired woman, entered and bowed. "Ohayo gozaimasu!" she called out. Everyone bowed and repeated in unison.

My eyes stung. "Ohayo gozaimasu" was how my grandmother and parents had greeted me each morning of my childhood. I didn't understand why the taiko teacher was saying "good morning" when the moon was already over the barn, but it gave me chills to hear it.

We stood over the tires and struck them with bachi, thick wooden dowels that filled my fists. Ichi! Ni! San! Shi! Counting the beats brought me back to the kitchen table of my childhood, reciting ichi, ni, san for my parents. Their glowing approval. I remembered Japanese vocabulary drills, how they'd point at things, and I'd name them in Japanese. It had been years since I'd used the language, especially since my grandmother had died. My arm vibrated, my bones feeling the impact of wood against the hard rubber tire. Its slight bounce.

We hit a basic beat. Right, left, right, left, right. Sensei struck an iron chime, and the metallic sound went through my teeth. Ichi, ni, san . . . hai! The drummers swirled and thundered between the drums. I kept my hands moving, faster and faster, rightleftrightleftrightleftright until my palms blistered, their bodies blurred and charged in front of my eyes, and the sound echoed huge under the rafters. The sensei kept hitting the chimes as if whipping a galloping horse, and everyone shouted the drummers on. Hahhhhh!

Soon I was dizzy, my hair and face streaming with sweat, my skin steaming.

I felt more in my body than I had in years. More than ever, maybe. It reminded me of when I gave birth to my daughters, immersing myself in waves of energy larger than myself. Suddenly unafraid to do things that girls aren't supposed to do. Hitting and yelling. Feeling exhilarated.

I returned the next week, and the next. I loved it, but I was not good at taiko. I was terribly inept. But the others applauded my attempts respectfully. They clapped their sticks together. The wood-against-wood sound made me happy.

I wondered if my poor coordination, my lack of kinesthesia, had anything to do with my premature birth, the lack of nutrition I had received in utero.

Sensei opened up a notebook and read to us. "Great taiko is said to resemble a mother's heartbeat as felt in the womb . . . babies are often lulled asleep by its thunderous vibrations." My eyes filled with sudden tears.

Here I had found a place for my rage and grief over my birth mother turning away. Here was a place I could be Japanese. I could hear the familiar language of my childhood. I planted my feet, straightened my spine. I felt the wooden sticks heavy and smooth in my fists. Donsu, donsu, donsu, doko don. *Don* means "hard," *su* means "soft." One on the back of the other, the blow followed by the caress.

One night, I arrived at the barn to see a husband-and-wife film crew. They unloaded video cameras, sound equipment, and enormous boxy lights. I noticed one of the taiko students holding an infant wrapped in flannel. I thought, *She has a baby? Why bring such a tiny baby to class?* Then I realized that the baby belonged to the woman working the video camera. The infant began crying, a distraught, thin sound. Its tiny fingers clawed the air.

I looked at the baby's mother. She was crouched low, her hands framing the monitor with the image of the drummers, their bodies turning like starfish. The taiko student walked back and forth between the cars, and the baby kept crying. The noise pierced me. I made a sympathetic face. "Maybe a different set of arms would help."

I walked the baby up and down the driveway, but she shrieked in my arms. Surely the mother would hear. Surely, she would rise from her stool and take the baby, unbutton her blouse, nurse the child to sleep. But the mother didn't turn around. She didn't flinch as her daughter wept, her hoarse little voice echoing against the tawny hills.

"Is she hungry?" we chorused. But the mother said no, the baby had been fed. She turned back to the camera. Her straight back, the long black braid resolutely said: I have work to do.

I jiggled the baby, a tangle of flannel and jerking limbs. It was cold; stars were brightening the sky.

The gong went off inside the barn, and the drumming started. "Listen, baby, listen," I said and tilted her toward the open door. Her eyes unclenched into black pools, wide and absorbing.

"Donsu doko don," I said to her and shifted my weight back and forth in time with the beat. Her lips came together. Her cheeks and nose smoothed into baby roundness, the wrinkles of rage melted away.

"Donsu doko don," I said, and the baby's weight settled. Suddenly she was heavy, relaxed, soft. We stood near the open doorway of the barn and a family of tiny bats, small as butterflies, swooped over our heads. The light around the hills was quickly melting away, and each time I looked up, I saw a new sprinkling of stars.

I held the baby for hours. She brightened each time the thunder of the drums began, and it held her attention until they fell silent. If she slept, it was a delicate, lacy sleep, broken by a dog's bark or a cold rush of wind across her face. What she liked best was darkness and drums. I stood in the shadows on the grassy slope behind the barn, away from the spotlights and bright windows. If light assaulted her face, she cried. If the drumming stopped, she cried. I tried to keep the beat up with my voice—don su don su doko doko.

Her beautiful Japanese mother, resolute in her work, did not come out of the barn. Her bearded father said wearily, "It's like this every night. She cries for hours."

I held her in my arms, this half-Japanese baby whose mother was deaf to her cries. She was eleven weeks old, the same age that I was when the hospital released me. I wondered if I made the same hoarse sounds as we rode together in the cab, my birth mother and I, on our way to our permanent separation.

I walked miles that night. I paced the figure-eight shape of infinity in the grass, cradling the baby until my arms and back ached. I was in a trance, the drums pounding against the night sky, the barn silhouetted in the darkness, its one amber window shining like a jar full of honey. The tiny bats swooping around the roof, sending out their silent calls. I was carrying a biracial baby, a baby girl soothed by thundering drums, a girl who found comfort in the arms of a stranger.

When the filming was finished, I took the sleeping child to her parents, and they took her back without questions or concern. My arms ached when I let her go. "Goodbye, sweet baby," I said and reached to grab my bachi for the last song. I asked her father what her name was.

"Mika," he said. "It's a Japanese name."

I cried as I drove home through the dark empty hills, for all the wrenching separations: releasing this small hanbun-hanbun girl whom I'd loved for three hours, the searing memory of loss, the beautiful unflinching Japanese mother, all of it breaking and falling around me like the bodies of burning stars.

PART 3

A SMALL HOLE

The surgical waiting area in Hackensack Hospital was fancy. No cheap vinyl chairs like the ones at Saint Luke's, where my father had had his first surgery. It was a classy, quiet place with thick gold upholstered sofas, comfortable enough to sleep on. And many people did. They slept a guarded, public sleep among strangers, their heads tucked into their folded-up jackets. Families took up residence, thumbing through thick, expensive magazines, letting their shoes slip onto the floor. They padded into the kitchenette and helped themselves to coffee. Abandoned coffee cups lay casually under the end tables, but not for long. The waiting room attendant, a round-faced woman in a navy blazer, glided through the room, picking up the trash, rearranging the magazines so that they sat square on the tabletop.

My mother and I, contingent of two, positioned ourselves on either end of a couch. It had been five years since my father's first surgery. We were veterans; we knew how it went. I read the *New York Times* Arts & Leisure section. She tapped her nails against the lemony wood.

The other family's surgeon entered, strangely intimate in his pajama-like scrubs suit, his puffy blue booties. He shook hands all around, saying, *Things went well.* He told them the patient was in *recovery.* He said they could go in one at a time. In forty-five minutes, he said, the patient would be moved *upstairs.*

The family members asked questions, but not many. They

searched the surgeon's face anxiously and brightened when he told them how well their loved one performed under anesthesia.

My mother and I watched seven doctors come in and give the same report to seven families. They got up, relieved, shaking crumbs from their clothing, detritus from the vending machine and the second-floor cafeteria. They made calls on the free phone. They said dramatically, "He was in there for over three hours." They made it sound as if that was a long time.

My mother and I tried not to count. But the numbers spun in our heads every time we heard the other families boasting. We knew, without looking at watches or clocks, that it had been ten hours since we kissed my father goodbye in the hallway outside this room. Eight hours and four minutes since the surgery had begun. But if he was still in there, it meant he was alive. So I read, and my mother tapped.

Finally, our doctor appeared. He knelt in front of the sofa as if to propose. I registered that his face was sad. His eyelashes stuck together in small, wet spikes. Something was wrong.

Before I could stand up and shout, *Excuse me, we will take another doctor, that bald overweight one with gold chains, the one who gives good news*—he had wrapped his hands around mine and he was saying, *He didn't make it.*

I felt as if I was falling from an airplane whose door had suddenly blown open. He held me with both hands. He kept me from plunging through clouds as my mother had plunged, flailing and writhing like a fish on the wide gold couch. She had fallen sideways, gasping.

They were both speaking at once, and their words whirled through a tunnel in my head.

My mother: "I don't believe it! I don't believe it!"

The doctor: "Sorry so sorry. So very, very sorry."

I could not speak. Or breathe. I stared at the surgeon's narrow, sorrowful face underneath his red bandana.

What happened?

He began to explain, his voice low and crumbling, and my

mother lurched away. She punched buttons on the free phone, calling Uncle Yo, my father's "kid brother."

"Yo? Yo! Masaji passed away."

She staggered back and landed on the couch. *Something unexpected, a terrible shock,* said the doctor. My mother punched at her face with a ball of tissue. A terrible wailing sirened out from the tissue. "What am I gonna do? What am I gonna do?"

I realized that the doctor had been speaking for a long time. I blinked and said, "Please. Say it again."

Of course, he said, infinitely gentle.

He took a pen from his pocket and began drawing on the fabric over his knee.

I pulled at him. Was he crazy? Don't write on your clothes!

It's all right, he said. He drew over his knee, the heart, its tubes leading here and there. Here were stitches, here were more squiggly lines. Here was a hole.

It was only two millimeters, he said. I heard the stunned shock in his voice. A little hole, too small to see.

The surgeon told the story. The operation, so long prepared for, so awaited and dreaded for all its intricacy and risk, had been finished. It was a success. My father had been closed up, put back together with little staples, and was being steered into Recovery, that gleaming forty-five-minute purgatory, that one-visitor-at-a-time place.

We knew all about Recovery. Go on, I said.

Our surgeon had pulled off his gloves. He had conquered the aneurysm, the deadly balloon. He had redrawn the vascular map inside my father's body. For eight hours, he embroidered my father's thorax.

He finished.

They stapled the patient together like a fat report.

That was when the machine beeped. The numbers stumbled downward, plummeting, lower than human numbers ever should be.

The nurse at my father's head gasped. Blood, red as the surgeon's bandana, leaked from my father's mouth. It spilled over the gurney's edge, a bright waterfall, puddling onto the floor.

The surgeon whirled back from the door, grabbed his scalpel and sliced again, searching for a door, a window, a clue for this torrent, riveting its way across the tiled floor. His gloved hands plunged into the lake of blood, his fingers grasping for a place to plug, to squeeze, to stop it from coming. The numbers stuttered into the single digits and hit zero.

My father's heart fluttered and stumbled, desperate for a few droplets to pump. There was nothing. Blood pressure: 0.

That 0 the size of the hole.

The surgeon pawed through the sticky remains until he found it. The hole-the-size-of-0 that had been hiding in secret. A little hole. Its formal name: Duodenal-arterial fistula. A hole the size of a sesame seed, through which a grown man's life slipped.

That was the moment our family shifted. I took charge. I called people. I planned a funeral and ordered platters of eggplant and meatballs from Casa del Sol. I went to one of the many nearby malls and bought myself a black suit. I wrote a program and chose photos and went to the copy store. I got a cardboard trifold display like for a science fair and covered it with photographs. My father as a boy in a sailor suit. A teenager, holding a raggedy, salty dog at Jones Beach. Handsome, proud soldier marching in Italy. In uniform on a park bench with my mother. Lifting me over the Atlantic Ocean in Florida. So many beach photos.

The funeral was packed, and the director presented a folded flag to my mother. "It's an honor to have one of those 442nd heroes here," he said. "An honor."

I became the person in charge of all the things. My mother was annihilated by grief and a fresh, shocking anger. She shouted, "This wasn't how it was supposed to happen!"

Nobody is supposed to die in surgery. Surgery is where one goes to be fixed. But her rage was over a broken promise. That they would one day "go together," whatever that meant. She didn't cry. She yelled. She felt utterly betrayed by him.

Her heart and her mind crumbled together. Over the next few months, she lost the ability to pay bills, to find her way from one part of town to the other.

She called me. "Susan. I'm in trouble."

She had gotten into a fender-bender at the mall. When an officer asked for her papers, they discovered that her drivers' license, vehicle registration, and insurance were all expired.

"You can't drive this car, ma'am."

"Then how am I supposed to get home?"

The cop made sure she had enough money to pay for a taxi and then impounded her car. She sounded like a child, three thousand miles away. It would take an army of acts of kindness from neighbors to get the car back, to renew the documents and pay the bills.

She could no longer live alone. For five years, she had been the brawn of the operation—taking care of all of my father's physical caregiving, hauling his wheelchair in and out of the car—but he had been the brains, selling souvenirs by phone from his hospital bed on the last day of his life.

We sold the house on Summit Street. Still protesting, she moved in with us. My mother came to us for good on Mollie's eleventh birthday. After picking my mother up from the airport, she helped me loosely wrap her from head to toe in gift wrapping paper and stick a bow on top of her head. She sat in the back seat of the minivan, and when I rolled into the carpool line at Mollie's school, I told her that a birthday present had arrived for her. She shrieked at the enormous, gift-wrapped lump in the back seat, with unmistakable white tennis shoes sticking out the bottom.

"Nana! The best present!"

My mother burst out of the paper and became a permanent member of our household for the next seventeen years.

SPIT

Thirty-four years after I met my birth mother, it was plain that she had no intention of telling me the identity of the man who had fathered me. Even the private investigator I'd hired more than a decade earlier had come up empty.

I had followed the trail of the man whose name my half sister, Mika, had mentioned as a wild guess. I had followed another set of breadcrumbs based on another speculation: a man I'll call Simon who seemed to fit the profile and had been a coworker of Yumi's the year I was born.

I found a photo of him, and his face looked familiar, with soft plump lips like mine. This could be the one! Further investigation revealed three children.

I followed Simon for years. He was alive, and I thought he was the one. Still, I was wary of contacting him. He appeared to be married to the same woman he'd been with since before I was born. I didn't want to divulge an infidelity or the fact of my birth mother's secret pregnancy. How could I find out the truth without revealing anything about myself or Yumi?

One of his sons was a writer, which I took to be another sign that we could be genetically connected. I subscribed to the son's online column and read everything he wrote. I found a photograph of him online and photoshopped it next to mine. I believed we had the same mouth, convinced he was my brother.

I plotted about flying to this man's town, following him to a restaurant or bar and pocketing a glass he'd marked with his DNA. This was how it was done on television crime shows, right?

Fact became stranger than fiction when I discovered that Simon was serving time in a federal prison. An elderly criminal! Maybe I could contact him without his wife knowing. I wrote him a cryptic letter indicating that we might be vaguely related and sent it to the prison by registered mail, but I never got a response. I continued to muse about tracking down his son the writer and wrenching a strand of hair from his head, but I never found the courage, or the insanity, to do it.

Eventually, deciding the search was beyond my capacity, I decided to hire a private investigator. Through a search engine, I found a kind-eyed, bearded man whose website said that he specialized in adoption searches. He was in the same area where my mother had lived when she was pregnant with me. He had facilitated dozens of post-adoption reunions. I was infinitely hopeful, but he sleuthed around for months and turned up nothing much. He admitted that the most reliable source of information was Yumi herself. He wanted to call her. At this point, she had not spoken to me in years.

"Go ahead," I said. "Talk to her. There's nothing to lose."

He called the next day. "I spoke with your mother," he said.

I stopped in my tracks, walking toward my peaked-roof cottage at Hedgebrook, a writing colony for women set on idyllic Whidbey Island. I had left my six- and ten-year-old daughters in the care of John and my mother so I could write unencumbered.

"You did?" My chest rattled. "How was she? How did she sound?" My heart smarted with the memory of her voice. *Suuuu-san.* At least she was still alive.

"She's fine. But listen."

"What?"

He cleared his throat with a barking note. "She doesn't want to say. Who he is."

"Well, I could've told you that."

The detective described her as smart and impressive.

"So that's it?" I threw up my hands.

"I'm sorry. I did what I could. I guess this is the end of the road."

I hung up. I was frustrated and furious. He was not supposed to give up. He was supposed to use all his investigative tools to find my birth father. But he was basically telling me we were done.

In 2005, I received a phone call from Beth Hall, an adoptive mother who had founded an organization called Pact, An Adoption Alliance. She held a perspective on adoption that I'd rarely heard from an adoptive parent. She championed openness—encouraging connections with birth families. She insisted that race mattered and that children needed to feel connected to their original cultures. She had adoptive parents do an exercise where they picked colored beads to represent extended family, neighbors, teachers, doctors, and others who had contact with their children. "Is your child the only brown bead in a sea of white?" she challenged. I admired her tremendously.

"Do you know anybody who might be a good fit as Pact camp director?" she asked me.

I thought about it for about five minutes. I loved organizing groups of people. At age twenty-five, I had coordinated the US-Nicaragua Colloquium on Health, bringing together hundreds of American health professionals and their Nicaraguan counterparts, an act of education and solidarity in the face of the US-backed contra war. I had organized educational and community service trips in Guatemala for groups of middle school girls. Planning events for groups of people was my jam.

As it turned out, Yumi also was a people organizer. I'd seen trips and events that she'd organized online. Maybe it was hereditary.

"I would," I said to Beth. "I would be a good fit. This job would be a dream."

I got the job. For the next seven years, it was my responsibility to pull together an ever-growing camp for adoptive families with children of color. It was some of the most fulfilling work of my life. What began as a weekend event with barely thirty families grew into an annual, week-long camp of hundreds. Kids got to play in the woods with young adult mentors who looked like them, often adoptees or former foster youth themselves. They got to talk "real talk" about their experiences. They got to wonder and think about their birth families. Parents, on the other hand, learned about the realities of raising children of color, understanding institutional racism, and making genuine connections with their children's birth family and culture. Some made decisions to move away from towns with little diversity. Most of the families were "transracial," where parents (mostly white) were raising children of a different race, although there were several parents of color as well.

Most of the expert speakers at camp were adopted adults themselves, who had endured racism or silences and secrets. They had grown into lauded professionals who conducted their own research or wrote their own narratives, in a space long dominated by adoptive parents or researchers without a personal connection to adoption. I listened to JaeRan Kim, the "Harlow's Monkey" blogger I had long admired, give a keynote talk about the "ambiguous loss" of adoption, and it struck a deep chord. I sat open-mouthed as Lisa Marie Rollins performed her solo show, *Ungrateful Daughter*, embodying the life of a transracial adoptee. It was electrifying. Afterward I rushed up to her and asked, "How did you learn how to do that?" I soon signed up for a solo performance workshop and developed my own show, *The Ice Cream Gene*. At Pact camp, I saw one of the first screenings of Angela Tucker's film, *Closure*, and Sue Harris O'Connor's moving monologues about racial identity development and her first birthday in foster care. I befriended another adoptee named Susan who was also a birth mother. I learned that her open adoption was unilaterally, heartbreakingly closed by her daughter's adoptive parents. At camp, I learned about the concept of abolition, envisioning a future where adoption did not perpetuate family separation because of poverty or the drive for profit.

These were my people.

In the evenings, we adult adoptees gathered in our own cabin, designated as the adult adoptee sanctuary, and shared stories over thermoses of wine and flaky fruit pies from a local produce stand. The table was strewn with coloring books and pipe cleaners. It helped to use our hands—to color intricate mandalas or twist fuzzy crowns—as we talked. It had been decades since I'd attended those ALMA support groups during college, and being with other adoptees was like coming home again. It was emotional to witness daily a camp full of young adoptees of color, from toddlers to teens, many of them echoing the issues and losses we knew all too well. Coming together on our own was crucial. These friends became my true home community.

I began learning about consumer genetics sites where adoptees and others could bypass the humans who were unwilling or unable to answer questions about their origins. I decided to pursue DNA testing to find the answers on my own.

I sent off my ninety-nine dollars and received my home testing kit. The process was more emotionally fraught than I'd expected. It felt subversive. I called Lisa Marie, one of my closest adoptee friends, and asked if she would be my witness and support person.

"Come on over, Sis." She opened the door with a hug and cleared a spot on her kitchen table for me to do the deed. We took deep breaths together.

It took longer than I had imagined to collect a few tablespoons of spit. The saliva rose up from the floor of my mouth, and it felt like a substantial puddle, but once I directed it into the plastic vial, it dissolved into bubbles and foam. I sucked the insides of my mouth, collected and dribbled until my spit finally reached the "fill to here" line.

I stared at the little tube in my hand. Would this finally provide me with the answer to that question, "What are you?" And even more important, "Who made you?" Lisa Marie applauded. We embraced after I sealed up the box and affixed the address label.

The post office was only a few blocks away. I sent off my saliva sample to 23andMe and later, to Ancestry.com and Family-TreeDNA. Each time, I spat into the provided tube, sealed it up, and deposited the little box into the mail.

A month later, I got my first results via email. *The moment you've been waiting for is here. Great news! Your AncestryDNA results are in.*

I clicked on the link, breathing hard: *Your DNA Story.* The first thing I saw was 47% Japanese. Even though I'd been told this my whole life, seeing it confirmed was an electric rush. Then the real news unfurled: 30% Scotland, 10% England and Western Europe, and 10% Wales. I stared at the map, at the glowing colors that told me: your people are from here. There was a small happy surprise of a nub: 3% Korean. I really was connected to all the Korean adoptees who had befriended me.

Finally, I could point toward a map when people asked about my other half. I could say, Scottish, English, and Welsh. Science had spoken.

I eagerly clicked on the tab for "DNA relatives," but quickly learned that fifth or sixth cousins were really, really, really far removed. I was as likely to be related to a random person in the grocery store as anyone else. There was no instant connection, no answers that declared "father" or "sibling." Every time I got an email saying, "You have new DNA relatives" my heart jumped, but the infinitesimal amounts of DNA never added up to anything substantial.

I turned my attention to the family in my house. My children were growing up, and my mother was growing needier. She had been officially diagnosed with dementia and attending to her needs was a full-time job.

Since she had moved in with us, she was increasingly confused and unhappy. She didn't remember that she had agreed to move cross-country. She complained to visitors that we had sold her house and her car and that she was trapped in California with "no family and no friends." It stung to hear her say that.

I threw myself into trying to find activities to occupy her, to help her feel less alone. I understood that it was bewildering to be in a new city, thousands of miles from home. I found her a local Japanese American church, but that only occupied her on Sunday mornings.

She had loved bowling since she was a teen and been part of a league for as long as I could remember. I heard about a league for Japanese American seniors, a "Go-Go" team (for those fifty-five and older). Most of the bowlers were well into their eighties and nineties.

I drove her to Albany Bowl, and we found the easily identifiable group of Asian seniors. The sound of balls barreling down the lanes, crashing into the pins, was comforting and familiar to both of us. I introduced my mother to a bespectacled woman with a clipboard. She waved the others in. "We have a new bowler! Everyone, this is Kiku."

They gathered close and said hello, offering handshakes and names. My heart surged with hope. She was going to have friends! She was going to have a little fun.

One of the men asked, "So, what camp were you in?" Everyone quieted and leaned in for the answer. *Camp* had become a sorting and bonding experience for nisei, who had once been reluctant to talk about what had happened during the war. But younger generations' activism had made it easier to share.

My mother shook her head. "I wasn't in camp."

"What!" The others couldn't believe it. "What do you mean? How can that be?"

"I lived in New York. We didn't go to camp." She shrugged.

The Californian nisei were stunned. Slowly, they drifted away. They didn't have much else to say to her.

Eventually, she made a few friends, but it was a challenge. It was hard to remember their names. They were all independent, driving their own cars, and she had to be picked up by her daughter. Sometimes she complained. "All those people want to talk about is camp, camp, camp."

She still loved watching sports on television. For Christmas, I surprised her with a pair of tickets to see the Golden State Warriors play basketball. John drove her to the game and said that she was happier and more animated than he'd ever seen her. We took the leap to get season tickets and for years, the two of them were constant companions at every home game. Multiple times a week, she bundled up in her overcoat and clapped her hands.

"Come on, John, we don't want to be late for tip-off!" It was a true source of joy for both of them. Throughout basketball season, they were either attending a game or watching on television. I was grateful to him for keeping her company, but unless one of our daughters was available, he and I were unable to leave her alone for a date night.

I kept searching for activities and people to occupy her days. When she was unable to follow instructions in a group sewing class at the Japanese community center, I took out an ad online for a "senior sewing tutor." Louise answered the call, and for the next eleven years, she came to the house to patiently help my mother piece together quilts. My mother chose the colors and patterns, and Louise did the math. My mother was able to work her sewing machine even when she couldn't remember where she was. Together, they made hundreds of quilts for my daughters' school and crew team fundraisers, for newborn babies of friends, for family shelters.

My mother was too stubborn and proud to ever agree to a formal caregiver. I had to be sneaky about it. I hired Alyson as a "personal chef," which we didn't exactly need, but she came to the house with bags of groceries and enlisted my mother as a sous chef to prepare dinner for the rest of us: John, me, and the girls. We were busy, hungry people, and we needed Alyson and my mother to chop vegetables. As far as my mother knew, she was providing a needed role for our family; but I was counting on Alyson to be a companion and friend. She was a stellar sneaky caregiver.

I lived with my parents for the first seventeen years of my life, and my mother lived with us for the last seventeen of hers. When I was a young adult, I never would have imagined that I could handle it. My mother and I had not been particularly close: we didn't share common interests. I was a bookworm and artist, and she was a short, rough-talking, Brooklyn-born athlete. At after-church basketball games, she was always chosen ahead of me. She laughed at my fear of the flying balls. "Whatsa mattah with you, Chicken Ito?"

In my twenties, I discovered a book that consisted of letters between mothers and daughters, some famous ones and others not as well known. I bought two copies and sent them to my adoptive and birth mothers one Mother's Day. I longed to exchange such letters, this "mingling of souls" with each of them, and I wrote an inscription that said so. Yumi responded with a polite thank-you note, but my adoptive mother was angry.

"What's wrong with the letters I write?" She tended to write superficial details about the weather, the neighbors, or the dog.

"I just . . . wanted to share more personal stuff."

She didn't understand what I meant, and it offended her. I should have sent a box of chocolate instead.

All my life, I had gravitated toward my father. He had been a source of unconditional love. When I entered a room, his face glowed with joy. "That's my girl! My rascal!" I never felt this way with my mother. But now he was gone. I sensed that he had moved aside to force my mother and I to find our way together. It took seventeen years.

At the start of our living together, we were irritable, resentful housemates. But over time, it changed. When I picked her up at the bowling alley, or came home from work, she perked up. "My daughter!" she exclaimed to anyone nearby.

At the insistence of my daughters, she began reluctantly accepting physical affection. For most of my life, she had been like the Lucy character in *Peanuts,* wiping off her kissed cheek and grimacing, "Dog germs!"

But now she opened her arms to us. "Hug?" she asked. And echoed back, "Love you," for the first time in my memory.

I WOULD MEET YOU AT
THE FERRY BUILDING

It was the day before Thanksgiving, and I was elbow deep in a bowl full of bread cubes and onions. Frying pans bubbled with butter and sausages, oysters, pecans. The phone rang, and I reached out a greasy hand. I almost dropped the receiver when I heard her voice.

"Su-saaaaaan?" Lilting, almost songlike. "It's Yumi!" Like she was a present about to be unwrapped. Years ago, she had vanished from my life. It had taken her years to cautiously return, saying that "life is too short to hold on to anger." We weren't as close as we had been in our earlier years of "reunion," but we had formed a fragile truce.

"Hi." I held my breath, waiting.

"I'm in California!" Her voice bounced, ebullient. I sighed. I was tired of being ambushed like this. Her phone call meant that I would drop everything: work, children, writing, schedules, my own dignity—to go and hide with her. To accept whatever moments or crumbs she was willing to dole out.

I sighed. It was a sigh of resignation, a sigh that echoed the swoons I used to swoon back in the early days. A sigh of impatience with my own self.

"Really." I tried to remain casual.

"We're babysitting Mika's dog while she's on vacation." The sting of another arrow. I flinched. Mika. My sister. My sister who lived nearby. Who still did not want to see or speak with me. Who had long ago disowned our siblingness.

Mika would be horrified to know that Yumi was calling me. Once again, I was the secret held by our mother. I was wilting under the weight of all the not telling. Still, I couldn't resist Yumi's siren call. I would crash on the rocks of her.

Yumi wanted to know if I was free. It was Wednesday, the day before Thanksgiving. We were expecting seventeen guests. I resisted the urge to throw the phone into the sink full of crusted pans.

I said, "I don't think today will really work." I closed my eyes. It was so hard for me to resist her.

"How about Friday?"

Friday. The day after Thanksgiving. We would still have out-of-town relatives, who would want to visit the holiday display at the zoo, or go sightseeing, or just hang around, like houseguests do. Could I leave them? I decided that I could, for a few hours. How often did these phone calls happen? How long would they continue? Any time could be the last time.

The morning after a full-bellied meal and walk in the park, I told my family I was going to San Francisco to meet my birth mother.

Emma had not seen Yumi since she was a baby; she was thirteen now. "I want to go! But only if Mollie does too." The last time Emma had seen this phantom grandmother, she had taken her first steps. Right into Yumi's outstretched hands. I told her that it probably wasn't a good idea.

Seventeen-year-old Mollie slept late, through my departure. Emma said, "You should bring pictures." She ran into her room and came out with a page of school photos. "How do you spell her name?"

My voice stuck in my throat. I whispered, "Y-U-M-I." I watched her write in tiny print. *To Yumi. From Emma, 8th grade, 13 years old.* I put the picture in an envelope along with one she had chosen of Mollie. "Stay with your cousins, Em, they really want to hang out with you."

My husband threw me a concerned expression. Don't do this,

he said without words. Don't put yourself in this situation again. He knew that any contact with Yumi could undo me. I turned my face away, defiant and ashamed.

My mother cornered me in the front hallway. "You're going to see Yumi?"

"Yes." I could barely look her in the face.

"Why doesn't she come here?"

I swallowed. "Well, she doesn't have a car."

She shook her head. "You should still invite her."

I didn't know what to say. I couldn't say, "She would never do that."

My mother pressed a crumpled bill into my palm. I unfolded it: a fifty-dollar bill. "What is this?" I asked, stupidly.

"It's for your visit. Have a nice lunch or something with Yumi." My nose prickled with tears. I hadn't told her much about the estrangement that had separated me from Yumi for years. Why Yumi had turned away from me, from all of us. For years, she had made a tradition of sending a giant poinsettia arrangement to my parents during the holidays. I knew that they had exchanged Christmas cards, and she had even visited their home a few times. They had been friends. When Yumi stopped speaking to me, the poinsettias and cards had also stopped. For a year or two, my mother commented on it. "The poinsettias didn't come. Yumi must be traveling or something." But then she stopped mentioning it, and we never discussed it.

I thanked my mother gruffly and grabbed my keys.

Yumi suggested meeting at the Ferry Building in San Francisco. It was thick with people on holiday, swarming the farmers market and gourmet food stalls. We'd agreed to meet on the pier overlooking the water. I arrived early and didn't see her.

I made my way to the public restroom. Looking at my reflection in the mirror, I realized I was wearing almost the identical outfit to the one I had been wearing the day I met her, twenty-seven years before: jeans, clogs, same haircut.

I remembered looking in the mirror in the Holiday Inn restroom that day, wondering what she would think of me. Today, I was wary, weary, and bruised. I applied lipstick and walked back to our meeting place.

Yumi was looking out at the water, her back to me. She was wearing a green suede jacket, a loosely knotted scarf, a black turtleneck, a stylish bag. Despite itself, my heart leapt when it saw her. I couldn't help it. I was awed by her good haircut, her easy way with fashion. My glamorous sort-of mother.

I approached her slowly. "Helloooooo."

She startled a bit, then turned and smiled her twinkly-star smile. We sidestepped back and forth, a slow awkward dance, then: Shall we go eat? Are you hungry? Yesssss!

Then we were walking side by side, bumping shoulders in the crowd, as if we did this every day, met for lunch, mother and daughter, scanning the menus for something good to eat. It felt so ordinary. And yet it was one out of maybe a dozen walks we'd had like this, one out of a dozen meals in decades.

I suggested a seafood bar and spotted an empty little round table with two chairs, tucked in a back corner. I nudged her. She nodded back, her eyes bright. The hostess, with seaweed-green fingernails, pointed the table out to a man standing in front of us. She told him, "You can sit there, or you can sit outside." Yumi and I whispered under our breath, an urgent, quiet chorus. "Outside! Outside!"

"We'll take the one outside," he said, and Yumi and I exchanged a look of triumph—a shared moment of *Yes! Score!* The hostess led us to the corner table.

We scanned the menu. Both of us chose oyster stew with crusty bread. A glass of wine. We often ordered the same dishes, swooning over our food. Sharing these moments brought me a swirl of happiness and anger.

This meeting was a microcosm of every time we had ever spent together. It was awkward, it was easy, it was funny and comfortable, tense and warm and terrible. It was secret. It was everything, and the weather between us shifted every thirty seconds.

Things went best when she was the one asking the questions. I told her about our family vacations, about my adoptive mother, the way she was settling into our household. But when I asked her questions, she often hesitated, and discomfort bloomed between us like a sour cloud.

I handed her the envelope with the pictures of the girls, remembering how photos had broken the ice at our first meeting together. She murmured nice things—"So pretty—so smart looking!" and handed the photos back to me.

I said, "No, they're for you. To keep."

She read what Emma had written. She looked happy but flustered. She wasn't sure what to do about these grandchildren who wanted to know her, who she held at an infinite distance.

When the bill arrived, I took out the crumpled fifty from my mother. "My mother said that this lunch is on her." This was maybe a tiny bit of a dig.

She looked taken aback for a second, and then said brightly, "Well, thank you, Kiku!" and put her wallet away.

I felt myself getting teary, laying the bill inside the leather folder, watching the waitress take it away. "My mom is doing really well these days," I said. "She's quilting, and bowling, and volunteering at Emma's school." I didn't mention her forgetfulness, the growing dementia, that she hadn't been able to drive a car in years.

After lunch we walked around and stopped at all the gourmet stalls. We picked up bamboo bowls and admired perfect produce. We tasted fancy olive oil on little cubes of bread. We walked, pointing out things that give us pleasure.

"I love the color of that plate."

"Same. It's gorgeous."

We sat on a bench near the water. We laughed a bit, the laughter floating off over the salty water, then evaporating. My phone vibrated inside my pocket. After three hours, the family was feeling my absence.

I reached for my purse. "I have my camera."

"I do too." We stood against the wooden railing out by the water and took pictures of each other. I showed her how I could twist the viewfinder of my camera around and hold it at arm's length. "See, we can take some of us together." We pressed our heads against each other, smiling.

It seemed clear that our time was over. I walked her to the train station and then followed her down the escalator. "You don't have to come all the way down here," she said, but she was smiling. I thought about how she had walked me to my bus stop in the snow at our first meeting.

"But I want to." And it was true. I didn't want it to end. This moment, our being together, the ease that we enjoyed for just a brief while.

Her train came roaring out of the tunnel, the first one to arrive. Before I could say anything, she jumped through the sliding doors and said, "I'm going to get the senior-citizen seat!" She sat right across from the train door in the section reserved for disabled people and seniors. Her face was alive with its mischievous, twinkly look. I snapped a final photo just before the doors closed and the train glided away.

I HAD AN AUNT

It had been years since I'd sent my spit off in a padded envelope, hopeful for a ping of connection. My friend Amber, a genetic genealogist, had been trying to help me make sense of it, drawing threads between my DNA and public family trees. Nothing had come of it.

Then one night I was cooking dinner when I glanced at my phone and saw an avalanche of text messages from Amber. WHERE ARE YOU? I FOUND SOMETHING!

A "close" match, or a second cousin, in genetic genealogy terms, was like hitting a vein of gold. While I was stir-frying onions, Amber had discovered I had a genetic connection with a man on someone's public family tree. He would have been in his late twenties the year I was born. She did more digging. His father was a mortician. From the same town where my birth mother had lived.

Amber typed, "I have some hard news, though. Sit down."

"Is it Simon?" The elderly inmate with the writer son.

I sat. I looked at my phone. "No, it's not."

She told me his name, someone I'd never heard of. "He passed away two years ago. I'm sorry."

Another missed chance. I wilted. But look! Amber quickly showed me a photo of his living sister, on Facebook. I gasped. A woman with round cheeks, and lips like mine, and a nose like mine. If pictures could tell a story, this was the story of a warm, connected, vibrant person. Who made quilts and supported refugees and seemed to laugh a lot.

"Susan. You need to call her."

"I don't know . . ." I was anxious. I remembered when Gina had called my birth mother.

"Come on. She looks so cool. She looks *great*. Susan, after all this time, you deserve to know this family."

Her number popped up when I searched online, and I decided to call the next morning.

I waited until I was alone in the house.

I didn't believe she would answer. I was expecting no answer at all, at best a voicemail message. And then what would I say? I dialed and waited. It rang five times. And then a bright, chipper voice said, "Hello?"

"Hello. Is this Elizabeth?"

"Yes . . ."

"Are you the sister of . . . ?" I spoke the man's name.

"Yes. Why, yes, I am." Her tone was perky, curious.

I took a deep breath. "I know this is surprising, but . . . I . . . I think your brother might be my father."

A momentary pause. "Whaaat?" Her voice rose a full octave.

"Um, I took this DNA test, and I got a match . . ."

"Whaaaat? Well, my dear, what's your name?"

"Susan."

"Susan! Well, dear, welcome to the family!"

Welcome to the family. In thirty-seven years of knowing my birth mother, she had never said anything like this. Once, in a burst of frustration and anger, she'd written, "It seems to me that you are determined to see yourself as a part of this family." Implying, of course, that I was not.

Elizabeth and I spoke for almost an hour. She had questions. I explained how I'd arrived at this connection, by putting together the DNA, the family trees, and the information I'd gotten long ago from the adoption agency.

"They said he was the son of a mortician."

"Well, bingo, you got that right!" she laughed.

She told me to call her Auntie. Auntie Liz. "I once played Auntie Mame on stage, did you know that?"

We spoke for hours over the next few weeks. We exchanged photographs and chatted on FaceTime. Of course, she wanted to know. "Who was your mother?" Her brother had never had any other children.

I was reluctant to say. But as soon as she saw my photo, she guessed.

"I have no doubt that you are my niece," she said. But we agreed that we needed undisputed confirmation, for the sake of her dubious family. I learned that Auntie Liz was the kind of person who would trust everyone and do anything for a stranger. I was virtually a stranger.

We took two separate independent DNA tests, and they came back with a ninety-nine percent probability of being niece and aunt.

She wrote, "I feel infinite, unconditional love for you. I am so happy. It's like having my brother come back to me again."

It turned out that my aunt and my birth mother had known each other. Auntie had been pregnant with her first son while my birth mother was secretly, invisibly pregnant with me.

It was incredible. My unmarried birth mother, hiding her pregnancy, living (unknowingly?) nearby her unborn child's pregnant aunt.

What about the married man my birth mother had told me about? The one with three children? That piece didn't match up. Auntie and I discussed it endlessly. Her brother had never had other children and wasn't married when I was born. He had married and divorced years later but, to his knowledge, was never a father.

Maybe she was in love with the man with three children, who she stayed in touch with, who thought to remember me. Maybe she thought he was the father. But it was undisputed; she had gotten pregnant by Auntie's brother. After decades of secret-keeping from me, it was possible that I finally knew more than Yumi did. And maybe it explained why her secret was so deeply kept. Maybe she hadn't even known.

On the plane, I drafted an email to my birth mother. The subject line was: News. I wrote that the question she'd evaded for so long had finally been answered and that I'd been warmly welcomed by Elizabeth and her family. I told her that Elizabeth and I would be nearby that week and that we'd like to meet with her.

I first stopped in Washington, DC, where I'd been invited to gather with thirty women for a speak-out for abortion rights. We had been invited to a television recording studio to tell our stories and to meet with congressional representatives. I couldn't help but think of my own birth mother, thirteen years before *Roe v. Wade*, pregnant and unmarried in a small town. She had told me that if abortion had been safe and readily available, she would have chosen that option. I thought about how she told me she didn't eat much during her pregnancy, how she didn't gain any weight. I wondered about how she didn't have the courage to seek an illegal abortion, but still she hoped her fetus wouldn't survive. But I did.

I understood the complicated and terrible situation she had been in. I didn't begrudge her wishing she could have had an abortion. Still, it saddened me that her pregnancy with me had brought shame, not joy.

I reviewed the email to Yumi and hit send. Immediately I felt nauseated. There was no taking it back.

I'd done an irrevocable thing. I'd found my birth father. I'd confirmed it. I'd contacted his family. That night, after hours of listening to intense and emotional abortion stories, I was exhausted. But I couldn't sleep. My mind wouldn't rest. *You've done it. You've really done it now.* Yumi was going to have a stroke over this news, and it would be my fault.

When the pro-choice delegation in the Capitol was over, I flew to the tiny airport closest to my aunt's home and rented a car. The small, tree-lined town square was surrounded by small businesses: a Mexican restaurant, a Subway, a bank, and antique stores. It was around the same size as Park Ridge, where I'd grown up. Maybe smaller.

The GPS on my phone announced: *You have arrived at your destination.* I pulled up in front of a sweet, dove-gray house with white trim, a little porch. Before I could brush my hair and smear lipstick on my mouth, she was out the front door, waving.

She wore a theater sweatshirt and black stretch pants, with soft Mary Janes. I got out of the car and climbed the wooden steps into her embrace. Her white hair tickled my cheek.

"Oh, my dear! You're here!" She was a pillow of love. I held her hand and followed her through the front door in a daze. I was there, in the town where I'd been conceived. With my birth father's sister. My aunt. She was excited and happy, showing me her handmade quilts. One with random squares on a white background, growing thicker and thicker until they merged into a solid field. This was what this journey had felt like: disparate puzzle pieces, floating singly for years, then decades, until finally they all pulled together and formed a picture, shocking in its completeness.

My aunt pointed out oval framed photos of her bearded great-grandfather, the Civil War general, his serious wife. "That's your great-great-grandfather," she said. I just stared. This stern white man in the Union uniform. Her words echoed in my heart. Your great-great-grandfather. When I thought about veteran relatives, it was always my nisei father and uncles, serving in the Japanese American 442nd regiment. My ancestral history until now had been truncated, only including people whose lives I could touch. I stared at this man in the blue cap. It was shocking to be confronted with the fact that not only did I have white relatives—something that had never really felt real to me—I had Civil War soldier ancestors. I didn't how to take it in.

We sat on the living room sofa, and I opened the email app on my phone. I had been avoiding it ever since I'd sent that email to my birth mother. I shuddered when I saw her reply. The first sentence: "The other shoe has finally dropped."

She said that she was filled with dismay and anger. The same anger she felt when my friend Gina had first contacted her, thirty-seven years ago. The phone was hot with her anger. I skimmed quickly. *You have opened a Pandora's box.* Now that I had found "family" (her quotes), we would both be free. She did not want to meet up with me or my aunt.

She wanted no further contact. Once again, she was done with me.

I turned my phone off and placed it gingerly on the coffee table.

"How are you feeling?" asked my aunt.

"I don't know," I said. But I was devastated. Just a few months prior, Yumi and I had spent time together when I'd been at a conference in her city. After we had shared a pleasant dinner, she'd asked to meet me for an early breakfast before my flight the next day. We had forged another tender alliance, and now it was destroyed. I had destroyed it.

I lugged my suitcase up a narrow staircase to the second floor. My aunt pointed out a room with blue wallpaper and patted the high, four-poster wooden bed. "This was your great-grandmother's bed," she said. "Your grandmother, my mother, was born in it." I was so stunned I didn't know how to react. Above the bed was a framed pen-and-ink rendering of a big house.

"That's the funeral home," she said. The funeral home: one of the adoption agency's "non-identifying" hints that had so long ago put me on the path that had led me here.

I couldn't stop staring. This house, or a three-story house very much like it, had been the setting of a recurring dream I'd had for more than ten years. In the dream, I kept climbing stairwells to the uppermost floor, where I found multiple bedrooms. Elizabeth told me that there were six bedrooms on the top floor of the house. I shook my head, incredulous.

We ate dinner at the Mexican restaurant on the square, and I snapped a selfie of us in front of a giant papier-mâché jalapeño. It was a festival of cheekiness, our faces echoing each other. Inside the restaurant, she exuberantly greeted the owner and several diners. Everyone knew everyone in this town, just like my birth mother had said. "This is my niece!" my aunt exclaimed to everyone in earshot.

"Oh, you look so alike!" said the owner. My heart quaked. Those were words I had hungered for my whole life. I wanted us to look alike. I wanted us to be family. And yet, every interaction felt tinged with betrayal. My birth mother's words, *Pandora's box*, echoed in my head. I imagined a network of lights snaking from house to house, street to street, until the entirety of the small town was flickering with news of my arrival, betraying my birth mother's secret. What had I done?

While I was in town, Elizabeth and her son, my cousin, showed me the building where she and my birth mother had worked long ago. When we stepped out of the car, I was dizzy for a moment.

"I was a fetus here." Yumi had walked these floors as I bobbed inside her. Elizabeth, also pregnant at the time, had been pressured into quitting work as soon as she began showing. It was considered unseemly for women to be in public, especially working, when they were expecting.

I tried to imagine my birth mother here, contracting her abdominal muscles underneath the rigid stays of a girdle to keep her secret safe. Me, kicking at her from the inside. Elizabeth's son had been born just a few weeks after I was.

Back in the car, my aunt pointed out the window. "I think that's where Yumi lived," she said. I stared at the modest two-story apartment building, wondering if this was where I had been conceived.

Then, she pointed out a neat white house with dormer windows. "That's where my brother and I grew up," she said, "before we moved into the funeral home." It was like a child's drawing of a house: square, with two windows on each side of the door, a chimney rising from the center of the roof.

"There's the root cellar." Her face drifted into memory. "We had so much fun in this yard." I was astounded that her entire life had taken place in this little town—not just her life and my father's but their ancestors going back to the Civil War as well. That she could drive a short distance from her house and touch the evidence of family history.

One morning during my stay, Auntie Liz brought out photo albums and boxes of loose photos. I'd been waiting for this all weekend. I snapped photos of photos with my phone.

"There's my mother, your grandmother, when she was just a little girl." I saw a mirror of my daughter's round cheeks in this sepia photo of a toddler in a white lace dress, a hint of wildness in her eyes. "There's my father." A stern man with heavy eyebrows. The pictures kept coming; the dining room table groaned underneath the images, the endless images of people, many of them no longer alive. She handed me a photo of my birth father in his forties, maybe, scruffy in a salt and pepper beard, a red flannel shirt. He was laughing in a particular way, and I was startled. I knew this expression, this configuration, this face. It was my face, and I had a photo of myself that matched it almost exactly.

Elizabeth gave me a handmade, spiral bound book that contained pages of letters, diary entries, family tree charts, photographs, and oral histories.

"Everything you want to know about our family is here," she said. I turned the pages, incredulous. I thought about the miserly index cards with the paltry information the adoption agency deigned to share with me. All the family details that Yumi kept from me. She had never even told me her parents' names. I was overwhelmed by the wealth of details in these pages.

"Let's show her that movie," said one of my cousins.

"Movie? What movie?" I was limp from emotional overload, but I didn't want to say no to anything. How many times would I be here, in this house? Would I ever come again?

The movie was a DVD compiled from years of home movies starting in the 1950s. Elizabeth had provided the voice-over. "Here's Christmas, here we all are in the funeral home, everyone's come over." They were a social family. People pouring in the door, jolly, holding casseroles and armloads of gifts.

"There's Billy. He has a toy. Jump, jump, jump!" Billy was a toddler, just three weeks younger than me. If he was a toddler in this movie, then I was a toddler too, riding a toy horse in New Jersey.

The camera panned to a dark-haired man sitting on a sofa. "There's my brother!" Elizabeth exclaimed. An electrical jolt went through my body. My father. I was seeing the man whose genes had created me, only a few years after it had happened. He was wearing a pullover sweater, opening a present. Those hands had touched Yumi. He unwrapped the paper and let it fall to the floor. The camera veered away, and I wanted to pull it back. *Stop. Show me. I want to see him.* Then another scene of him playing cards with his nephews. I watched him fly a kite in the backyard and open a beer. "He was in such good shape then," said Elizabeth. The camera followed the kite up into the sky where it got stuck in a tree. Below, my birth father laughed. I wished I could hear the sound.

That night, I lay awake in the four-poster bed, unable to sleep. I opened the Ancestry app on my phone and started adding names and images. My family tree, bare for so long, began bursting with leafy green hints as the branches expanded and grew. Census records, birth and death certificates, photos, and stories poured into my hands.

On my last day with them, my aunt took me to visit the cemetery where my father was buried. She and I and her grandchildren piled into my rental car and went to Walmart, where I chose a small bouquet, including a chrysanthemum, my silent acknowledgement of my adoptive mother back in California. Her name, Kiku, means "chrysanthemum" in Japanese, but I didn't mention this to anyone. Holding her namesake flower in my fist tethered me to home. We drove another short distance to the town cemetery. Everything in the town was a five-minute drive from everything else.

The cemetery was sprawling, different from the tightly packed neighborhood where my adoptive family members were buried in New Jersey. We drove on a narrow road until we reached a prominent boulder.

"There it is!" I followed Elizabeth to the large, weathered stone carved in giant block letters: CRANE. "We are descended from Cranes," she said. Underneath the grass lay the bones or dust of humans whose genetic codes were linked to mine. We walked around the miniature village of headstones, pointing out names and dates from the 1800s, 1910s. Elizabeth "introduced" me to her parents: my grandparents. What would they have made of me, a half-Asian bastard child?

"I wish I had known about you," my aunt sighed. "I could have raised you. I would have. You and my son could have been like twins, born just a few weeks apart."

My heart split.

On one hand, her welcoming kindness: she would have taken me in!

On the other hand, my entire life, growing up with my Japanese American family, swept away. My childhood vanished. The mint green house on Summit Street. I was in a tsunami, floating away from the foundations of my known life. Her words were kind, but my heart was shattered. It showed just how random my life was. How I could have so easily not existed at all if only Yumi had had the resources and courage to find an abortionist, or how I could have ended up being raised by a completely different family, my genetic family—or by someone, anyone, else. I had believed that I was meant to be an Ito—but this reminded me that I could have gone anywhere, been with anyone. My adoptive parents could have taken that Japanese boy in the swing. The randomness of adoption was stunning.

"You know, you don't really look Asian to me at all! You look like one of us!" These words shocked me. For my entire life, all I had known were my Japanese parents and my Japanese birth mother. My European roots had always been a cloudy, theoretical mystery. But I couldn't deny that their features mirrored mine.

I'd befriended so many transracial adoptees: Black, mixed, Latino, and Asian friends adopted from foster care or other countries, raised by white families, separated from anyone who might mirror them, growing up in what they called Whitesville. This place felt like Whitesville. But unlike my friends who are more visible adoptees of color, I knew I could pass as white. This knowledge saddened me. When she said, "You don't look Asian to me," I glimpsed the life that might have been. If she had raised me. If I had grown up as a Crane descendant whose ancestors fought in the Civil War. I might have just been a funny-looking white kid, whose features might evoke the question, "What are you?" I would have been steeped in the European-rooted generations that lived and were buried in this small town. I would have had no knowledge or connection to my Japanese kin, either adoptive or biological. The thought of it bruised my heart.

I approached the flat grave marker where my genetic father had been buried only three years earlier. A simple rectangle of pale, flecked gray marble. I traced his name with my fingers. It stabbed at me that his death date was no longer than an arm's length into the past. I had come so close to knowing him. Thirty-seven years of searching, only to miss him by thirty-six months. What would he have done with the news of my existence? Maybe it was just as well. It could have been a crushing disappointment. Maybe it was best this way, to be embraced by my enthusiastic aunt, a relative who had no secret past, no shame or regret. Still, I felt a swirl of overwhelmed emotion and numbness as I knelt in

the damp grass. I unwrapped the cellophane from the chrysanthe-
mums and lay them down next to his name. The harsh wind bit
through my fleece coat. I didn't say anything out loud, but inside
my head, I said hello and goodbye.

Back at the house, I noticed a white porcelain crane hanging from a
knob on a kitchen cabinet. I smiled. "I'm folding a thousand cranes
for my daughter Mollie's wedding."

"Really!" she exclaimed. "That's so exciting! Well, you know,
because of our ancestors, I love anything with a crane shape."

I remembered how I had struggled to learn origami at the Tule
Lake internment camp pilgrimage. Back then, I'd believed it was
because I wasn't Japanese enough to accomplish it, but really it
was a lack of clear instruction and practice. A young surfer dude
on YouTube had one of the best tutorials I'd seen, and his patient
step-by-step had given me the skills to fold hundreds of flawless
cranes.

"I'll teach you," I said. She clapped her hands and called her
daughter-in-law and grandson into the kitchen.

I cut sheets of printer paper into white squares and laid them
out on the table. I demonstrated each step slowly. First you make a
triangle, then a kite, then a boat. After a few minutes, a quartet of
paper cranes was lined up on the table. Everyone was delighted.

"Look!" Elizabeth exclaimed. "The Cranes have made some
cranes!" The wild synchronicity of it all.

When it was time for me to leave, my aunt pointed out her
brother's ancient microscope, heavy and solid, beautiful as a table
sculpture. My throat tightened with sudden tears. The strange
and mysterious threads of nature were undeniable. I marveled
at the way my multiple strands of identity echoed these origins.
I was a physical therapist, a science major, a writer, a teacher, and
a performer. One daughter was a biology major, the other one a
health professional and artist. Suddenly, these choices felt less than
random.

Elizabeth handed me the microscope, and its solid metal weight pulled my arms down. "It's yours if you want it," she said. "It's one of the only things he left behind. There wasn't much."

She offered me a few other assorted objects—his little spiral notebook, a packet of ID cards wrapped in a rubber band. I tucked them into my suitcase and wrapped the microscope in a sweater. It was strange to me how this piece of metal endured while the man who gazed through its lens was no longer. His sister said he never knew of my existence. I thought about him peering into a drop of pond water, seeing the infinite life floating there, and never imagining the strands of his own DNA swimming inside my birth mother, transforming into me.

My aunt and I spoke at least once a week. We discussed presidential candidates, our favorite shows on Netflix and Hulu, our heartaches and worries, our bodies and hair and favorite foods and family. We were in sync. I loved her boisterous laugh coming out of my phone. "Hey, honey bunch!"

I had always disliked my nose, until I saw it on her face. It wasn't like any nose I'd ever seen. A short-term boyfriend had once compared it to an acorn. But when I saw her acorn nose, I fell in love with it. It had popped out of a mold, and it was the same as mine.

When I learned she had cancer two years later, I was shattered. It felt grossly unfair that we would have so little time together. I wept and screamed and broke things. I raged at my birth mother who had kept my father's family hidden so that I hadn't discovered them until after he died. Who cut off communication with me when I told her about the DNA results that led me to them. I feared that when Elizabeth was gone, the rest of her family would float away, and once again I would be unmoored.

The last time I visited her, she was dwindling. She slept most of the day and had trouble eating. I made her soft fried eggs on her favorite kind of toast, and she ate them sitting up in bed, watching endless episodes of *Law and Order: SVU*. I told her that this was my adoptive mother's favorite show too. They would have liked each other a lot.

My aunt loved my eggs. They were soft and buttery and easy to swallow. I was so happy to bring the plate to her bed and to see her eat with pleasure.

She sat propped up on pillows and mused about what music she wanted played at her funeral. She sang a few lines, conducting cheerfully with her finger. It pained me to think about it, but she wanted a say in her memorial. "I love your artwork," she said. "Will you design something for the cover of the program?" I promised that I would.

As I was leaving for the airport, she remarked, "I love that top you're wearing. Where did you get it?" It was from a Japanese boutique in northern California's wine country. I stripped it off on the spot and handed it to her.

She and I laughed in our bras near the front door. She wriggled into my shirt, loose with abstract indigo ovals like giant amoebas, a crisscrossing of red like barbed wire. It looked fabulous on her.

"I love it," she said.

I told her she could have it. It was one of my favorite pieces of clothing.

"Just—if you ever don't want it or need it, would you save it for me?" I unzipped my suitcase and took out another top to wear to the airport. She was overjoyed. I looked at her, happy in my clothes. I didn't want to think that it was the last time. "I'll come back in January," I promised. But she died in November.

Auntie Liz's last words to me, four days before she died, came in a voicemail: "Don't worry about me. Should I worry about you? Are you okay?" I wasn't okay. She sensed through my text messages and my voice that I was drowning in anticipatory grief.

They did include me, when she died, in all the ways that mattered. Her daughter, my cousin a few years younger than me, called to let me know of her sudden decline, that she had been transferred to hospice and that the end was soon. I crumpled over my phone, my heart broken. My aunt died two days later.

John came with me to the funeral, but as soon as we landed, he was stricken with the flu. I went alone to the cemetery and sobbed as the minister led prayers over a pitcher filled with flowers made from her colorful quilting scraps. Her pre-engraved headstone was just steps away from my birth father's.

During the church service, I met more cousins I'd never known, second and third and twice-removed. Most of them had an acorn nose. All of them embraced me.

When I returned to her house after the funeral, the top I'd given her was hanging in her closet in a dry-cleaner bag, waiting for me. When I wear it now, I feel her body against mine. I love that she once inhabited my clothing, that this fabric enveloped us both. I see us laughing in her living room, topless. "I'd give you the shirt off my back," I said to her, and I did.

It feels cliché to say that two years were better than nothing. But those years were suffused with love. Every interaction echoed *you belong.* Knowing my aunt for those two years healed a lifetime of erasure, secrecy, and denial.

I designed the cover of her funeral program, just as she'd asked me to. It was a watercolor painting of her house, its triangle-on-a-box shape resembling a child's classic drawing of a house. I drew a tiny figure of her on the front porch, her arms akimbo, in the classic welcoming pose. This is how I will always remember her, saying, *welcome—welcome home.*

GOT OBC?

Forty years after I'd begged the social worker at the adoption agency to give me the records of my birth and adoption, a FedEx envelope showed up in my mailbox. I was sixty years old.

I'd once performed a one-woman show about finding my birth mother, *The Ice Cream Gene*, at a New York–based adoption conference that was sponsored by the same agency. One scene dramatized my earlier standoff with Nancy, the social worker who had doled out crumbs of "non-identifying" information to me when I was a college student. Two young women approached me afterward and identified themselves as Spence-Chapin employees. They wiped away tears and told me how powerful the performance was, how moved they were by my story.

My heartbeat quickened. I had won them over!

"So," I said hopefully, "does this mean I can have my records now?"

They exchanged glances. "Um, so sorry," said one of them. "Records are still sealed."

It didn't matter how moved they were. It didn't matter that they cried. I still didn't have the right to my own original birth certificate, even if I knew the information it held.

I bought a T-shirt imprinted with the logo *Got OBC?* mimicking the Got Milk? ad campaign popular in the nineties. Most people outside of the adoption community did not know what *OBC* stood for. The back of the shirt explained: *Whose birth certificate is it anyway? Help adult adoptees access their Original Birth Certificates.*

I wore the shirt for the remainder of the conference weekend, hoping to run into those women so I could flash it in their faces.

The majority of states, including New York where I'd been born, sealed adoption records and original birth certificates and kept them from adult adoptees. This is what had led me to the subterfuge of asking my adoptive parents to lie about my adoption papers in order to get a copy, to masquerade as a pregnant woman and steal my hospital records from an unwitting gynecologist. It took years, often decades, of relentless activism to convince state lawmakers to unseal the records. Many adopted people died waiting to get their vital records. Many are still waiting.

In 2019, then–New York Governor Andrew Cuomo signed a paper decreeing that adult adopted people could access their birth certificates and other vital records. On a winter day, in early 2020, I received a FedEx envelope from New York State Vital Records.

I found my *Got OBC?* T-shirt in a bureau drawer and affixed a Post-it note below it on which I'd scribbled "NO." I took a selfie. Then I tore open the envelope and affixed a "FINALLY, YES!" Post-it in its place.

There were six sheets of paper inside.

The first was a Judgment of Adoption from the Bergen County Court.

In the Matter of the Adoption of a child by Masaji Ito and Kikuko Ito . . . They have had the child MIKA NOGUCHI under their constant care in their home since November 30, 1959. The said MIKA NOGUCHI was born in New Rochelle, New York; the natural parents of the said child surrendered the custody and control of the child to the SPENCE-CHAPIN agency for the full term of her minority."

The next paper was the official finalization of my adoption, four years after my birth. Why did it take four years to finalize?

I lifted out the Live Certificate of Birth: my original, unaltered birth certificate. By now, neither my original name nor my birth mother's name were secrets to me. I had uncovered them long ago. Still, I pored over every detail. I noted that all of the data had been filled in by typewriter, except my own original name. Someone (my birth mother?) had hand-printed "Mika" on that line. I wondered if it had been blank and filled in later. Another mystery. But it was something solid that told me that I had existed. I was real. I had been born, and someone had witnessed it.

I recognized the obstetrician's name from an early conversation with my birth mother. Tracing his signature on my birth certificate brought a surge of emotion. He had been kind, she'd told me, and treated her compassionately, instead of adding to her already intense shame. I searched for his name and on his obituary, I read that he "was an early advocate of birth control and safe abortion, a spirited proponent of quality healthcare for all women and served on the Medical Board of Planned Parenthood." I was glad that she'd had the good luck to have been attended by him instead of someone who would've judged her.

The next page in the envelope was the Information for Birth Certificate by Adoption form. My adoptive parents' names and addresses were listed, along with their ages and occupations (sales representative, housewife). I gasped at my father's familiar handwriting, where he'd filled in "Yellow" in the space asking for their color.

Finally, a brief letter from my parents' lawyer, requesting a birth certificate "suitable for adoption" so I could be registered for school. This meant an altered document, which stated that my adoptive parents had given birth to me.

It was a paltry sheaf of paper, mostly containing information I'd found on my own long before. But they were my papers. I was practically a senior citizen before I'd been allowed to lay eyes on these pages, pages that reflected the fact that I had not been born to my adoptive parents.

This lie, perpetuated by the infamous "baby thief" Georgia Tann, became standard practice in the 1930s, after she colluded with corrupt judges, doctors, and law enforcement to take babies from poor women and then sell them to wealthy would-be parents across the country. Sealing records, changing adopted children's names, and altering birth certificates were all ways of covering up evidence. The true crime was blocking adopted people from the truth of our very existence.

I finally had my papers. They were paltry, but they were mine. I gathered them around me, like I collected the tiny green "hint" icons on my Ancestry family tree. The branches grew and grew, and clicking on the green leaves became a self-soothing activity. The tree expanded to thousands, in every direction. In an unexpected discovery, I found a surprise on John's paternal tree: the Cranes of Texas. I whooped aloud.

LOOK AT THE BABY

The COVID-19 virus showed up just as our first grandchild was due to be born. This invisible, deadly threat was spreading across the country. Our state issued a mandatory shelter-in-place order. Bottles of hand sanitizer, boxes of gloves and surgical masks, paper towels and rubbing alcohol piled up on the kitchen counter, and our jobs abruptly transitioned to staring at our computer screens. The five of us—me, John, Emma, Mollie, and her husband, Michael—plus three dogs, hunkered down together.

Mollie was burstingly pregnant and planning a home birth. Thirty years prior, I had dreamed of giving birth in our woodsy A-frame cabin, but my preeclampsia attack and the loss of our first child had made me afraid. I tried to remain calm, but along with my joy, I worried about her, worried about the baby. Mollie invited me to meet her serene and wise midwife, who patiently listened to my fears.

My emotions were often triggered by pregnancy and newborns. Seeing my daughter's basketball-sized orb up close recalled Yumi's pregnancy with me: how she had managed to carry me without anyone noticing, how she had hidden me within the confines of a rigid girdle. The unbearable loneliness of her secret pregnancy haunted me. Now that I had walked the streets Yumi had walked while pregnant, now that I had spent time in the tiny town where she lived as an unmarried, Japanese woman in 1959, I recognized even more profoundly the shame and stigma she had endured.

Every morsel of joy over our coming grandchild reminded me of my birth mother's likely opposing emotions. Our family fol-

229

lowed the fetus's growth on a phone app that displayed its size as a fruit or vegetable each week. Our grandchild was now the size of a lemon! A grapefruit! A melon! We cheered as the produce icons grew in size. Decades earlier, Yumi had squeezed her belly down, praying I would be no more visible than a walnut.

Mollie and Michael had shared their news with me and John by wrapping takeout burritos in black ultrasound photographs. They watched closely as we unwrapped them. What was this black paper? A discount flyer or an ad for the burrito store? As the shiny dark paper unfurled, I saw the curled fetus image, and slowly began to understand what I was seeing. It was startling, funny, and then wildly thrilling. I screamed out loud. "Baby!!"

When did Yumi realize her own condition? There were no home pregnancy tests then. She would not have trusted a small-town doctor to keep her confidence. She had no friends or family she could tell. There was no celebrating.

Mollie's labor happened surreptitiously, under my nose. Two days after we began sheltering in place, she walked gingerly through the kitchen and stopped to lean on the counter.

"This hurts more than period cramps," she remarked. Then she asked if she could take a bath in our tub with Jacuzzi jets. I thought it was only the beginning, but not much later, I heard a full-throated wail coming from her room. The front door opened, and the midwife's clattering footsteps rushed in.

Less than a minute later, John's face lit up. "I hear a baby!"

"Are you sure?" I couldn't believe it. Then I heard it too: the unmistakable high, insistent voice of a newborn. Sequoia had arrived seconds after the midwife entered the house. Later on, we—the new grandparents and auntie—were ushered into the room, which felt like a womb itself, warm and darkened. The little human was perfect.

My granddaughter had burst into the world in the very room where my mother had lived for seventeen years. Sequoia had been born in this space that I associated so keenly with my mother's presence. Here is where she fell on the floor. And here. Here is where she sat every morning, affixing bobby pins to her hair. Here is where she cried for my father. *Masaji! Where are you?* Now, here, this tiny creature had appeared.

After so many years of living with us, it had eventually become clear that my mother needed more care than we could provide. The stairs in our home were unmanageable. So eventually she moved to a small neighborhood care home with doting caregivers who sang to her and braided her hair. On basketball nights, they all donned bright yellow Warriors shirts and cheered at the television. For years, she and John had trekked across the parking lot at the Oakland coliseum where they held a pair of season tickets. When she could no longer manage the games in person, she followed her beloved Warriors onscreen. The caregivers prepared her favorite ochazuke with pickled plum umeboshi. I taught them how to say *dai joubu*, the Japanese phrase for comfort, when she became confused or fretful.

My mother finally met her great-granddaughter on Mother's Day. We drove to the care home and rang the doorbell, carrying Sequoia in her car seat. A sign saying NO VISITORS was taped to the door. The caregivers opened the curtains and wheeled my mother to the window.

We hoisted the car seat with the sleeping baby up to the screened window. My mother, inside, was happy. "Cheeks!" she exclaimed, pointing. She asked the baby's name and then forgot it within seconds.

"Sequoia," we repeated. *Tsukoya?* she asked. *Nihongo name? Sequoia, Sequoia. Pretty name.*

Then she called out, "Susan! My husband is gone. He's the only fella I ever went with. What shall I do?"

I didn't know what to say. All I could do was hold up the baby, yawning and cooing.

"Look at the baby," I said. She looked, and her sadness evaporated. We have these losses. Things change, and people vanish from our lives. What can we do, except focus on the things that bring us joy?

I remembered the Mother's Day when my parents and grandmother had first met Yumi, so many years before when we had all shared lunch in a sushi restaurant in Manhattan, and I fought a restless impulse to order flowers for Yumi. I wanted her to know that she had a great-granddaughter too. For decades, I had sent her flowers on Mother's Day. They were a way for me to say, thank you for my life. They said, I still care about you, in spite of everything. They said, thank you for letting me live so that I could have my parents. So that I could be a mother and a grandmother. But I remembered what she had said when I'd found my paternal family: *I want no more contact.*

Sequoia was eight weeks old that Mother's Day weekend. I carried her to the mirror and said, "Who is that baby?" I said, "I am your Nana." We looked at each other and ourselves in the mirror. There were moments when I cradled the little warm bundle of her that I felt overwhelmed by grief. I had been alone at eight weeks old. I had had no family. A baby who never cried. Because crying was useless. All of these feelings crowded into my heart. My sweet darling granddaughter. My baby self. My birth mother, so far away, so done with me.

Mollie told me, "Sequoia sleeps with her foot tucked into my belly button." It was stretched and deepened from pregnancy, and Mollie believed that it comforted the baby to tuck her foot into her grounding spot. The place where Mollie was connected to me, in my own womb. My own umbilical spot, where I attached to Yumi over sixty years ago, was dried and tiny. It was nearly invisible now.

THE MOST JAPANESE
PERSON IN THE FAMILY

Over the course of the pandemic, our family scattered. My mother's beloved companion dog died at sixteen and a half, and she moved into a small neighborhood care home. Mollie and Michael and Sequoia moved out of state to be in a more affordable environment. Emma moved into an apartment in the neighborhood where I'd first met John and acquired a tiny, golden cat. Our once-full house was down to just John and me.

For ten months, we kept a distance from my mother, to save her, to save ourselves. She didn't understand. She gestured at me through the window. "Come in. Please come inside and sit with me."

She held her arms out to me like a child does. "Hug?" she said. I stepped in for a quick, masked embrace and then slathered my hands and arms with sanitizer in the car.

After months of watching her dwindle through the window, I asked the caregivers to wheel her out to the back porch. We sat at a distance. I brought her treats—chocolate donuts and miniature cans of Coke. It was never close enough. She pawed at her blue mask. "I don't like this thing."

I often drove away sobbing. My mother had softened into a human who wanted nothing more than to love and be loved. All her years of complaining and bitterness had vanished. Her eyes lit up when I appeared, just as my father's once had.

"My daughter," she called, pointing at me, and I answered, "My mother." I realized that my long bitterness had also melted.

All I wanted was for her to be comfortable. To be happy. To be well. My long years of struggle were over. I loved her.

I thought about my birth mother, also elderly now, also vulnerable. I wondered if she was healthy. I wondered if anyone would tell me if she was not.

At the start of 2021, my mother fell ill and was hospitalized. It was a week of agony, when she was alone, confused, and terrified. A nurse propped up a tablet on an iPad and left it near her bed. My disembodied voice tried to comfort her as she wailed for her family, for her long-dead brother, for me. *Dai joubu, Mommy. Dai joubu.* She couldn't hear me. I wept, watching her suffer. There was nothing I could do.

She made a brief improvement, and they sent her back to the care home but said she wouldn't fully recover. Her heart was failing, and her oxygen levels fell lower each day. Hospice service began, and, for the first time in a year, they allowed me through the front door. I sat next to her bed, and we held hands without distance. "Mommy," she murmured at me.

She lasted only four more days. It was late, a storming night when the hospice nurse called and said she was "close." Emma and I sat near her while John and Mollie watched on FaceTime. A double layer of masks under plastic face shields kept us safe from—what? I patted her hands while Emma rubbed her feet.

"I love you, Mommy," I said. "You'll be seeing Papa soon. Mas."

I thought of my father waiting at the curb with his car, holding the door open for her. "Iku, Kiku" he liked to say. His shorthand affection for *Ikimashouka*: let's go.

"Iku, Kiku," I said to her. "Papa's waiting."

Ten minutes after we arrived, she let out a long soft sigh. This must be what obituary writers mean when they say someone "died peacefully, surrounded by loved ones."

I sat with her until she cooled. I took a picture of her still self, curled like a shrimp in her pink flowered nightgown, a worn stuffed dog in the crook of her arm. I stroked her feet in their purple socks with white dogs. For days after, I stared at this image on my phone, not believing it was true.

My husband and I sat alone in the empty house in our grief. Nobody came. Nobody could come. It was a strange and terrible way to mourn. For six weeks, her body lay in limbo. The cremation waiting list was long because of COVID-19. We waited and waited, and finally they said it was her turn and we could go. We could witness the cremation if we wanted.

How could I say no? It was all we had. No wake, no visitation, no funeral. We wouldn't have a service at the Japanese church, wouldn't serve sushi or fold cranes to give away, like I'd seen at other funerals. There wouldn't be a table in the foyer for the koden ladies to collect the condolence envelopes in a basket.

I learned that koden was traditionally given in worn dollar bills, never new (that was for weddings). I learned that you were supposed to send a card written in pale gray ink to signify that your tears were watering down the pigment. I learned that in thanks for koden, bereaved families sent back a small token, like postage stamps, to the givers. I ordered a stack of thank-you stamps from the post office and wrote letters in gray ink for all the food, the flowers, the gifts, the koden that had come in so many forms.

John and I dressed in black.

They told us we could bring things if we wanted, to put in the crematorium with her. I brought her sticky, tattered photo album with pictures of Sequoia. My mother had signed it in ballpoint on the cover, her swooping, wobbly signature *K*. We brought a photo of her with my father on their wedding day, ducking heads from flung rice, rushing to their honeymoon. Iku, Kiku. Let's go.

I brought the stuffed dog she had stroked furless. I brought a chrysanthemum-shaped cookie one of my friends had commissioned. I imagined her Brooklyn voice, "What, I died and you get cookies? I don't even get one?" *Here you go, Mom.*

A blonde funeral worker in a black blazer and a fake flower in her hair led us to the witness room. "I'm Shannon," she said. She gestured at a sofa facing a glass window with red velvet curtains and then said, "Actually, you can come inside if you want."

Did we want to come inside? John and I looked at each other's eyes above our masks and we said yes. We went through the door into the cremation room. A long cardboard box lay atop a wheeled stretcher. My mother had been in there for six weeks, waiting her turn.

I arranged the book, the picture, the dog, the cookie on the lid of the box.

"Do you want to push the button?" Shannon asked.

I didn't know what the button did. I said no.

A man pushed a button on the wall and the oven opened its mouth. Inside was a roaring, a color, an orange abyss. He slid the box inside, and the dog toppled into the fire. He pushed the button again, and the door closed.

A week later, they called me and said I could pick up her ashes. A box in a velvet drawstring bag. I put it in the family room next to her favorite chair, with a view of the television, so she could watch the Warriors.

I was now the most Japanese person remaining in our family. It filled me with a grief that was larger than losing just my mother. She had been my anchor to our Japanese heritage, and I felt suddenly unrooted. Now we were a family of one biracial Asian, one white man, and two quarter-Japanese daughters. It shocked me to think that my granddaughter was only one-eighth Japanese. Now it was up to me to be the anchor.

We started watching the Japanese series *Midnight Diner,* and it brought me a strange comfort. It grounded me to listen to the actors speaking Japanese, and I repeated every word that was familiar to me. When I heard them say "dai joubu," I wept.

"Did you hear that?" I called out to John on the couch. "Dai joubu! It's gonna be okay!" I frantically scribbled all the words I knew, words I remembered from my grandmother, dead now for almost thirty years. The opening acoustic song with the man singing in Japanese soothed me like a lullaby.

It had been four years since I'd last been in contact with Yumi. The last thing she had said to me, when I'd notified her of the DNA match with my genetic paternal family, was that "we should no longer be in contact." I had agonized over this. I hated the thought that our last communication would be so painfully final. "You and I may be biologically tethered," she wrote, "but this relationship has always been fraught." I couldn't argue that point. She had been ambivalent at best about my finding her, forty years earlier.

But when my adoptive mother died, I was consumed by the desire to tell my birth mother. She was my last surviving parent. They had known each other, and for many years had retained a kind of friendship. Yumi had expressed tremendous surprise and relief that I'd been adopted by Japanese parents. I needed to tell her that my mother was gone.

I didn't think about it. I just sent an email, quickly, before I could talk myself out of it. I said simply, "I have been trying to honor your request to not be in contact. I don't know if you would want to know this or not, but Kiku passed away in February." I attached her obituary and a photo of Sequoia.

She responded within hours. She thanked me for letting her know the sad news and said that Sequoia was beautiful.

She was back. Once again, we were on the other side of anger. I kept a respectful distance, but occasionally I reached out and she always responded. Our tone remained cordial. I sent her a birthday greeting and she answered with a festive photograph of herself, blowing out candles on a cake. She was as stylish and beautiful as ever. My birthday, falling on the calendar the following week, went unmentioned. And I understood that we would probably never see each other again.

EPILOGUE

For months after my mother's death, I found it unbearable to visit the trio of rooms where she had lived alongside our daughters. But over time, John and I made changes to our finally empty nest. We installed new carpeting, replacing years of human and canine stains. We repainted the rooms. Silver Sage. Mascarpone. Grey Owl. Gradually, the rooms transformed into a suite of writing spaces: beds and desks surrounded by trees. My friends now come and write alongside me in the quiet.

I named my mother's original room, where Sequoia was born, the Cherry Blossom room. It no longer breaks my heart to be there. I carry a wide-bottomed coffee mug from my biological cousin's theater company to the room, and sip while I write at the desk.

Family mementos surround me. My mother's chrysanthemum quilt covers the bed, her hope chest against the wall. A pair of carved stone fish that Yumi gifted me long ago. A short, fat stick that my granddaughter handed me on a walk, worn smooth in my pocket. My father's 442nd "Go for Broke" army medal, the hand holding the torch. Framed artwork from Auntie Liz's room, beautifully ornate Italian calligraphy, hangs above the bed. My biological father's microscope sits on a shelf. The generations surround me as I sit at this desk, full of questions still left unanswered.

Occasionally, Yumi emails with chatty news. She inquires after Sequoia and responds, "So adorable!" when I send photos. I agree.

Sometimes she vanishes for weeks or months at a time, and

a fear grips me, that one day she will disappear for good, and nobody will tell me.

This fragile, tenuous relationship is in its final season. She is a nonagenarian now, and I am in my sixties. I pray that our relationship will come to a close with a gentle truce, bonding over our mutual adoration of our grandchild/great-grandchild. My time of asking questions is done. There are so many things I will never fully know or understand.

At so many points during the past forty years, I tried to complete this book. Thousands of pages clutter my computer hard drives and landfills. I was always paralyzed by fear that the actual telling of it would mean an end to my relationship with Yumi. I wrote. Then when I reread what I had written, I panicked and set it aside, at times for months or years. I slipped back into the guise of the good, silent adoptee. Then, the burning need to say "I exist" would overcome me, and once again, I'd turn to the manuscript.

I began a conversation about publishing with my editor during a time that Yumi and I were estranged. I felt I had nothing left to lose.

But once again, my birth mother and I are in each other's orbits. We exchange cautious, affable messages. There is a sense of peace between us.

Two days before the manuscript is due, anxiety floods my body. What am I doing? I bury my head in my hands. Is another flood of anger, a final separation, worth it? I spent decades carefully tiptoeing around the landmines. But at the same time, I was carrying my own bomb, in the form of manuscript pages, and it was strapped to my body.

Since the start of my life, I have been a secret, my existence a wild inconvenience. The first poem I ever wrote was titled "The Closet," typed on a sheet of onionskin paper in my college room. I wrote about how it felt being hidden in another person's closet. From the inside, I could hear the muffled sounds of her life, but no one could hear me. I was afraid to make a sound. For decades, I held my birth mother's secret.

But this story is not hers alone. That girl in the closet has waited a lifetime to open the door and claim her own truth.

Inked up, scribbled manuscript pages litter my desk. I take one, cut it into a square, and then fold it by heart, the steps embedded into my hands now. A crisp crane, its wings peppered with words, balances on my palm, ready to fly away.

ACKNOWLEDGMENTS

Infinite thanks: first, to editors Kristen Elias Rowley and Joy Castro, who believed in my story, deeply understood it, and encouraged me as I labored to birth it. To book cover artist Nathan Putens, who so beautifully captured its spirit in the cover art. To Tara Cyphers, Samara Rafert, and everyone at the Ohio State University Press who worked on this book, thank you for being an incredible team.

I have a profound desire to express my gratitude to every single person who had some part in supporting me over the thirty years it has taken to complete this book. It has been a long, long journey, and there are too many people to name everyone. Please know I could not have gotten here without you. To all of you who have encouraged me, read my pages, bolstered my confidence, and kept me going, thank you.

Adopted friends have been a lifelong source of support, solace, and understanding. Your solidarity and infinite narratives continue to sustain and ground me. At ALMA, I met one of my first adopted friends, Pam Hasegawa. She gave me room to share my adoption experience for the first time at age eighteen. PACER, Pact, and #AdopteeTwitter have buoyed me and made me feel like I wasn't alone.

Beloved adoptee friends have sat with me, stood with me, been with me. When I've been in it, you've been there for me: June Edelstein, Lisa Marie Rollins, JaeRan Kim, Angela Tucker, Vaishali Lerner, Laura Callen, Susan Dusza Guerra Leksander, Chinyere

Oparah, Mary Going, April Dinwoodie, Sue Harris O'Connor, and Alison Larkin. You get me.

Thank you to the adoptee writers who've inspired me with your honest and powerful poems and stories: Florence Fisher, Betty Jean Lifton, Jenny Heujin Wills, Lee Herrick, Nicole Chung, Jackie Kay, Matthew Salesses, Rebecca Carroll, Kit Myers, Susan Devan Harness, Shannon Gibney, Jane Jeong Trenka, J. S. Lee, Jennifer Kwon Dobbs, Megan Culhane Galbraith, Sun Yung Shin, and many others.

To the many first/birth and adoptive parents who have been friends and allies, thank you for reaching across the adoption constellation. Particular thanks to Beth Hall, director and founder of Pact, and the staff members, counselors, board members, and adoptive families who embrace the hard work. Thanks to Paul Weber, Tom Calarco, Carla Birnberg, and Ronda Slater. I am indebted to Amber Decker, whose genetic genealogy skills helped me discover my paternal birth family.

This book has taken decades to write, and countless friends, mentors, writing groups, and communities have journeyed with me as I've navigated its pages. From my late third-grade teacher, Florence Sharff, the first person to encourage me to write, to my current writing group (Elmaz Abinader, Faith Adiele, and Tara Dorabji), who spurred me to finally cross the finish line. My dear friend, Lisa Lerner, was my first writing pal when we were undergraduates in Ithaca. My Mills MFA comrades—Leanna James Blackwell, Audrey Ferber, and Wendy Williams: we continued meeting monthly for years after graduation, and we are still the original fab four. Thank you to my *Ghost at Heart's Edge* anthology coeditor, Tina Cervin, for recognizing the power in adoption narratives. Special appreciation for the 18th Street Writers, particularly Michael Alenyikov and Andrew Chen, for making the magic that comes from writing together in a shared space.

Mills has been a source for so many connections. Kathryn Reiss and I have shared many cups of tea, and she's nudged me to finish this book since I began. Karen Su's Asian American

Women Writers class made us want to become Asian American women writers ourselves, and thus the Rice Papers group was formed, with members ranging from nineteen to eighty-one years of age, including Patricia Wakida, Sasha Hom, Rose Mark, Christine Hyung-Oak Lee, and Melanie Hilario, and many others. I fondly remember the late Khartar Dhillon and Mary Suzuki. I am grateful to dear Mills colleagues Natalee Kēhaulani Bauer, Brinda Mehta, and Kim Magowan.

It's been life-changing to be part of the Writers Grotto. It's kept me immersed in a large community of talented and dedicated writer friends, including Zahra Noorbakhsh, my original office mate, Anisse Gross, Alice Wu, Grace Loh Prasad, Vanessa Hua, Bonnie Tsui, Dominic Lim, Heather Bourbeau, Susanne Pari, Sarah Pollock, Lindsey Crittenden, Maw Shein Win, and Ethel Rohan. It's where I had the opportunity to co-organize Rooted & Written, the first free writing conference for writers of color, with founder Roberto Lovato, Jesus Sierra, Aditi Malhotra, J. D. Beltran, and others.

Thanks to Jeff Greenwald and Joy Johannessen for invaluable editorial feedback. Thanks to Caroline Grant and Literary Mama for publishing my "Life in the Sandwich" column, about living in a multigenerational household with my mother and offspring. Thanks to Laura Fraser for publishing "The Mouse Room" for SheBooks and to the many editors who included versions of "Just a Bee Sting" in their publications. Recently, I am grateful to Meilan Carter-Gilkey for her calm and steadfast support. Thanks to Kathleen Caldwell, bookseller extraordinaire at a Great Good Place for Books, for her amazing support for me and this book.

There are friends who can't be categorized in one kind of way. I live so many Venn diagrams of identity in my existence that I'm often in-community in infinite ways and with incredible people. I want to acknowledge them: Julie Lythcott-Haims, Leah Korican, Lisa Factora-Borchers, Marie Myung-Ok Lee, Ilana deBare, Monica Wesolowka, Lily Aguas, Nikki Trufant-Wade, Fanshen Cox, Ericka Lutz, Alison Teal, Caroline Grant, Sari Botton, Michelle Valladares, Masha Hamilton, and Elizabeth Crane.

Parts of this story existed as a solo performance piece titled *The Ice Cream Gene,* and I owe gratitude to my mentors, friends, and directors at the San Francisco Solo Performance Workshop. Thanks to W. Kamau Bell and Martha Rynberg for helping me bring these words to the stage.

I am grateful to the generous residencies that offered me precious space and time to write: Hedgebrook, the MacDowell Colony, the Blue Mountain Center, and the Mesa Refuge.

To my students from UC Berkeley Extension, the Writers Grotto, Bay Path University, and Mills College: you inspire me.

To the friends of my youth and beyond: Gina Eaton, Ken Weeden, Tom Mesevage, Cathy Pagano, Ken Shiotani, and Jean Anne Zollars.

To my parents, Masaji and Kikuko Ito. I miss you both and my grandmother, Asano Inouye, forever. To my Ito relatives, especially my aunt Mary Ito, thank you for being my family.

To my paternal birth family, whom I discovered late in my life, thank you for welcoming me so openly. Getting to know Kay, Jeannie and Bob, Betsy, Sara and John, Steve and Melanie, Phil and Cindy, Nancy, Abby, Theresa, Beth, Lois, Emily and Landon, and the rest of the family has been a gift. I treasure our friendship as well as our shared DNA.

In spite of our ever-shifting relationship, I never regret meeting and knowing my birth mother. I wish her peace.

To my wonderful extended family of in-laws, I hit the jackpot when I married into your clan. I am especially grateful to my dear late uncle-in-law O. C., a fellow writer who cheered me on as long as I knew him.

To my dear family: Mollie, Emma, Michael, and Sequoia, I love you.

Finally, thank you to my beloved partner, John, who completely believed in me from the beginning, read every page multiple times, and wiped every tear that I shed over this book. It would not have been possible without you.

ABOUT THE AUTHOR

Susan Kiyo Ito is the coeditor of the literary anthology *A Ghost at Heart's Edge: Stories and Poems of Adoption*. Her work has appeared in numerous literary magazines and anthologies. A MacDowell Fellow, she has also been awarded residencies at the Mesa Refuge, Hedgebrook, and Blue Mountain Center. She has performed her solo show, *The Ice Cream Gene*, around the US and adapted *Untold Stories: Life, Love, and Reproduction* for the theater. She writes and teaches in the Bay Area.

MACHETE

Joy Castro, Series Editor

This series showcases fresh stories, innovative forms, and books that break new aesthetic ground in nonfiction—memoir, personal and lyric essay, literary journalism, cultural meditations, short shorts, hybrid essays, graphic pieces, and more—from authors whose writing has historically been marginalized, ignored, and passed over. The series is explicitly interested in not only ethnic and racial diversity, but also gender and sexual diversity, neurodiversity, physical diversity, religious diversity, cultural diversity, and diversity in all of its manifestations. The machete enables path-clearing; it hacks new trails and carves out new directions. The Machete series celebrates and shepherds unique new voices into publication, providing a platform for writers whose work intervenes in dangerous ways.

I Would Meet You Anywhere: A Memoir
SUSAN KIYO ITO

Birding While Indian: A Mixed-Blood Memoir
THOMAS C. GANNON

Chi Boy: Native Sons and Chicago Reckonings
KEENAN NORRIS

We Take Our Cities with Us: A Memoir
SORAYYA KHAN

The Sound of Memory: Themes from a Violinist's Life
REBECCA FISCHER

Finding Querencia: Essays from In-Between
HARRISON CANDELARIA FLETCHER

Eating Lightbulbs and Other Essays
STEVE FELLNER

The Guild of the Infant Saviour: An Adopted Child's Memory Book
MEGAN CULHANE GALBRAITH

Like Love
MICHELE MORANO

Quite Mad: An American Pharma Memoir
SARAH FAWN MONTGOMERY

Apocalypse, Darling
BARRIE JEAN BORICH